African American Women Playwrights

Crtitical Studies in Black Life and Culture
Volume 31
Garland Reference Library of the Humanities
Volume 1996

Critical Studies in Black Life and Culture

C. James Trotman, *General Editor*

Richard Wright
Myths and Realities
edited by C. James Trotman

The Rhetoric of Struggle
Public Address by African American Women
edited by Robbie Jean Walker

Ntozake Shange
A Critical Study of the Plays
by Neal A. Lester

From Harlem to Hollywood
The Struggle for Racial and Cultural Democracy, 1920–1943
by Bruce M. Tyler

The Black Underclass
Critical Essays on Race and Unwantedness
by William A. Darity, Jr., and Samuel L. Myers, Jr. with Emmett D. Carson and William Sabol

The Great White Way
African American Women Writers and American Success Mythologies
by Phillipa Kafka

Langston Hughes
The Man, His Art, and His Continuing Influence
edited by C. James Trotman

Toni Morrison's Fiction
Contemporary Criticism
edited by David L. Middleton

African American Women Playwrights
A Research Guide
edited by Christy Gavin

African American Women Playwrights

A Research Guide

Edited by
Christy Gavin

GARLAND PUBLISHING, INC.
A MEMBER OF THE TAYLOR & FRANCIS GROUP
New York & London
1999

Published in 1999 by
Garland Publishing Inc.
A Member of the Taylor & Francis Group
19 Union Square West
New York, NY 10003

10 9 8 7 6 5 4 3 2 1

Library of Congress Cataloging-in-Publication Data

Gavin, Christy, 1952-
African American women playwrights : a research guide / edited by Christy Gavin.
p. cm. — (Critical Studies on Black life and culture ; v. 31) (Garland reference library of the humanities ; vol. 1996.)
Includes bibliographical references and index.
ISBN 0-8153-2384-0 (alk. paper)
1. American drama—Afro-American authors—Bio-bibliography. 2. Women and literature—United States—Bibliography. 3. Afro-American in literature—Bibliography. 5. Women dramatists, American—Bibliography. 6. Afro-American dramatists—Biography. I. Title. II. Series: Garland reference library of the humanities ; v. 1996.
PS153.N5G29 1998
812'.54099287'0899073—dc21 98-40865
CIP

Printed on acid-free, 250-year-life paper
Manufactured in the United States of America

Contents

For my mother
Camille Gavin
a kindred soul

General Editor's Preface

Critical Studies in Black Life and Culture is a series devoted to original, book-length studies of African American developments. Written by well-qualified scholars, the series is interdisciplinary and global, interpreting tendencies and themes wherever African Americans have left their mark. The ideal reader for the series is one who appreciates the combined use of scholarly inquiry with a focus on a people whose roots stretch around the world.

Critical Studies is also a window to that world. The series holds out the promise of fulfilling the ideal of all scholarship by uncovering and disseminating the sources of a people's life-line. In relationship to this series, the untranslated Ghanaan narratives offering the earliest perspectives on African life and thought illustrate a scholarly need in this area. If and when they are published, we might have a clearer view of the past and of the consciousness of blacks in antiquity. The clarity would almost certainly contribute to a more detailed basis for understanding what the roots of "culture" and "civilization" are for African Americans in particular and for all of us in general.

Sometimes, however, the scholarly works published in Critical Studies remind us that the windows have not always been open or, if they were, the shades were pulled down, making it difficult if not impossible to see in or out. The series reaffirms forerunners who, by talent and determination, refused to be unseen or unheard: Phillis Wheatley, Anna Julia Cooper, Frederick Douglass, William E.B. DuBois, Zora Neale Hurston, Langston Hughes, and Ralph Ellison. They laid the aesthetic and intellectual foundation for Ralph Bunche, Albert Luthuli, Desmond Tutu, Martin Luther King, Jr., Wole Soyinka, and Toni Morrison to be awarded Nobel prizes. In addition to individual achievements, the outstanding examples of organized and permanent group life are to be found in the historic black church, black colleges and universitites, and the NAACP;

none of these, I might add, has received a comprehensive historical treatment, leaving sizable gaps in any effort to conceptualize a total picture if multicultural America.

All of these achievements suggest a promising future in African American developments, pointing to a great deal of activity—some from those who have successfully peeked around pulled-down shades to look out, while others have found ways to peep in. Critical Studies in Black Life and Culture is committed to publishing the best scholarship on African American life.

C. James Trotman
West Chester University
1999

Preface

This volume documents the scholarship of ten black American women playwrights. These writers represent two major periods that greatly influenced the work of black dramatists: the Harlem Renaissance (roughly 1920–1940) and the period between the 1950s and the 1970s. Underlying both eras is the acute awareness of black pride and women's rights. Highly supportive of black women writers, the Harlem Renaissance produced several prominent playwrights whom scholars have recently re-discovered and who are represented in this volume: Marita Bonner, Mary Burrill, Angelina Weld Grimké, Zora Neale Hurston, Georgia Douglas Johnson, and May Miller. The form, content, and conventions of the dramas of these early playwrights anticipated the dramatic writing of black women writers who began their careers after World War II. Four of the latter are included in this bio-bibliography: Alice Childress, Lorraine Hansberry, Adrienne Kennedy, and Ntozake Shange.

These ten playwrights were selected because they have attracted sufficient attention from theater and literary scholars to warrant charting the critical reception and breadth of interest in their work. The purpose of this bio-bibliography is threefold: to introduce students to the life and work of these dramatists, to provide serious researchers with a starting point from which to begin their analyses, and to encourage scholars to continue to explore new areas of the dramatist's canon.

Each of the ten chapters in this volume is devoted to one playwright and includes the following information:

- a brief biography of the playwright
- a list of plays
- production information (unless otherwise indicated all references are to initial productions in a New York City theater)
- plot summaries of major plays

- playscripts
- an annotated bibliography of profiles, interviews, general criticism, and, for selected plays, performance reviews and formal criticism; plays for which there is little extant scholarly documentation are listed at the end of the chapter.

The scope of the volume is large but not all-inclusive. Emphasis is on English-language monographs, chapters in books, Festschriften, and articles in the popular and scholarly press. Excluded are doctoral dissertations, book reviews, films, audiocassettes, and Internet sources. All items included in the bibliography have been verified.

Theater and drama present a unique challenge to the researcher. Other disciplines have sophisticated tools that allow easy access to the primary and secondary literature. However, the bibliographic control of information for theater and drama is chaotic. These disciplines lack a comprehensive access tool that indexes production reviews, critical studies, interviews, and biographies in performing arts and allied magazines and journals. Thus deprived of a systematic research approach, the researcher must employ a variety of tools and methods to acquire information about individual plays and playwrights.

To gather the material for this book, pertinent retrospective bibliographies were consulted as well as several on-line book catalogs. Because so much of the information on these playwrights is concentrated in popular and scholarly periodical literature, several periodical indexes and electronic databases were searched. These include*MLA Bibliography, Humanities Index, Reader's Guide to Periodical Literature, Access: The Supplementary Index to Periodicals, Alternative Press Index, Arts and Humanities Citation Index,* and *Index to Periodicals By and About Blacks*. To obtain additional reviews of play productions, general newspaper indexes such as *Black Newspapers Index, Ethnic News Watch, National Newspaper Index, Newspaper Abstracts* and *Newsearch* were consulted, as well as the indexes to individual newspapers such as the *New York Times, Christian Science Monitor, Los Angeles Times, Wall Street Journal,* and *Washington Post.*

African American Women Playwrights

Chapter One
Marita Bonner

Brief Biography

According to Margaret Wilkerson, *The Purple Flower* by Marita Bonner (1898–1971), is "perhaps the most provocative play" created by a black woman in the early part of this century. Critics have observed that in this work Bonner anticipates the dramatic expressionism of Adrienne Kennedy and Ntozake Shange. Unlike the genteel plays of Angelina Weld Grimké, Bonner's race dramas, with their distinctive second-person narration, reflect her unflinching rage toward racial injustice. In her prescient essay "On Being Young-A Woman-and Colored," Bonner wrote, "[Whites] have never had petty putrid insult dragged over them-drawing blood-like pebbled sand on your body where the skin is tenderest. . . . You long to explode and hurt everything white; friendly; unfriendly. But you know that you cannot live with a chip on your shoulder." Lorraine Roses and Ruth Randolph (1.8) report that Charles T. Copeland, Bonner's writing instructor at Radcliffe, encouraged her to write "but not to be 'bitter'—a cliché to colored people who write."

Born in Boston, Bonner attended Brookline High School. In 1922 she graduated from Radcliffe and went on to teach school in Virginia and Washington, D.C. While in Washington, she became part of the S Street Salon, a group of writers and intellectuals founded by the writer Georgia Douglas Johnson. During this period Bonner wrote three plays: *The Pot Maker, The Purple Flower,* and *Exit, an Illusion;* the latter two won first place in contests sponsored by *The Crisis,* a black magazine. A fourth drama, *Muddled Dream,* has been lost. Although Bonner joined the Krigwa Players, a theatrical group based in Washington, D.C., the company did not perform any of her plays. According to Jennifer Burton, the players were unaware of her dramas. In1930 Bonner married William Occomy, a graduate of Brown University, and the couple moved to Chicago. After her marriage, Bonner apparently ceased writing drama and concentrated on fiction and raising her children. In 1941 she ceased writing altogether. Some critics surmise that she quit because of her union with the First Church of Christ Scientist, but Roses and Randolph point out that writing is not anathema to the church's philosophy.

None of Bonner's plays was produced during her lifetime.

Burton and others speculate that Bonner's plays went unproduced because their uniqueness set them apart from other contemporary plays written by blacks and because they would have been perhaps technically too complex to stage. Yet, as Elizabeth Brown-Guillory notes, Bonner's plays "were read and savored . . . by some of the finest [Harlem Renaissance] artists, including Georgia Douglas Johnson, May Miller, and Langston Hughes."

Profiles and General Criticism

Brown-Guillory, Elizabeth. *Their Place on the Stage: Black Women Playwrights in America.* New York: Praeger, 1990.

While focusing on later black women dramatists, Brown-Guillory includes discussions of several female playwrights active during the Harlem Renaissance: Bonner, Burrill, Grimké, Johnson, and Miller.

Burke, Sally. *American Feminist Playwrights: A Critical History.* New York: Twayne, 1996.

Burke agrees with Perkins's (1.6) opinion that Bonner's work influenced the expressionistic plays of Adrienne Kennedy. She also points out that Bonner anticipated Shange's use of drumbeat, dance, and song: "Bonner pressed the boundaries of the drama, providing new ways of depicting age-old struggles."

Burton, Jennifer. "Introduction." In *Zora Neale Hurston, Eulalie Spence, Marita Bonner, and Others: The Prize Plays and Other One-Acts Published in Periodicals.* Edited by Henry Louis Gates, Jr., xix-lx. New York: G.K. Hall, 1996.

Burton's solid introduction to the plays of early women playwrights provides background on Bonner and briefly explores each of her plays. The introduction is accompanied by extensive notes and a bibliography.

Flynn, Joyce. "Marita Bonner Occomy." In *Dictionary of Literary Biography:* Vol. 51, *Afro-American Writers from the Harlem Renaissance to 1940.* Edited by Trudier Harris. Detroit: Gale Research, 1987.

Flynn, co-editor of Bonner's collected works, provides a basic introduction to the life and work of Marita Bonner. Accompanying the essay is a photo of Bonner and reproductions of pages from her journal. See also *Frye Street & Environs: The Collected Works of Marita Bonner.* Edited by Joyce Flynn and Joyce Occomy Stricklin. Boston: Beacon, 1987.

Miller, Jeanne-Marie. "Black Women Playwrights from Grimké to Shange: Selected Synopses of Their Works." In *But Some of Us Are Brave: Black Women's Studies.* Edited by Gloria T. Hull, P.B. Scott, and Barbara Smith, 280–290. Old Westbury, N.Y.: Feminist Press, 1982.

Miller surveys the work of several African-American women whose plays "offer a unique insight into the Black experience," including Angelina Weld Grimké, Marita Bonner, Georgia Douglas Johnson, Mary Burrill, Lorraine Hansberry, Alice Childress, Ntozake Shange, Adrienne Kennedy, Sonia Sanchez, J.E. Franklin, and Martie Charles.

Perkins, Kathy A. *Black Female Playwrights: An Anthology of Plays Before 1950.* Edited by Kathy A. Perkins, 189–190. Bloomington: Indiana University Press, 1990.

Perkins maintains that Bonner's importance lies in the fact that she rejected dramatic realism. Her plays anticipate the surreal and expressionistic plays of Adrienne Kennedy thirty-five years later.

Peterson, Bernard L. *Early Black American Playwrights and Dramatic Writers: A Biographical Directory and Catalog of Plays, Films, and Broadcasting Scripts.* New York: Greenwood, 1990.

The entry on Bonner includes a brief biography, plot summaries, staging history, and list of secondary sources.

Roses, Lorraine Elena, and Ruth Elizabeth Randolph. *Harlem Renaissance and Beyond: Literary Biographies of 100 Black Women Writers, 1900–1945.* Boston: G.K. Hall, 1990.

The entry on Bonner provides brief biographical information and selected list of primary and secondary sources.

———. "Marita Bonner: In Search of Other Mothers' Gardens." *Black American Literature Forum* 21 (Spring-Summer 1987): 165–83.

Although the authors limit their discussion to Bonner's short fiction, their introduction to her life, based on her papers and interviews with her family, is highly relevant to a study of Bonner's drama.

Shafer, Yvonne. "Marita Bonner." In *American Women Playwrights, 1900–1950,* 428–432. New York: Peter Lang, 1995.

Shafer provides a basic introduction to Bonner and her work. Included are brief synopses and analyses of Bonner's plays.

Exit, An Illusion

(Won first prize for best play in the *The Crisis* magazine contest, 1927; unproduced during Bonner's lifetime)

Playscripts

Black Female Playwrights: An Anthology of Plays Before 1950. Edited by Kathy A. Perkins, 187–199. Bloomington: Indiana University Press, 1990.

"Exit, an Illusion." *The Crisis* (Oct. 1929): 335–36, 352.

Frye Street & Environs: The Collected Works of Marita Bonner. Edited by Joyce Flynn and Joyce Occomy Stricklin, 47–56. Boston: Beacon, 1987.

Zora Neale Hurston, Eulalie Spence, Marita Bonner, and Others: The Prize Plays and Other One-Acts Published in Periodicals. Edited by Henry Louis Gates, Jr., 126–132. New York: G.K. Hall, 1996.

Summary of Play

Asleep in a shabby flat, amid a mess of clothes, dishes, lacy lingerie and red kid pumps, is Buddy, a black man, and Dot, a half black, half white woman. They are neither brother and sister nor husband and wife. Dot, who is ill with an unspecified disease, awakes and announces to Buddy that she has a date with Exit Mann, a man she has known all her life. They argue. Buddy's jealousy of Exit, whom he believes is white, is complicated by the fact that he is angry that Dot can pass for white. Buddy threatens that if Exit comes for Dot, Buddy will shoot both of them. Suddenly, Exit appears. Buddy screams at him for taking Dot away. Dot implores Buddy to say he loves her. Instead, Buddy rejects her and she goes to Exit. Buddy fires a shot that hits a light and the stage goes dark. Buddy strikes a match. He sees Dot lying prostrate as Exit turns to reveal his true self—the "hollow eyes and fleshless cheeks" of Death. Buddy awakes as if from a dream, realizes Dot is dead, and cries, "I love you."

Criticism

(No criticism on *Exit; An Illusion* is available)

The Pot Maker (A Play to Be Read)

(Published, 1927; unproduced during Bonner's lifetime)

Playscripts

Frye Street & Environs: The Collected Works of Marita Bonner. Edited by Joyce Flynn and Joyce Occomy Stricklin, 17–29. Boston: Beacon, 1987.

"The Pot Maker." *Opportunity: A Journal of Negro Life* (Feb. 1927): 47–56.

Wines in the Wilderness: Plays by African American Women from the Harlem Renaissance to the Present. Edited by Elizabeth Brown-Guillory, 1–10. New York: Greenwood, 1990.

Zora Neale Hurston, Eulalie Spence, Marita Bonner, and Others: The Prize Plays and Other One-Acts Published in Periodicals. Edited by Henry Louis Gates, Jr., 107–114. New York: G.K. Hall, 1996.

Summary of Play

Elias has been called from the fields by God to preach the Gospel. He rehearses his sermon to his family, including his parents, Luke and Nettie, his wife, Lucinda, and her lover, Lew Fox. As he begins, his family constantly interrupts him with comments and criticisms, especially his frustrated wife. Elias tells the parable of the maker of earthenware pots. The pot maker tells the pots that if they do as he says, they will be transformed into pots made of gold, silver, brass, iron, or tin. The pots will be filled, according to the pot maker, and must remain upright even though the room will darken and terrifying noises will erupt. Some of the pots complain of cracks. The pot maker mends the cracks. As the room darkens, the pots react in different ways—some fall over and they turn to tin; some hang their heads, but "settin' up" they turn to silver. Others try to deceive the pot maker by acting as if they are upright; for their boldness, the pot maker turns them to brass. Those that remain standing are turned to gold. Elias concludes that the pots symbolize people. If they "keep settin' on the truth" of God, they will be rewarded. Following Elias's parable, Lew leaves the house. Shortly thereafter, Lucinda attempts to follow him but is prevented by her mother-in-law. Lucinda loses her temper and screams at her husband for his irresponsibility — "Ain't no woman so in love with her man's mother she wants to live five years under the same roof with her like I done." Meanwhile, Lew, outside waiting for Lucinda, falls down the well. Elias prevents Lucinda from saving him. She breaks loose and runs to Lew. Elias yells that they are both "tin." Suddenly he realizes he also has cracks. He runs to the well and attempts to save Lucinda, but he drowns as well. The play ends with the playwright commenting, "A crack has been healed. A pot has spilled over on the ground. Some wisps have twisted out."

Criticism

Harris, Will. "Early Black Women Playwrights and the Dual Liberation Motif." *African American Review* 28, no. 2 (1994): 205–221.

Harris asserts that important to the plays by black women dramatists in the earlier part of the twentieth century were raising racial consciouness and staging strong, independent roles for women. However, *The Pot Maker* differs from other plays by women of the period by its refusal to celebrate race or women's independence. According to Harris, "Lucinda's direct criticism of her husband Elias violates the rule of silence on the subject of black men held by the other female salon playwrights. Lucinda's affair (that is, her rejection of the racially defined terms of the egalitarian commitment) results in her own death, her lover's, and her husband's."

Wines in the Wilderness: Plays by African American Women from the Harlem Renaissance to the Present. Edited by Elizabeth Brown-Guillory, 1–10. New York: Greenwood, 1990.

Brown-Guillory observes that Bonner depicts "poor and middle class black women who defend themselves against gender-based, societal constraints." *The Pot Maker* reflects Bonner's concerns with resisting the romanticization of the South, portraying poverty and immorality and dramatizing the devaluation of women. Bonner could have reduced the central female character, Lucinda, to a one-dimensional adulteress. However, Bonner empathizes with Lucinda's rage and frustration toward her husband, who is oblivious to her emotional and financial needs. Brown-Guillory contends that Bonner influenced the work of future writers such as Flannery O'Connor's "Christocentric" fiction of the 1950s, which "resembles . . . emphasis on redemption and saving grace."

The Purple Flower: A Phantasy That Had Best Be Read

(Won first prize for best play, *The Crisis* magazine contest, 1927; unproduced during Bonner's lifetime)

Playscripts

Black Female Playwrights: An Anthology of Plays Before 1950. Edited by Kathy A. Perkins, 187–199. Bloomington: Indiana University Press, 1990.

Black Theater U.S.A.: Forty-Five Plays by Black Americans, 1847–1974. Edited by James V. Hatch and Ted Shine, 201–207. New York: The Free Press, 1974.

Black Theatre USA: Plays by African Americans, 1847 to Today. Rev. Ed. Edited by James V. Hatch and Ted Shine, 206–212. New York: The Free Press, 1996.

Frye Street & Environs: The Collected Works of Marita Bonner. Edited by Joyce Flynn and Joyce Occomy Stricklin, 30–46. Boston: Beacon, 1987.

Modern Drama by Women 1880s-1930s: An International Anthology. Edited by Katherine E. Kelly, 309–317. London: Routledge, 1996.

"The Purple Flower." The Crisis (Jan. 1928): 9–11, 28–30.

Zora Neale Hurston, Eulalie Spence, Marita Bonner, and Others: The Prize Plays and Other One-Acts Published in Periodicals. Edited by Henry Louis Gates, Jr., 115–125. New York: G.K. Hall, 1996.

Summary of Play

The play takes place "here, there or anywhere-or even nowhere" during the time of "the middle-of-things-as they-are." Two groups fill the stage: the ubiquitous White Devils, whose characteristics combine those of angels and devils, "artful little things with soft white eyes . . . soft hair that flops around their horns"; and The Us, who can be "as white as the White Devils, as brown as the earth, as black at the center of a poppy." The White Devils live in Somewhere and use their tricks to prevent The Us, who live below in the valley that lies between Nowhere and Somewhere, from ascending the hill to where the purple Flower-of-Life-At-Its-Fullest grows. The Us, after many years of struggle, of laboring, of educating themselves, realize that these factors alone cannot help them to overcome the oppression of the White Devils. What is needed is a revolution, "new blood for birth so the NEW MAN can live." Finest Blood, sent by The Us, confronts the leader of the White Devils and says, "White Devil! God speaks to you through me!-Hear Him!-Him! You have taken blood; there can be no other way. You will have to give blood! Blood!" The curtain falls with all participants listening and the playwright asking, "Is it time?"

Criticism

Abramson, Doris E. "Angelina Weld Grimké, Mary T. Burrill, Georgia Douglas Johnson, and Marita O. Bonner." *Sage* 2, no. 1 (Spring 1985): 9–13.

Abramson points out that Bonner's call for revolution sets up a paradigm for later plays. In *The Purple Flower,* Bonner presents a "battle cry that is a question—for Bonner asked in 1928 not, will there be a revolution, Black versus white, but 'is it time?'" The focus of revolution is the purple flower that appeared in Bonner's earlier work, the short story "Nothing New." The color purple for Bonner, trained in the classical tradition, connotes wealth and power. Furthermore, purple "is 'colored' or 'stained' as if by blood. . . . It is a perfect color for the flower so jealously guarded and so desperately desired, symbolizing as it does both power and blood."

McKay, Nellie. "'What Were They Saying?': Black Women Playwrights of the Harlem Renaissance." In *The Harlem Rennaissance Re-examined.* Edited by Victor A. Kramer, 129–147. New York: AMS, 1987.

According to McKay, Bonner is the "most interesting black woman dramatist during the years of the Harlem Renaissance." Bonner is important for her expressionistic forms, her view of the inevitablility of a racial revolution, and her placement of "black American oppression within the framework of world oppression based on the hierarchy of race." With the exception of W.E.B. Du Bois, no one was the equal of Bonner, who "articulat[ed] . . . the political and economic connections between the almost world-wide white domination of colored peoples across the globe and the situation of Afro-Americans in this country." McKay also briefly discusses Bonner in her article "Black Theater and Drama in the 1920s: Years of Growing Pains." *Massachusetts Review* 28 (Winter1987): 615–626.

Sullivan, Esther Beth. "Marita Bonner and the Harlem Renaissance." In *Modern Drama by Women 1880s-1930s: An International Anthology.* Edited by Katherine E. Kelly, 309–317. London: Routledge, 1996.

Second-person narration and allegory, which are used extensively in *The Purple Flower,* are hallmarks of Bonner's dramatic works. According to Sullivan, Bonner's use of the allegorical form closely approximates modern art forms such as expressionism and symbolist drama. *The Purple Flower* also responds to the call by Du Bois to develop drama that is "propagandistic with a vengeance."

Chapter Two
Mary Burrill

Brief Biography

Very little is known about the life of Mary Burrill (1879–1946). Following her graduation from Emerson College of Oratory (Emerson University), she taught high school English for several years before returning in 1929 to Emerson College where she obtained a second bachelor's in literary interpretation. She then went on to direct the School of Expression at the Conservatory of Music in Washington, D.C. According to scholars, two other contemporary women playwrights were known to Burrill: writer May Miller was a student of hers, and scholar Gloria Hull suggests that Angelina Weld Grimké was a close friend, if not a lover.

Burrill wrote two explosive plays: *They That Sit in Darkness* (1919) and *Aftermath* (1928). Unlike Angelina Weld Grimké's genteel drama of racial despair, Burrill's folk dramas were revolutionary in confronting problems facing impoverished blacks living in America. In *Aftermath,* she advocates for blacks' proactive stance in overcoming white injustice. In *They That Sit in Darkness,* Burrill argues for empowering women with the information they need to control their pregnancies.

Burrill's significance lies in her central positioning of poor blacks in her dramas and her provocative solutions to race oppression. Elizabeth Brown-Guillory suggests that Burrill's *Aftermath* "initiates a host of plays that would advocate Hammurabi's code of an eye for an eye." Furthermore, her authentic black dialect negates the idiom put into the mouths of "darkies" by white writers. As James V. Hatch and Ted Shine remark, Burrill's rendition of the black dialect "reveal[s] that there is more to capturing folk language than a substitution of d's for t's."

Profiles and General Criticism

Brown-Guillory, Elizabeth. *Their Place on the Stage: Black Women Playwrights in America.* New York: Praeger, 1990.

While focusing on later black women dramatists, Brown-Guillory includes brief discussions on several female playwrights active during the Harlem Renaissance: Bonner, Burrill, Grimké, Johnson, and Miller.

Burton, Jennifer. "Introduction." In *Zora Neale Hurston, Eulalie Spence, Marita Bonner, and Others: The Prize Plays and Other One-Acts Published in Periodicals.* Edited by Henry Louis Gates, Jr., xix-lx. New York: G.K. Hall,1996.

Burton's solid introduction to the work of early women playwrights provides background on Burrill and briefly explores each of her plays. The introduction is accompanied by extensive notes and a bibliography.

Miller, Jeanne-Marie. "Black Women Playwrights from Grimké to Shange: Selected Synopses of Their Works." In *But Some of Us Are Brave: Black Women's Studies.* Edited by Gloria T. Hull, P.B. Scott, and Barbara Smith, 280–290. Old Westbury, N.Y.: Feminist Press, 1982.

Miller surveys the work of several African-American women whose plays "offer a unique insight into the Black experience," including Angelina Weld Grimké, Marita Bonner, Georgia Douglas Johnson, Mary Burrill, Lorraine Hansberry, Alice Childress, Ntozake Shange, Adrienne Kennedy, Sonia Sanchez, J.E. Franklin, and Martie Charles.

Peterson, Bernard L. *Early Black American Playwrights and Dramatic Writers: A Biographical Directory and Catalog of Plays, Films, and Broadcasting Scripts.* New York: Greenwood, 1990.

The entry on Burrill includes a brief biography, plot summaries, staging history, and list of secondary sources.

Roses, Lorraine Elena, and Ruth Elizabeth Randolph. *Harlem Renaissance and Beyond: Literary Biographies of 100 Black Women Writers, 1900–1945.* Boston: G.K. Hall, 1990.

The authors provide brief biographical information on Burrill and a selected list of primary and secondary sources.

Aftermath

(Published 1919; Krigwa Players, Baltimore, 1928)

Playscripts

"Aftermath." *Liberator* (April 1919): 55–61.

Black Female Playwrights: An Anthology of Plays Before 1950. Edited by Kathy A. Perkins, 55–66. Bloomington: Indiana University Press, 1990.

Black Theatre USA: Plays by African Americans, 1847 to Today. Rev. Ed. Edited by James V. Hatch and Ted Shine, 175–182. New York: Free Press, 1996.

A Century of Plays by American Women. Edited by Rachel France, 55–61. New York: Richards Rosen Press, 1979.

The Roots of African American Drama: An Anthology of Early Plays 1858–1938. Edited by L. Hamalian and James V. Hatch, 134–151. Detroit: Wayne State University Press, 1991.

Zora Neale Hurston, Eulalie Spence, Marita Bonner, and Others; The Prize Plays and Other One-Acts Published in Periodicals. Edited by Henry Louis Gates, Jr., 13–24. New York: G.K. Hall, 1996.

Summary of Play

John, a World War I hero, returns home to his family's cabin in South Carolina to learn that a mob of whites have killed his father and step-brother. Enraged at the injustice of his father's murder and that the whites were not punished, John exclaims, "Them w'ite devuls send me miles erway to suffer an' be shot up fu' the freedom of people I ain't nevah seen, while they're burning and killin' my folks here at home!" Grabbing his war pistol, John disappears into the darkness to confront the men guilty of lynching his father.

Criticism

(No published criticism of *Aftermath* is available)

They That Sit in Darkness

(Published, 1919; revised and retitled *Unto the Third and Fourth Generations,* 1930; published in Emerson College's yearbook and awarded the Best Junior Play of the Year; no record of productions)

Playscripts

Black Female Playwrights: An Anthology of Plays Before 1950. Edited by Kathy A. Perkins, 67–79. Bloomington: Indiana University Press, 1990.

Black Theater U.S.A.: Forty-Five Plays by Black Americans, 1847–1974.

Edited by James V. Hatch and Ted Shine, 178–187. New York: The Free Press, 1974.

Black Theatre USA: Plays by African Americans, 1847 to Today. Rev. Ed. Edited by James V. Hatch and Ted Shine, 182–187. New York: The Free Press, 1996.

"They That Sit in Darkness." *Birth Control Review* (Sept. 1919): 5–8.

Zora Neale Hurston, Eulalie Spence, Marita Bonner, and Others; The Prize Plays and Other One-Acts Published in Periodicals. Edited by Henry Louis Gates, Jr., 25–33. New York: G.K. Hall, 1996.

Summary of Play

Malinda Jasper, frail after giving birth to ten children, is exhausted after completing the day's washing with the help of her seventeen-year-old daughter Lindy, who will be leaving shortly for Tuskegee Institute. That evening, Nurse Elizabeth Shaw visits and scolds Malinda for working after recently giving birth. Malinda feels trapped because she and her husband need money for food. Malinda should be "careful," says Shaw, and not have any more children. But Malinda asks her how. "You got'a be tellin me sumpin' better'n dat, Mis' Liz'beth," she says. While Shaw tells Malinda that she empathizes, she is bound by the oath of a nurse not to inform her about birth control options. Shortly thereafter, Malinda dies. Consequently, Lindy must give up her career aspirations and assume her mother's duties of taking care of her siblings.

Criticism

Abramson, Doris E. "Angelina Weld Grimké, Mary T. Burrill, Georgia Douglas Johnson, and Marita O. Bonner." *Sage* 2, no. 1 (Spring 1985): 9–13.

Abramson observes that Grimké's *Rachel* and Burrill's *They That Sit in Darkness* are similiar in that they both "share a concern for children, the future of the race." Their differences lie in the choice each protagonist makes concerning childbirth. In *Rachel,* the main character chooses not to have children because of the treatment they receive from whites. On the other hand, Burrill's Malinda and her husband, out of ignorance of birth control methods, have too many children to care for responsibly.

Burke, Sally. *American Feminist Playwrights: A Critical History.* New York: Twayne, 1996.

They That Sit in Darkness was published in a special issue of Margaret Sanger's *Birth Control Review* devoted to "The Negroes' Need for Birth Control, As Seen by Themselves." According to Burke, Sanger and Burrill both realized that women, especially black women, were kept ignorant about birth control. The play focuses on the consequences of this ignorance: birth defects, hungry children, parents' exhaustion, and unfullfilled aspirations. Burrill's race drama, Burke points out, is also important for its genuine dialect, "which countered the sometimes unintelligible attempts of white playwrights to write black dialect."

McKay, Nellie. "'What Were They Saying?': Black Women Playwrights of the Harlem Renaissance." In *The Harlem Renaissance Re-examined.* Edited by Victor A. Kramer, 129–147. New York: AMS, 1987.

Burrill's play illustrates the intersection of race, class, and sex. Poor black women are oppressed and limited by the fact of their race, gender, and income status. Unlike wealthier women, poor black women do not have access to health care and information concerning birth control; they must rely on tax-supported health agencies, which participate in the suppression of health information. Furthermore, wealthy women "have done little to alleviate the political pressure that deprives poor women of similar access." McKay points out that "contrary to some beliefs commonly held by some people in the rest of the society, [*They That Sit in Darkness*] points out that the women caught in this situation are neither oblivious to nor passive in their attitudes to it. They are anxious to change it."

Chapter Three
Alice Childress

Brief Biography

Before Alice Childress (1916–1994), black female playwrights focused on racial inequities experienced by blacks of both genders. Childress, also committed to exposing racial oppression, placed her female characters center stage. She is considered to be a transitional writer whose plays anticipated the work of contemporary dramatists such as Ntozake Shange.

"Uncompromising" is a descriptor of Alice Childress that frequently appears in interviews, discussions, and critiques about her art and aesthetic as a playwright. She is considered uncompromising in the sense that she singlemindedly dedicated herself to writing plays that dramatized the black experience as unvarnished truth, not truth tempered to ease the conscience of white audiences. But Childress paid a high price for adhering to the truth as she saw it—she remained on the fringe of mainstream theater. Two of her plays, *Trouble in Mind* (1955) and *Wedding Band: A Love/Hate Story in Black and White* (1966) may have had Broadway openings if she had been willing to make the changes requested of her by white producers. But she was not. As playwright-author Mitchell aptly observes, "Miss Childress represents a figure that is not unknown to students of the American drama—a major talent that is rarely produced" (Mitchell, *Black Drama,* 169).

Alice Childress was the great-granddaughter of a slave. She was born on October 12, 1916, in Charleston, South Carolina, but spent most of her youth growing up in Harlem; she died of cancer in Manhattan on August 14, 1994. At the time of her death she was living with her husband, the musician-teacher Nathan Woodard, who wrote the music for Childress's play *Gullah.*

During the 1940s Childress began her professional development in the theater as an actress with the American Negro Theatre. She performed in *On Striver's Row* (1940), *Natural Man* (1941), and the hit *Anna Lucasta*

(1944). Participating in the American Negro Theatre grounded her in all aspects of the theater, both onstage and off. Besides acting, she directed, coached other actors, ran the personnel office for a while, and finally wrote plays.

Her experiences with the American Negro Theatre greatly impressed upon her that most plays produced dealt with male-oriented issues. The paucity of scripts about women's issues challenged Childress to become a dramatist. In addition to feminism, Childress's plays reflect her passionate interest in the intersection of race and class. Like Ntozake Shange and Lorraine Hansberry, Childress wrote about the lower middle class, traditionally the invisible people in drama. She believed that writers should not ignore those experiences that show blacks in a less positive light—"Black writers cannot afford to abuse or neglect the so-called ordinary character who represents a part of ourselves, the self twice denied, first by racism and [then] by class indifference."

Unlike the works of black experimentalists such as Ntozake Shange and Adrienne Kennedy, Childress's experimentations were in content rather than form. Her plays conformed to the conventions of realism. Childress's innovations were grounded in character and themes. As Elizabeth Brown-Guillory points out, Childress was instrumental in bringing new images to the stage for females, avoiding the typecast roles of the black woman as fallen woman, frigid, domineering, or helpless. Gayle Austin emphasizes that Childress's plays are important in the study of feminist critical theory because of her refusal to express relationships (black/white, male/female, North/South) in binary oppositions, "with their implications that one is superior to the other."

Childress accumulated many awards and accolades for her work as a playwright. She won an Obie for *Trouble in Mind.* In 1968 she received a Radcliffe Alumnae Graduate Society Medal for Distinguished Achievement, and in 1977 she was awarded the Paul Robeson Medal of Distinction for "Outstanding Achievement in Theater Arts by the Black Filmmakers Hall of Fame in 1977. In 1993 she received the Lifetime Career Achievement Award from the Association for Theater in Higher Education.

Like so many other women playwrights, Childress published in other venues. She wrote several young adult novels, including *A Hero Ain't Nothin' But a Sandwich* (1973), *Rainbow Jordan* (1981), and *Those Other People* (1989), as well as the adult novel *A Short Walk* (1979), and a collection of short stories, *Like One of the Family . . . Conversations from a Domestic's Life* (1986).

Profiles

"Alice Childress." In *Interviews with Contemporary Women Playwrights.* Edited by Kathleen Betsko and Rachel Koenig, 62–74. New York: Beech Tree Books, 1987.

Childress is included in this landmark volume of thirty interviews of international women playwrights who have been successful in the commercial theater. Childress's interview focuses on her views of race relations, especially the critics' response to *Wedding Band,* her play about interracial relationships. On feminism, she says, "I am a black woman and I am a black woman playwright. I'm neither proud nor ashamed of it. This is our fight and our struggle. I'll take the responsiblity on." This interview is a must for anyone studying Childress's aesthetics and feminism.

Brown-Guillory, Elizabeth. "Alice Childress: A Pioneering Spirit." *Sage: A Scholarly Journal on Black Women* 4, no. 1 (Spring 1987): 66–68.

Brown-Guillory encourages Childress to talk about the forces that shaped her passion for reading and writing, such as her grandmother Eliza ("She wasn't your typical grandmother"), the Salem Church in Harlem ("I remember how people . . . used to get up and tell their troubles to everybody"), her teacher Miss Thomas, and her access to the library. Childress also reminisces about her start in the theater and articulates her creative processes and the work she is currently doing.

Childress, Alice. "But I Do My Thing." *New York Times* (Feb. 2, 1969): D9.

Childress's article is part of a group of pieces by well-known black theater artists, each of whom addresses the dilemma for many black artists of whether to concentrate their creative efforts on developing a theater in the black community or to focus their energies on Broadway and Off-Broadway venues. Alice Childress seems to say that black artists should not be restricted to either realm but urges them to "Cope! cope anyhow, anywhere you can, to the best of your ability."

———. "For a Negro Theatre." *Masses and Mainstream* 4 (Feb. 1951): 61–64.

Childress articulates the need for a black theater to nurture the creative talents of black artists and to develop an aesthetic for black playwrights and other theater artists. Blacks working in the theater, Childress asserts, do not get the necessary training or education from white schools and theater classes, whose curriculum is based on the cultural heritage of the white man. As Childress remarks, "The Negro people's theater must study and teach not only what has been taught before but found and establish a new approach to [the] study of the Negro in the theater." See related articles by Childress in *Negro Digest* (Jan. 1968): 36, 85–87, and *Black Women Writers (1950–1980): A Critical Evaluation.* Edited by Mari Evans, 111–116. Garden City, N.Y.: Anchor Books, 1984.

———. "Keynote Address." In *International Women Playwrights: Voices of Identity and Transformation—Proceedings of the First International Women Playwrights Conference, October 18–23, 1988.* Metuchen, N.J.: Scarecrow Press, 1993.

Childress remarks that women writers will "create new forms, not to be stylish, but because they have to find the best way to express themselves without asking permission. We have to learn how *not* to put down ourselves." Through negative training, women have been conditioned to minimize themselves. "Soon," says Childress, "we will begin to understand that formally uneducated women are not fools and are waiting in the past for present interpretation."

———."Knowing the Human Condition." In *Black American Literature and Humanism.* Edited by R. Baxter Miller, 8–9. Lexington: University Press of Kentucky, 1981.

Childress urges black writers to address the truth as they see it, despite increasing pressure to please mass audiences. She encourages writers to cover all segments of the black experience, not just those that promote a positive image of the black community.

Contemporary Authors: A Bio-Bibliographical Guide. Vol. 3, New Revision Series. Edited by Ann Evory, 122–124. Detroit: Gale Research, 1981.

The entry includes a biographical sketch and general comments on her work by critics and by Childress herself.

Contemporary Literary Criticism: Excerpts from Criticism of the Works of Today's Novelists, Poets, Playwrights, and Other Creative Writers. Vol.12. Edited by Dedria Bryfonski, 104–109. Detroit: Gale Research, 1980.

Curb, Rosemary. "Alice Childress." In *Dictionary of Literary Biography:* Vol. 7. *Twentieth Century American Dramatists.* Edited by John MacNicholas, 118–124. Detroit: Gale Research, 1981.

This extensive introductory essay on the life and work of Childress includes a primary and secondary bibliography. See also Trudier Harris. *Dictionary of Literary Biography:* Vol. 38. *Afro-American Writers After 1955: Dramatists and Prose Writers.* Edited by Thadious M. Davis, 67–79. Detroit: Gale Research, 1985.

DeVine, Lawrence. "Playwright Childress Has 'A Certain Following.'" *Detroit Free Press* (March 11, 1993): 1F, 3F.

Childress is profiled on the occasion of the Detroit Theatre Company's dramatization of selected monologues from Childress's novel *A Hero Ain't Nothin But a Sandwich.*

Downey, Maureen. "Alice Childress: Blacks Must Write About All Issues." *Atlanta Constitution* (March. 27, 1986): C1–2.

Downey reports on Childress's participation in "Black Women: Images, Styles and Substance," a seminar sponsored by Georgia State University. Childress reflects on her life and her work as a novelist and playwright.

Holliday, Polly. "I Remember Alice Childress." *Southern Quarterly* 25, no. 3 (Spring 1987): 63–65.

Polly Holliday, who played the part of Annabelle in Joseph Papp's production of Childress's *Wedding Band* at the Public Theatre in 1972, fondly reminisces about working with the playwright during rehearsals.

Maguire, Roberta. "Alice Childress." In *The Playwright's Art: Conversations with Contemporary American Dramatists.* Edited by Jackson R. Bryer, 48–69. New Brunswick, N.J.: Rutgers University Press, 1995.

This is a substantial and insightful interview with Childress that builds upon an earlier Childress interview by Kathleen Betsko and Rachel Koenig ("Alice Childress." In *Interviews with Contemporary Women Playwrights.* New York: Beech Tree Books, 1987. *See Chapter 3, Profiles, Betsko and Koenig*).

Childress talks about the problems she encountered in staging some of her plays, such as *Trouble in Mind* and *Wedding Band.* She addresses the lack of politics in contemporary plays and notes that critics have told her that they admire her work but that it is "too political." Childress remarks that critics have deliberately missed political implications in her plays. For example, in *Wedding Band,* Childress claims that critics failed to address the John C. Calhoun speech delivered by Herman; they gloss over it by referring to it as Herman's "creat[ing] a scene in the backyard." The interview also touches upon Childress's feminist views and artistic vision, as well as the playwriting process.

Peterson, Bernard L. *Contemporary Black American Playwrights and Their Plays: A Biographical Directory and Dramatic Index,* 106–108. Westport, Conn.: Greenwood, 1988.

Peterson provides a biographical sketch and a brief staging history of Childress's plays.

Wright, Sarah E. "Alice Childress: 'This Little Light of Mine, I'm Gonna Let it Shine.'" *N.Y. Amsterdam News* (Aug. 27, 1994): 12, 33.

Wright highlights the achievements of Childress.

Additional Biographical Entries

Black Writers: A Selection of Sketches from Contemporary Authors. Edited by Linda Metzger, 100–103. Detroit: Gale Research, 1989

"Alice Childress" *The Call and Post* (Aug. 25, 1994): 3B.

Contemporary American Dramatists. Edited by K.A. Berney, 93–96. London: St. James Press, 1994.

Contemporary Dramatists. 3rd Edition. Edited by James Vinson, 87–88. New York: St. Martin's, 1982.

"Alice Childress" *Ebony* 14 (Apr.1959):

Wright, Sarah E. "Celebrities Remember Alice Childress with Love." N.*Y. Amsterdam News* (Nov. 19, 1994): 22, 50

"Alice Childress" *The Weekly Journal* (Sep., 8, 1994): 17.

General Criticism

Brown-Guillory, Elizabeth. *Their Place on the Stage: Black Women Playwrights in America.* New York: Praeger, 1990.

Brown-Guillory's landmark study situates the position of black female dramatists within a sociopolitical context. Her major focus is on the major plays of three significant writers: Alice Childress, Lorraine Hansberry, and Ntozake Shange. These three playwrights, observes Brown-Guillory, "are crucial links in the development of black playwriting in America from the 1950s to 1980s. It is because of their dogged determination to have their voices heard that these black women dramatists have been able to carve an indelible place for themselves on the American stage."

Burke, Sally. American Feminist Playwrights: A Critical History. New York: Twayne, 1996.

Burke includes a survey of Childress's plays in the first sociohistorical examination of American feminist dramatists. Burke credits Childress for bringing "feminist drama from the 1940s to tomorrow, igniting possibilities inherent in the future for her sister dramatists."

Fabre, Genevieve. *Drumbeats, Masks and Metaphor: Contemporary Afro-American Theatre.* Cambridge, Mass.: Harvard University Press, 1983.

Fabre examines contemporary black theater writing within a sociocultural context. She categorizes black theater as militant theater and theater of experience; she asserts that both are based on a quest for identity. Although she reserves her extensive discussions to black male dramatists, she briefly mentions the work of Alice Childress, Ntozake Shange, Adrienne Kennedy, Sonia Sanchez, and Micki Grant.

Hay, Samuel A. "Alice Childress's Dramatic Structure." In *Black Women Writers (1950–1980): A Critical Evaluation.* Edited by Mari Evans, 117–128. Garden City, N.Y.: Anchor Press, 1984.

Hay observes that Childress is fundamentally a traditionalist in terms of dramatic structure—that is, her plays have a beginning, a middle, and an end. Each episode builds upon the preceding ones, and she avoids experimental devices. However, unlike the conventional episodic frameworks used by Eugene O'Neill, Tennessee Williams, and Arthur Miller to dramatize psychological characterizations, Childress exchanges characterization for theme. Consequently, according to Hay, "the substitution strains the traditional structure because Childress does not reveal the theme through characterization but through argumentation." Of Childress's seventeen plays, Hay analyzes *Florence, Trouble in Mind, Wine in the Wilderness,* and *Mojo: A Black Love Story.*

Jennings, La Vinia Delois. *Alice Childress.* New York: Twayne, 1995.

This is the first full-length examination of Childress's work. Jennings describes Childress as a transitional writer whose female-centered plays anticipated the work of Ntozake Shange and Sonia Sanchez. The book provides a good introduction to the life and work of Childress as well as analyses of each play and discussions of the main themes and influences within sociohistorical contexts. Substantial discussions are provided for *Mojo, String, Trouble in Mind, Wedding Band,* and *Wine in the Wilderness.* See also Jennings's entry on Childress in *Contemporary Poets, Dramatists, Essayists, and Novelists of the South.* Edited by Robert Bain and Joseph Flora, 104–116. Westport, Conn.: Greenwood, 1994.

Miller, Jeanne-Marie. "Black Women Playwrights from Grimké to Shange: Selected Synopses of Their Works." In *But Some of Us Are Brave: Black Women's Studies.* Edited by Gloria T. Hull, P.B. Scott, and Barbara Smith, 280–290. Old Westbury, N.Y.: Feminist Press, 1982.

Miller surveys the work of several African-American women whose plays "offer a unique insight into the Black experience," including Angelina Weld Grimké, Marita Bonner, Georgia Douglas Johnson, Mary Burrill, Lorraine Hansberry, Alice Childress, Ntozake Shange, Adrienne Kennedy, Sonia Sanchez, J.E. Franklin, and Martie Charles.

———. "Images of Women in Plays by Black Playwrights." *CLA Journal* 20, no. 4 (June 1977): 494–507. Reprinted in *Women in American Theatre.* Edited by Helen Krich Chinoy and Linda Walsh Jenkins, 256–262. New York: Theatre Communications Group, 1987.

Miller discusses the position of the black woman in selected plays of several African-American playwrights, including Childress's *Trouble in Mind, Wedding Band, Wine in the Wilderness,* and *Florence.*

Florence, A One-Act Play

(Committee for the Negro in the Arts, Harlem, 1950)

Playscripts

"Florence." Masses and Mainstream 3 (Oct. 1950): 34–47.

Wines in the Wilderness: Plays by African American Women from the Harlem Renaissance to the Present. Edited by Elizabeth Brown-Guillory, 111–121. New York: Greenwood, 1990.

Summary of Play

Childress wrote *Florence,* her first play, overnight to win a wager she had with some of her fellow actors from the American Negro Theatre, among them Sidney Poitier, who believed that in a play about blacks and whites, only a "life and death thing like lynching is interesting on stage" (Abramson, 189).

This one-act dramatizes the interaction of two women, one black, the other white, in a Jim Crow railway station in a small Southern town. The play opens with the two women separated by a low railing: The black woman, Mrs. Whitney, sits in the "Colored" section, and Mrs. Carter sits in the section reserved for "Whites." The women talk, most of their discussion centering on Mrs. Whitney's daughter Florence, an aspiring actress who is trying to break away from playing the "maid" roles in professional New York theater. During the course of their conversation, Mrs. Carter's self-described liberalism is exposed for what it is: racist stereotyping.

Florence, the unseen daughter who attempts to break from a "hostile world" to pursue a lifestyle of her choosing, prefigures the positive images of black women in Childress's later plays, as well as in the plays of Lorraine Hansberry and Ntozake Shange.

Criticism

Abramson, Doris E. *Negro Playwrights in American Theatre, 1925–1959.* New York: Columbia University Press, 1969.

Abramson comments that although *Florence* is a "static" play, it is strong enough to "prove that everyday situations can be dramatized." Furthermore, this one-act demonstrates that Childress has a good ear for dialogue and a "fine sense of characterization."

Brown-Guillory, Elizabeth. "Black Women Playwrights: Exorcising Myths." *Phylon* 68, no. 3 (Fall 1987): 230–238.

According to Brown-Guillory, Childress, like Hansberry and Shange, wrote plays that "present a vital slice of [black] life." She offers realistic images of the black experience that differ markedly from the perceptions of male writers, both black and white. Brown-Guillory demonstrates how Childress employs the image of the evolving black woman in *Florence.* Florence, whose husband died at the hands of whites, represents a positive image of black womanhood because she refuses to rely on racism to justify her victim status and pursues her dream of making it as an actor in the New York theater.

Mitchell, Loften. *Black Drama: The Story of the American Negro In the Theatre.* New York: Hawthorn Books, 1967.

Mitchell briefly discusses *Florence* and *Gold Through the Trees.*

Gold Through the Trees

(American Negro Theatre, Club Baron Theater, 1952)

Writer and director Loften Mitchell lauded *Gold Through the Trees* as a "highly successful . . . beautifully mounted [play, which] enjoyed pleased audiences." *Gold* marks the first play written by an African-American woman to be produced professionally. Childress dramatizes blacks' oppression historically, that is, their enslavement in America, as well as their struggle in South Africa. Woven into the play are traditional African dances, modern dance, blues rhythms, Harriet Tubman, and the civil rights movement. *Gold* signifies Childress's commitment to write meaningful dramas relevant to the black experience.

Criticism

Abramson, Doris E. *Negro Playwrights in American Theatre, 1925–1959.* New York: Columbia University Press, 1969.

Abramson sees this play as an attempt "to make American Negroes proud of their past history" and as "further proof of Miss Childress' creative talent in the theatre."

Jefferson, Miles M. "The Negro on Broadway 1951–1952—Another Transparent Season." *Phylon* 13 (3rd Quarter 1952): 205.

Jefferson includes the Club Baron's production of *Gold Through the Trees* in his annual assessment of Broadway and Off-Broadway productions.

Mojo: A Black Love Story

(New Heritage Theatre, 1970)

Playscripts

Best Short Plays of the World. Edited by Stanley Richards, 126–137. New York: Crown Publishers, 1973.

Mojo and String: Two Plays. Dramatists Play Service, 1971.

"Mojo." Black World 20 (April 1971): 54–82.

Summary of Play

Director Ernie McClintock considers *Mojo* and Childress's *Wine in the Wilderness* as two of the classic dramas of contemporary black theater. *Mojo* is a story about Teddy and Irene, who are no longer married but who have shared a special bond over the years. The play opens as Teddy, a man in the "numbers business," is getting ready to go out when he is interrupted by Irene, who shows up unexpectedly after a long absence. She visits him—after learning that she has cancer and must face an uncertain operation—to settle some "unfinished business that [they] may have." While sharing memories of their past lives, Irene reveals that she divorced him all those years ago because she felt that he "didn't seem to love [her] like [she] loved [him]." Moreover, she informs Teddy that she gave up their baby, which he didn't know about, to a "professional" couple. By the end of the play, Teddy and Irene are closer and Irene "feels great" and that she's ready to let a "white man in a white suit . . . stick a knife in [her]."

Criticism and Performance Reviews

Bailey, Peter A. "Stage: Contemporary Black Classical Theatre." *Black Collegian* 14 (Jan./Feb. 1984): 34.

Bailey briefly discusses *Mojo* and *Wine in the Wilderness.*

Brown-Guillory, Elizabeth. "Black Women Playwrights: Exorcising Myths." *Phylon* 68, no. 3 (Fall 1987): 230–238.

The black male in search of his manhood is a theme that appears in several of Childress's plays. In *Mojo,* for example, Teddy represents the black man who does not allow oppression and poverty to become "fragmented" or "abusive." He overcomes the pain of being black in a white society to become a "fine black man."

Kupa, Kushauri. "Close-Up: The New York Scene." *Black Theatre* 6 (1972): 38–40.

Although Kushauri liked the production of *Mojo* by the New Heritage Theatre, he contends that the play should have more action to counteract the excessive talking and criticized Childress for contrived scenes: "that old formula of playwriting which takes the characters through all sorts of conflicts and emotional changes before finally bringing them to rest in the arms of a happy ending."

Lowell, Sandra. *Los Angeles Times* (Oct. 13, 1978), sec. 4: 28, 29.

The Inner City Cultural Center performed two Childress one-acts, *Mojo* and *String.* Lowell's assessment of the plays is lukewarm. She contends that while both deal with pain, the characters do not communicate their pain well; they and Childress "attack the pain too hard for us to deal with easily."

Mahoney, John C. "*Mojo* at the L.A. Cultural Center." *Los Angeles Times* (May 18, 1982): sec. 6: 3.

Mahoney delivers a much more positive review of *Mojo* than Lowell did in 1978. The production, directed by Beah Richards at the Los Angeles Cultural Center, "is no mentholated waterfall romance of television commercial mannequins, but a love story of survivors in a hostile world, who are even more apprehensive about expressing their tender feelings than the rest of us."

Richardson, Alice. "Two Childress One-Acts at Hadley Players." *N.Y. Amsterdam News* (New York) (March 12, 1988): 33.

Richardson provides no critical information about this production of *Mojo* and *Wine in the Wilderness,* as performed by the Hadley Players of Harlem. She does comment that *Mojo* centers on the importance of roots and echoes Malcolm X, "A people without history is a people without roots."

Moms: A Praise Play for a Black Comedienne

(Hudson Guild Theater, 1987)

Playscripts

(No published playscripts are available)

Summary of Play

Childress wrote *Moms* to honor the legendary comedienne Jackie "Moms" Mabley. Mabley, played by Clarice Taylor, weaves jokes, songs, and dance with bittersweet memories of her life to an audience of two: her maid and confidante, Epatha Merkerson, and Grenoldo Frazier, her foil and piano accompanist. As Mel Gussow points out (3.47), nothing escaped her ridicule, including herself. Mingled with her recollections are "the earthly, impudent, broadly satiric routines" that Moms performed largely in black-owned nightclubs and theaters and later in films and on television. The music was written by Alice Childress, her husband, Nathan Woodward, and Grenoldo Frazier.

An interesting note about *Moms* is Childress's lawsuit against Clarice Taylor, who won an Obie for her performance in Childress's play. Taylor later starred in a version of *Moms* that was subtitled "The First Lady of Comedy," which was written by Ben Caldwell and produced at the Place Theater in 1987. Childress accused Taylor and her associates of infringement of copyright: "They took my play, redid it a little and put someone else's name on it. I'm not concerned with money. I just want my play back." Taylor countered that she could not be sued for copying Childress's play because she and Childress coauthored the work. The U.S. Federal District Court later ruled in Childress's favor. See "Author of *Moms* Sues Actress over Copyright." *New York Times* (Oct. 22, 1987): C17; "Author of Play About Jackie 'Moms' Mabley Obtains Summary Judgment in Copyright infringement Action. *Entertainment Law Reporter* (March. 1991): 5–6; Squiers, Deborah. "Author of 'Moms' Mabley Play Prevails in Copyright Claim. *New York Law Journal* (Nov. 30, 1990): 1, 31.

Performance Reviews

Beaufort, John. "*Moms* Pays Tribute to Black Comedienne." *Christian Science Monitor* (Feb. 13, 1987): 28.

Moms is more than a "fragmentary life story" of an entertainer; "affection and admiration" coalesce in the writing as well as the performance of Moms by Clarice Taylor.

Feingold, Michael. "Mother Complex." *Village Voice* (Feb. 17, 1987): 100.

Feingold praises *Moms* as a sketch of the turbulent life of Moms Mabley. Childress manages to avoid the "and-then-I-played" kind of lecturing that plagues so many theatrical biographies of entertainers. Between the jokes, songs, and dances, Childress offers the audience a glimpse of Moms as a complex woman. But Feingold wishes that Childress would have explored the depths of that complexity. "It would be nice to see more historical detail, more inner expression" he writes. Although Childress hints at Moms's lesbianism in the play, he maintains that she fails to explore the nature of it. Feingold wonders if it was "a by-product of vaudeville's casual mores, or a revulsion of men [having been raped at age eleven]." Furthermore, he questions how it influenced her work and her relations in the male dominated theater. But Feingold concedes that this is a "praise" play and not intended as a penetrating character study: "Its random strokes make a good pencil portrait of a beloved artist."

Gussow, Mel. "The Stage: *Moms*." *New York Times* (Feb. 10, 1987): C16.

Gussow writes that Childress "shrewdly gives Moms center stage and lets her comic sensibility speak for itself." He disagrees with the popular sentiment that Moms was a vulgarian but rather "a humorist who used earthiness as an armament as part of a considerable arsenal." Unlike other reviewers, Gussow thought that Clarice Taylor was "not entirely secure as Moms." Although he found her delivery to be "disarming" he notes that she seemed on the "verge of forgetting her lines."

Oliver, Edith. "Moms." *New Yorker* 63 (Feb. 23, 1987): 105.

Oliver finds the play's routines and jokes "very funny—not a dud among them . . . and the scenes, Miss Childress's contribution, are firm and telling." Childress "writes with considerable tact, with just enough story to keep things moving and varied and to display the best of Moms' wares."

Sinclair, Abiola. "Childress, Taylor Triumphantly Mother *Moms.*" *Amsterdam News* (New York) (Feb. 28, 1987): 32.

The play's success predicated on Taylor's portrayal and Childress's talents as a playwright. "Seeing a Childress play is a lesson in playwriting," Sinclair writes.

String

(Adapted from Guy de Maupassant's "A Piece of String," Negro Ensemble Company, 1969)

Playscript

String. New York: Dramatists Play Service, 1969.

Summary of Play

The action revolves around an old man who is invited to a picnic. While there, he picks up a piece of string. Shortly afterwards, a wallet is missing and someone recalls seeing the old man pick up something. The old man unsuccessfully tries to convince the picnickers that his find was string, not the wallet. Meanwhile, the wallet is found behind a tree. Everyone believes he planted it there and "graciously or contemptuously, agrees to forget the incident." He protests his innocence but to no avail—his denials "do not make the slightest dent in their crass magnanimity."

Criticism and Performance Reviews

Barnes, Clive. "Theater." *New York Times* (April. 2, 1969). Excerpted in *Contemporary Literary Criticism: Excerpts from Criticism of the Works of Today's Novelists, Poets, Playwrights, and Other Creative Writers.* Vol.12. Edited by Dedria Bryfonski, 104–109. Detroit: Gale Research, 1980.

Barnes observes that *String* fails to measure up to Guy de Maupassant's "A Piece of String," from which the play is adapted. According to the critic, "the play drags out."

Contemporary Literary Criticism: Excerpts from Criticism of the Works of Today's Novelists, Poets, Playwrights, and Other Creative Writers. Vol. 12. Edited by Dedria Bryfonski, 104–109. Detroit: Gale Research, 1980.

Kerr, Walter. "So They Will Live Together." *New York Times* (April 13, 1969): sec. 2: 1, 20.

This review of *String,* as performed by the Negro Ensemble Company, is not well written, and Kerr's comments are not clearly supported. He seems to not like the play, finding fault with its staging. Kerr remarks that the "actor [unclear as to which actor he is referring to] has been given nothing to do except poke feebly at the various points of escape, pawing the ground like an invisibly reined horse."

Lowell, Sandra. "Young, Old Facing Up to Death." *Los Angeles Times* (Oct. 13, 1978): sec. 4: 28, 29.

In her review, Lowell claims that although *String,* at the Inner City Cultural Center in Los Angeles, engages the audience with comical characters, the play ultimately fails because the "old man doesn't communicate his pain when his little world falls apart."

Oliver, Edith."Off Broadway." *The New Yorker* 45 (April 12, 1969): 131.

Oliver considers *String* to be the best of the third season of the Negro Ensemble Company's "Evening of One Acts." She "enjoyed the comic byplay—hurt feelings and hasty amends and bitchery lightly overlaid with daintiness" in the otherwise somber play.

Pasolli, Robert. "Theatre: An Evening of One Acts." *Village Voice* (April 10, 1969): 47.

Pasolli's lukewarm review praises *String* as an "entertaining, conventional character drama."

Trouble in Mind: A Comedy-Drama in Two Acts
(Greenwich Mews Theatre, 1955)

Playscripts

Black Drama in America: An Anthology. Edited by Darwin T. Turner, 291–346. Washington, D.C.: Howard University Press, 1994.

Black Theater: A 20th-Century Collection. Edited by Lindsay Patterson, 135–174. New York: Dodd, Mead, 1971.

Plays by American Women: 1930–1960. Edited by Judith E. Barlow, 469–542. New York: Applause, 1994.

Summary of Play

Trouble in Mind, for which Childress won an Obie in 1956, was her first play to be performed Off-Broadway. Unfortunately, this production did not move to Broadway, despite positive notices, because Childress refused to make changes in interpretation to appease white audiences.

In the work, Childress mocks the so-called liberal theater's attempt to address racial prejudice in America. The action takes place during the 1950s when a group of black actors and a white director are rehearsing a Broadway play, written and produced by whites, about a lynching in the South. Art mimics life: the black actors find themselves not only playing stereotyped roles but also deferring to "the man." They are advised to "be pleasant. Do what you're told without question. Don't make waves." In short, if they do not play by the rules, they will not survive. As Sheldon, one of the black actors who plays the game very well, tells the protagonist, Wiletta, "Yeah, we all *mind* [about playing stereotyped roles], but you gotta swallow what you mind. 'Mind' don't buy beans."

The tension grows between the director and Wiletta, a veteran actress of stereotyped roles. Wiletta questions the authenticity of the roles, especially hers as a black mammy. She tells the director that a black mother would never relinquish her son to white authorities in the name of white justice. She asks,"Why can't he escape?" To which the director replies, "We don't want to antagonize the audience." Childress dramatizes what British reviewer Michael Billington describes as the "clash of egos and priniciples in which authentic black experience confronts the Great White Way."

Criticism and Performance Reviews

Abramson, Doris E. *Negro Playwrights in the American Theatre, 1925–1959,* 189–205. New York: Columbia University Press, 1969. Excerpted in *Contemporary Literary Criticism: Excerpts from Criticism of the Works of Today's Novelists, Poets, Playwrights, and Other Creative Writers.* Vol.12. Edited by Dedria Bryfonski, 104–109. Detroit: Gale Research, 1980.

Unfortunately, Abramson devotes much of her discussion to summarizing *Trouble in Mind* rather than offering a critical examination of the play. Although she allows that the primary significance of the work is that the majority of the roles are for blacks, she pinpoints several problems associated with the play. First of all, Childress's characters lack individuality and depth because of her constant "assaults on racial prejudice." Second, Childress's manipulation of her characters is overt; the audience is "very much aware of the author pulling strings." And third, although the characters and dialogue are "interesting," they "ring false whenever they are saturated with sermonizing."

Austin, Gayle. "Alice Childress: Black Woman Playwright as Feminist Critic." *Southern Quarterly* 25, no. 3 (Spring 1987): 53–62.

Austin concurs with Rosemary Curb (3.83) and others who feel that Childress has been neglected by theater scholars. Austin attributes this neglect to the fact that Childress was "ahead of her times in the combination of subject and treatments." One of Childress's major contributions, according to the author, is that her plays portray realistic images of blacks and whites; they dispel several "binary oppositions so prevalent in Western society—black/white, male/female, north/south, artist/critic—with their implications that one is superior to the other." Thus Childress's ideology and aesthetics are important to modern criticism and feminist critical theory. Austin analyzes *Trouble in Mind* and *Wine in the Wilderness* within the context of what she sees as the three stages of feminist literary criticism and discusses how these plays employ the "concept of absence."

Billington, Michael. *"Theatre: Trouble in Mind." The Guardian* (Oct. 14, 1992): Features, 4.

Billington reviews the premiere of *Trouble in Mind* at the Tricycle Theatre in London. Childress's message of the artist's responsibility to protest racial inequities far outweighs the play's weaknesses, which include "one of those 'memory' speeches . . . the blight of American drama." As Wiletta, Carmen Munro "delivers her lines with just the right angry, purposeful conviction."

Evans, Donald T. *Black World* 20 (Feb. 1971): 43–45. Excerpted in *Contemporary Literary Criticism: Excerpts from Criticism of the Works of Today's Novelists, Poets, Playwrights, and Other Creative Writers.* Vol. 12. Edited by Dedria Bryfonski, 104–109. Detroit: Gale Research, 1980.

Evans points out that Childress "shows the difficulty of working in *the man's* theater and maintaining one's integrity and identity." *Trouble* explains why the black arts movement emerged so that it could counter "the half-human creatures [whites] created and maintained in asinine comedy after comedy."

Gelb, Arthur. "Theater." *New York Times* (Nov. 5, 1955): 23.

Childress's portrayal of the dilemma confronting black actors playing stereotyped roles is "witty" and he praises her "avoid[ance] of any impassioned sermonizing."

Jones, Rick. "Pathos and Revolt." *Evening Standard.* (Oct. 13, 1992): 42.

According to Jones, "Crude it may be, but [*Trouble,* Tricycle Theatre, London] is ultimately one of the more affecting dramas currently playing." Childress exploits the plot's satiric potential to the fullest. However, Jones feels that the entrance of the new actor serves no usefulness "apart from boosting the numbers of patronising whites." The time and space could be better used to enlighten the spectators as to the plot of the inner play. But for these faults, "it is a tragedy that *Trouble* has not been seen before in this country."

Keyssar, Helene. "Foothills: Precursors of Feminist Drama." In *Feminist Theatre: An Introduction to Plays of Contemporary British and American Women,* 31–31. London: Macmillan, 1984.

Keyssar acknowledges that Childress is one of the first female playwrights to write complex roles for women. While *Trouble in Mind* is about race relations, it is also a play "*about* roles in which female stereotypes are acknowledged and jarred."

Killens, John O. "The Literary Genius of Alice Childress." In *Black Women Writers (1950–1980): A Critical Evaluation.* Edited by Mari Evans, 129–133. Garden City, N.Y.: Anchor Books, 1984.

Killens celebrates Alice Childress, whom he refers to as "a tremendously gifted artist who has consistently used her genius . . . to change the image we have of ourselves as human beings, Black and white." He briefly discusses Childress's *Trouble in Mind* and *Wedding Band.*

Kingston, Jeremy. "Black Comedy Finds Its Roots." *The Times* (London) (Oct. 15, 1992): Features.

Kingston praises *Trouble* (Tricycle Theatre), which he contends is the first Childress play to be produced in London. He commends this "fascinating and spirited play" for its unique way of using farce to dramatize racial prejudice. As Wiletta, Carmen Munroe's parody of all her past "gushin' and grievin" roles is "sublimely comic and socially astute." Childress's dialogue is "rich in irony." Childress is weak only in the scenes in which multiple conversations occur.

Koyama, Christine. *"Trouble: A Lack of Truth." Chicago Tribune* (Apr. 5, 1984): sec. 5: 10.

This production of *Trouble in Mind* by the Kuumba Theatre Company totally misses the mark, according to Koyama. This "humorless and heavy-handed" version reduces Childress's play to melodramatic stereotypes. For example, David Cromer, who plays Al Manners, is a "petulant, prancing Caligula," and director Chuck Smith has transformed the rehearsal scenes into "bad turn-of-the-century melodrama: broad gestures, booming voices, and not an ounce of truth." Koyama finds this a disappointing production for such a "landmark" play.

Richardson, Alice. *"Trouble in Mind: Being Black and a Performer." N.Y. Amsterdam News* (June 13, 1987): 29.

Richardson reviews the production of *Trouble in Mind* by the HADLEY Players of Harlem and finds that the "beauty" of this play-within-a-play is its dramatization of how blacks survive in the theater world as well as in the world at large. Childress has "brilliantly laced her play with insight and meaning" of black survival, which entails "not displaying their intelligence, even when they are a thousand steps ahead of their components." Richardson sees the characters as "symbols of ones who fear they must perform even in a distortion, even in something that they know is not real and not rote in order to survive." See also the review by Abiola Sinclair, "Alice Childress' Terrific *Trouble in Mind." N.Y. Amsterdam News* (June 17, 1987): 20.

Sommer, Sally R. *Village Voice* (Jan. 15, 1979): 91. Excerpted in *Contemporary Literary Criticism: Excerpts from Criticism of the Works of Today's Novelists, Poets, Playwrights, and Other Creative Writers.* Vol.12. Edited by Dedria Bryfonski, 104–109. Detroit: Gale Research, 1980.

Sommer observes that *Trouble* anticipates the "tough" naturalistic black plays of the 1960s that "hit hard, inset with sermon-like arias for solo performers." The play's strength lies in its multiple levels of language and "seething, funny role-enactments." Sommer says that the play-within-a-play structure has its weaknesses. The form seems to work well on paper in juxtaposing appearance versus reality, but the "playing of it [is] cumbersome and unwieldy."

Stephens, Judith L. "Anti-Lynch Plays by African-American Women: Race, Gender, and Social Protest in American Drama." *African American Review* 26, no. 2 (Summer 1992): 329–339.

Stephens's purpose "is to establish a critical framework for the study of the anti-lynch play as a primary site of struggle against dominant racial and gender ideologies of late nineteenth and early twentieth century America." Her critical approach is to employ both feminist theater and black feminist literary criticism, because the former traditionally has privileged gender over race and class. According to Stephens, "Anti-lynch plays are of particular value to [the struggle against oppression] because they are based in a social protest movement which revealed the role of white women in maintaining a system of racial oppression. The Anti-Lynch Movement also revealed how the exploitation of black men and women and white women were interdependent and vital to an ideology of white-male supremacy." The plays Stephens includes are Angelina Weld Grimké's *Rachel,* Georgia Douglas Johnson's *A Sunday Morning in the South,* and Alice Childress's *Trouble in Mind.* See also Stephens's earlier article, "The Anti-Lynch Play: Toward an Interracial Feminist Dialogue in Theatre." *Journal of American Drama and Theatre* 2, no. 3 (1990): 59–69.

Turner, Darwin T. "Negro Playwrights and the Urban Negro." *CLA Journal* 12, no. 1 (Sept. 1968): 19–25.

Turner briefly discusses Childress's *Trouble in Mind.*

Wardle, Irving. "The Truth in Several Slippery Forms." *The Independent* (Oct. 18, 1992): 21.

Wardle applauds Childress's *Trouble* as performed at the Tricycle Theatre in London: "[F]or once, the theatre is telling the truth about itself. [This piece] is a humane and well-characterised study of artistic compromise." However, Wardle complains of a few "schematic drawbacks." For example, Childress belabors her meaning by "dragging in a parallel with Irish Home Rule, and the unwisely prolonged lynch-melodrama scenes bankrupt its credit as a Broadway property."

Williams, V.A. "Alice Childress: An Uncompromising Playwright." *Afro-American* (Oct. 14, 1988): 4–5.

Williams reports on a press conference held by Childress prior to a performance of *Trouble in Mind* by the Takoma Players of Washington, D.C. Childress talks about her plays (especially *Trouble in Mind* and *Wedding Band*), as well as issues confronting the American theatre, such as color-blind casting. Childress comments that she has turned down many profitable projects, having rejected them because "she refused to write romanticized or untrue things about . . . heroines of Black History."

———. "*Trouble in Mind* Has a Message." *Afro-American* (Oct. 7, 1988): 5.

Williams presents a brief, but favorable review of *Trouble* as performed by Washington, D.C.'s Takoma Players.

Wedding Band: A Love/Hate Story in Black and White

(New York Shakespeare Festival, Public Theatre, 1972)

Playscripts

The New Women's Theatre: Ten Plays by Contemporary American Women. Edited by Honor Moore, 255–337. New York: Vintage Books, 1977.

Wedding Band: A Love/Hate Story in Black and White. New York: French, 1973.

Summary of Play

Set in 1918 in South Carolina, the play concerns Julia Augustine, a black dressmaker, and her white, common-law husband of ten years, Herman, a baker. Julia and Herman cannot marry because of South Carolina's law forbidding interracial marriage. They have remained in the South because of Herman's responsibility to his mother and sister. To complicate matters, Herman's mother dislikes Julia because she is black and persists in alienating Herman's affections toward Julia. Herman plans to go North with Julia so that they can marry. However, before they can execute their plan, Herman succumbs to influenza, which has spread with a vengeance throughout the country.

Wedding Band was optioned for Broadway several times, yet the play went unproduced. Childress said that some of the producers had the money but lacked the nerve. Herman's death at the end of the play was problematic for several producers. According to Childress, Joe Papp told her, "You know, we'd be on Broadway . . . if it wasn't Julia's play—if it became more of Herman's play." But Childress refused to rewrite the play to focus on Herman.

Criticism and Performance Reviews

Barnes, Clive. "Theater." *New York Times* (Oct. 27, 1972): 30. Excerpted in *Contemporary Literary Criticism: Excerpts from Criticism of the Works of Today's Novelists, Poets, Playwrights, and Other Creative Writers.*

Vol.12. Edited by Dedria Bryfonski, 104–109. Detroit: Gale Research, 1980.

Barnes writes that despite the play's sentimentality, Childress skillfully captures "black consciousness, as well as the strength of white bigotry." The critic also observes that it is difficult to judge the realism of black speech and thought in 1918 because Americans have had "black stereotypes thrust upon them" by the white media.

Bennett, Susan. "Wedding Band." *Contemporary American Dramatists.* Edited by K.A. Berney, 720–721. London: St. James Press, 1994.

Assessing both the black and white critics' dissatisfaction with this play, Bennett observes that the blacks wanted Childress to focus on positive black role models, while the whites criticized the white male protagonist as being too weak. While Bennett concedes that the play drives home the notion that an individual's happiness is dependent on sociopolitical conditions, the protagonists' relationship "is perhaps less convincing."

Childress, Alice. "Why Talk About That?" *Negro Digest* 16 (April 1967): 17–21.

Childress's title refers to the controversial racial issues raised in her play *Wedding Band,* controversial because at the time of this article, there were few plays produced on Broadway that dramatized society as perceived by African-Americans. Childress talks about the genesis of *Wedding Band* and the state of black theater.

Clurman, Harold. "Theater." *Nation* 215 (Nov. 13, 1972): 475–476. Excerpted in *Contemporary Literary Criticism: Excerpts from Criticism of the Works of Today's Novelists, Poets, Playwrights, and Other Creative Writers.* Vol.12. Edited by Dedria Bryfonski, 104–109. Detroit: Gale Research, 1980.

Clurman praises the play for its humor, pathos, and "touching thumbnail sketches." He observes that the play's relevancy is not diminished although attitudes toward interracial marriage have loosened somewhat: "[T]he divisions and tensions that *Wedding Band* dramatizes still exist to a far more painful extent than most of us are willing to admit."

Curb, Rosemary. "An Unfashionable Tragedy of American Racism: Alice Childress' *Wedding Band.*" *Melus* 7, no. 4 (Winter 1980): 57–68.

Curb views *Wedding Band,* a play about the tragic consequences of miscegenation laws, as Childress's "finest and most serious piece of literature." The play dramatizes the playwright's concern for the racist as well as "anti-woman" laws that oppress the characters of the play. Childress's greatness lies in the fact that she does not portray them entirely as innocent victims—they too have their defects. The protagonists, Julia and Herman, do not represent martyrs in the cause of civil rights but rather "are weak, confused, superstitious, lonely, and impatient." However, the integrity of the lovers shows in their willingness to defy the laws of miscegenation to pursue their relationship.

Dillon, John. "Alice Childress' *Wedding Band* at the Milwaukee Repertory Theater: A Photo Essay." *Studies in American Drama, 1945–Present* 4 (1989): 129–141.

Accompanying this article are nine photographs depicting scenes from the Milwaukee Repertory Theater's 1989 production of *Wedding Band.* Dillon discusses the play within a historical context.

Epstein, Helen. *Joe Papp: An American Life.* Boston: Little, Brown, 1994.

In Epstein's biography of Papp, the founder of the New York Shakespeare Festival, Papp remarks that Childress's language in *Wedding Band* "is so authentic and rich, it's like the loam in the earth . . . . By itself, that is literature to me."

Gottfried, Martin. *Women's Wear Daily* (Oct.10, 1972). Reprinted in *New York Theatre Critics' Reviews,* 33 (Dec. 4, 1972): 163–164.

Gottfried charges that while *Wedding Band* works well as a "folk history . . . it abruptly nosedives into the familiar patterns of current black rhetoric." Furthermore, Childress fails to develop the potentially interesting secondary characters.

Kauffmann, Stanley. "Stanley Kauffmann on Theater." *New Republic* 167 (Nov. 25, 1972): 22, 26.

According to Kauffmann, *Wedding Band* "is a very mixed bag: of dramaturgic lumps, orated themes, and engaging contextual material." Although the dialogue is awkward and the ending is "irrelevant pathos," much of the play is "rich and flavorful."

Kerr, Walter. *New York Times* (Nov. 5, 1972): sec. 2: 5, 14. Reprinted in *New York Theatre Critics' Reviews,* 33 (Dec. 4, 1972): 163–164.

According to Kerr, *Wedding Band* is an honest portrayal of life in 1918, but as drama it is weak. The play's message is already known: "that intermarriage, especially in redneck districts, is apt to be opposed." For opposing opinions on the play's relevancy, see the following reviews: Clurman, Harold. "Theater." *Nation* 215 (Nov. 13, 1972): 475–476 Eder, Richard. "Stage: *Wedding Band* by Alice Childress." *New York Times* (Jan. 11, 1979): C17.

Mitchell, Loften. *Crisis* (April 1965): 221–223. Excerpted in *Contemporary Literary Criticism: Excerpts from Criticism of the Works of Today's Novelists, Poets, Playwrights, and Other Creative Writers.* Vol.12. Edited by Dedria Bryfonski, 104–109. Detroit: Gale Research, 1980.

Mitchell applauds the play as a "well-written, humorous, dramatic piece, positive in its approach." Childress's perceptiveness reflects her belief that race relations is a "family fight, but not in the sense that a Dixiecrat would claim the problem in the South is the South's alone."

Molette, Barbara. "They Speak: Who Listens?" *Black World* 25 (April 1976): 28–34.

Molette believes that the reason few African-American women playwrights have their works produced is because they "are at the mercy of various media brokers," the producers and publishers (usually white men) who "will not present informative entertainment or the exposition of truths that might be of some use to an oppressed group of people in reducing their oppression." Molette argues that whites are uncomfortable with the realistic portrayals of blacks and the issues they engender. To substantiate her accusation, the author cites the example of a few black women playwrights, including Alice Childress. According to Molette, Childress's *Wedding Band,* a play about the romantic relationship between a black woman and a white man, never fulfilled its scheduled run at the Atlanta Municipal Theatre because "white folks were not ready to deal with the issue [of miscegenation]." To rectify the situation, Molette suggests that women concentrate on moving into the administrative areas of the theatrical community and that black artists develop "regional Black theaters . . . to produce plays that are talking to Black people . . . and Black women in particular." Molette also discusses Angelina Weld Grimké, May Miller, Mary Burrill, and Lorraine Hansberry.

New York Theatre Critics' Reviews 33 (Dec. 4, 1972): 163–164.

A collection of reprinted reviews from selected New York newspapers.

Oliver, Edith. *The New Yorker,* 48 (Nov. 4, 1972): 105. Excerpted in *Contemporary Literary Criticism: Excerpts from Criticism of the Works of*

Today's Novelists, Poets, Playwrights, and Other Creative Writers. Vol.12. Edited by Dedria Bryfonski, 104–109. Detroit: Gale Research, 1980.

Oliver maintains that Childress creates an impressive ambiance of life in 1918, but after the "splendid" first act, the play weakens. The characters seem to talk "straight to the audience."

Simon, John. *New York* 5 (Nov. 13, 1972): 134.

Although "there is a play in all this," Simon criticizes Childress for clumsy plotting, one-dimensional characters, and "undistinguished" dialogue.

Watt, Douglas. "Theater." *New York Daily News* (Nov. 27, 1972). Reprinted in *New York Theatre Critics' Reviews* 33 (Dec. 4, 1972): 163–164.

A collection of reprinted reviews from selected New York newspapers. While "nicely written," *Wedding Band* is an "inconsequential little period play about miscegenation. "[N]othing much comes of it and it winds up being pat and superficial."

Watts, Richard. "Theater." *New York Post* (Nov. 27, 1972). Reprinted in *New York Theatre Critics' Reviews* 33 (Dec. 4, 1972): 163–164.

Watts finds that the couple's problems "are never more than mildly dramatic . . . and the ending, while touching, was less moving than it could have been."

Weathers, Diane. *Black Creation* 4 (Winter 1973): 60.

Weathers finds that *Wedding Band's* "sense of tragedy is never quite conveyed and left [her] feeling no sadness or bitterness but a good deal of boredom instead."

"Wedding Band." *Variety* (Dec. 20, 1972): 58.

The reviewer hails Childress as a "powerful and poetic writer." She is answering in her fierce depiction of an era when injustice was accepted with resignation modern audiences many have forgotten."

Wiley, Catherine. "Whose Name, Whose Protection: Reading Alice Childress's *Wedding Band.*" In *Modern American Drama: The Female Canon.* Edited by June Schlueter, 184–197. Rutherford, N.J.: Fairleigh Dickinson University Press, 1990.

Wiley's reading of *Wedding Band* emphasizes a feminist approach rather than one that focuses on interracial heterosexual politics. She bases her decision on the fact that the play is concerned more with the relations of black women and relations between black and white women than miscegenation.

Additional Performance Reviews

Christon, Lawrence. "Wedding Band at Inner City." Los Angeles Times (June 15, 1977): sec. 4: 17.

Lowell, Sandra. "Stage Beat." *Los Angeles Times* (May 20, 1977): sec. 4: 22, 23

———. "Stage Beat." *Los Angeles Times* (May 12, 1978): sec. 4: 25

Mahoney, John C. "Stage Beat." *Los Angeles Times* (Feb. 25, 1983): sec. 6: 9

Wine in the Wilderness

(New Dramatists, 1971–1972)

Playscripts

Black Theater U.S.A.: Forty-Five Plays by Black Americans, 1847–1974. Edited by James V. Hatch and Ted Shine, 713–736. New York: The Free Press, 1974.

Black Theatre USA: Plays by African Americans, 1847 to Today. Rev. Ed. Edited by James Hatch and Ted Shine, 752–770. New York: Free Press, 1996.

Plays by and About Women. Edited by Victoria Sullivan and James Hatch, 379–421. New York: Vintage, 1973.

Wine in the Wilderness: A Comedy-Drama. New York: Dramatists Play Service, 1969.

Wines in the Wilderness: Plays by African American Women from the Harlem Renaissance to the Present. Edited by Elizabeth Brown-Guillory, 122–149. New York: Greenwood, 1990.

Summary of Play

The action takes place in Harlem during the summer of 1964, following the riot there. The protagonist, artist Bill Jameson, awaits the arrival of his neighbors, Cynthia and Sonny-man, who are bringing a prospective model,

Tommy, to pose for the third panel of Bill's triptych. Waiting for their arrival, Bill explains to Oldtimer the images of the completed panels. The first image is of a girl who represents innocence. The woman in the second panel represents "Mother Africa, regal, black womanhood." The last painting, he says, will depict the opposite of the noble African woman: "She's ignorant, unfeminine, course, rude . . . vulgar . . . there's no hope for her." Cynthia and Sonny-man arrive with Tommy, who appears rather gauche. Tommy admits to Cynthia that she is attracted to Bill, but Cynthia tries to discourage her. After the couple leave, Tommy overhears Bill talking on the phone and describing the second painting of the African queen, and Tommy believes it is she he is describing. Her confidence improves, Bill overlooks her gaucheries, and they spend the night together. However, Tommy learns the truth from Oldtimer that she is to be the "messed up chick" of the triptych. Tommy reproaches Bill, Sonny-man, and Cynthia for their hypocrisy toward blacks. Bill is shaken by Tommy's condemnation. Consequently, Bill repaints the triptych to reflect his new attitude.

Criticism and Performance Reviews

Anderson, Mary Louise. "Black Matriarchy: Portrayal of Women in Three Plays." *Negro American Literature Forum* 10 (Spring 1976): 93–95.

Anderson examines the role of the black matriarch, which "white society has forced" on the black woman, in three plays: Lorraine Hansberry's *A Raisin in the Sun,* James Baldwin's *The Amen Corner,* and Childress's *Wine in the Wilderness.* Anderson describes the stereotyped black matriarch as religious; as one who identifies strongly with her role as mother, nurturer, and protector and who teaches her children to accept the condemnation of whites. Furthermore, the black matriarch is often portrayed as being responsible for the black man's inability to exercise his masculinity. In *Wine in the Wilderness,* Anderson examines how a black man confronts the stereotype of the black maternal figure, and how he ultimately recognizes that "the beauty of the Black matriarch is long past due."

Bailey, Peter. "Stage: Contemporary Black Classical Theatre." *Black Collegian* 14 (Jan./Feb. 1984): 34.

According to Bailey, director Ernie McClintock considers *Wine in the Wilderness* a classic piece of contemporary black theatre.

———. "Annual Round-Up: Black Theater in America." *Black World* (April 1977): 4–7.

Bailey, in his annual review of black theater, calls *Wine in the Wilderness* a "beautiful" play and a "superb" production by Roger Furman's New Heritage Theatre.

Brown, Janet. *Feminist Drama: Definition and Critical Analysis.* Metuchen, N.J.: Scarecrow Press, 1979.

Brown's work is one of the earliest in-depth studies of feminist theater criticism. She addresses the question, "What is feminist about a play?" Brown's exploration hinges on her idea of feminism, or the "feminine impulse," which she defines as "a woman's struggle for autonomy against an oppressive, sexist society." In addition, the author employs Kenneth Burke's literary theory that all fictive works have a rhetorical or persuasive motive. Brown argues that for a play to qualify as feminist, it must have as its central rhetorical motive a woman grappling for independence in the dominant patriarchal society. To illustrate her methodological approach, Brown analyzes several plays, including Childress's *Wine in the Wilderness.*

Brown-Guillory, Elizabeth. "Contemporary Black Women Playwrights: A View from the Other Half." *Helicon Nine* 14/15 (Summer 1986): 120–127.

Brown-Guillory, a prolific writer on black women dramatists, asserts that Lorraine Hansberry, Alice Childress, and Ntozake Shange "are crucial links in the development of black women playwriting in America." These dramatists consciously avoid the stereotypical images of black women that are found in the plays of their black male counterparts and white playwrights. Brown-Guillory observes that one image that dominates the plays of these women is the "evolving black woman," a phrase that "embodies the multiplicity of emotions of ordinary black women for whom the act of living is sheer heroism." For the evolving women in Childress's *Wine in the Wilderness* and Shange's *for colored girls who considered suicide/when the rainbow is enuf,* the men in their lives have been shattered. Rather than wallowing in self-pity or engaging in man-hating, these women "become independent because of their fear of being abused physically and/or emotionally in subsequent relationships."

Childress, Alice. "Negro Woman in Literature." *Freedomways* 6 (Winter 1966): 14–19.

Black writers have portrayed "strong, matriarchal" women in their plays, yet underlying many of these portrayals is the assumption that the strength of these women somehow diminishes their femininity and is responsible for the emasculation of black men. Childress defends the position of black women and explains the historical circumstances that demanded assertiveness and independence. The playwright also summarizes several racist and sexist laws that deeply affected black women; for example, Childress points out that a black woman "came out of bondage with the burden of the white and black man's child," because a law was passed that stipulated that children born of a black woman during slavery "shall be known as the legitimate children of *their mother only.*" Thus, both white and black men were released of any responsibility. Realistic depictions of the black woman in literature, says Childress, will happen only when "those of us who care about truth, justice, and a better life tell her story."

Hatch, James V., and Ted Shine. *Black Theater, U.S.A: Forty-Five Plays by Black Americans,* 737. New York: The Free Press, 1974. Excerpted in *Contemporary Literary Criticism: Excerpts from Criticism of the Works of Today's Novelists, Poets, Playwrights, and Other Creative Writers.* Vol.12. Edited by Dedria Bryfonski, 104–109. Detroit: Gale Research, 1980.

Hatch observes that the role of Tommy reflects a new black heroine that challenges the stereotype of the traditional black matriarch.

Kupa, Kushauri. "Close-Up: The New York Scene." *Black Theatre* 6 (1972): 38–40.

Although impressed with *Wine's* humor and irony, Kushauri maintains that the "authoress got hung up on making preachments and creating contrived situations," which caused her work to falter.

Schroeder, Patricia R. "Re-Reading Alice Childress. In *Staging Difference: Cultural Pluralism in American Theatre and Drama.* Edited by Marc Maufort, 323–337. New York: Peter Lang, 1995.

Schroeder assumes that materialist feminist drama critics ignore Childress because of her reliance on realism, a dramatic form materialists dismiss because it is grounded in patriarchal ideology. However, by analyzing *Wine in the Wilderness,* Shroeder attempts to show how Childress is in fact a materialist feminist. This play, according to the author, "reflect[s] her attention to material culture, to unequal power relations, to the relationships between race, class, and gender, and to political activism."

Additional Performance Reviews

Weiner, Bernard. "Theater." *San Francisco Chronicle* (Jan. 19, 1983): 55.

Other Plays by Alice Childress

The African Garden

Playscript

"A Scene from The African Garden." In *Black Scenes,* 137–146. Garden City, N.Y.: Zenith Books, 1971.

Gullah

(Revised version of *Sea Island Song,* University of Massachusetts, Amherst, 1984)

Just a Little Simple

(Based on material from Langston Hughes' *Simple Speaks His Mind,* Committee for the Negro in the Arts, Club Baron Theatre, 1950)

Let's Hear It for the Queen

(Children's play)

Playscript

Let's Hear It for the Queen. New York: Coward, McCann & Geoghegan, 1976.

A Man Bearing a Pitcher

(Unpublished)

When the Rattlesnake Sounds

(Children's play)

Playscript

When the Rattlesnake Sounds. New York Coward, McCann & Geoghegan, 1975.

Reviews

"Reviews." *Horn Book Magazine* (June 1976): 300–303.

"Reviews. *Bulletin of the Center for Children's Books* (May 1976): 139–140.

The World on a Hill

(Childrens' play)

Playscripts

Plays to Remember. Edited by Henry B. Maloney, 103–125. Toronto: Macmillan, 1970.

The World on a Hill and Other Plays. Compiled by Karen Press. Cape Town: Oxford University Press, 1994.

Chapter Four
Angelina Weld Grimké

Brief Biography

Poet and playwright Angelina Weld Grimké (1880–1958) chose to expose racial injustice through the "best type of colored people." She wanted to cancel out the ubiquitous stereotypes of blacks prevalent on stage and in the media. According to James Hatch and Ted Shine (4.7) *Rachel* (1916) was the first play written in the twentieth century by a black that was publicly performed with an all black cast. It was also the first work used by the National Association for the Advancement of Colored People (NAACP) to raise the issue over racial inequality and "to enlighten the American people relative to the lamentable condition of ten million . . . colored citizens in this free Republic." After its initial production in 1916, *Rachel* was staged in New York City and Cambridge, Massachusetts, but subsequent productions have been few. For many, the play is too depressing, sentimental, and melodramatic for modern tastes. However, as Hatch and Shine observe, "A reader who approaches *Rachel* with a historical perspective and an open heart should not be ashamed if occasional lumps rise in his throat. Angelina Grimké was a sensitive and delicate artist. She wrote poetry about herself."

Angelina Weld Grimké, not to be confused with her white great aunt, the feminist and abolitionist Angelina Grimké Weld, was born into a comfortable, biracial, middle-class background. According to Gloria T. Hull, Grimké's genteel background "encouraged her to concentrate on the 'talented tenth' and to produce work that was correct, conservative, and highbrow."

Like her lawyer father, Grimké was highly educated. She graduated from Boston Normal School of Gymnastics and took courses at Harvard. She began writing poetry at an early age and continued while attending college and teaching high school in Washington, D.C. She remained unmarried and childless, having resolved to devote her life to writing and to her father. Hull has suggested that Grimké might have been lesbian but remained deep in the closet, and "probably continued to desire women, in silence and frustration."

With the death of her father in1930, Grimké stopped writing. According to Hull, "Clearly, for reasons personal to her, Grimké lost the requisite motivation, mentality, and industry for writing and did so at a time that roughly coincided with and was to some extent influenced by the external conditions that ended the Harlem Renaissance." In addition to *Rachel,* Grimké wrote one other play, *Mara,* unpublished and unproduced, which also dealt with lynching.

Profiles and General Criticism

Brown-Guillory, Elizabeth. *Their Place on the Stage: Black Women Playwrights in America.* New York: Praeger, 1990.

While focusing on later black women dramatists, Brown-Guillory includes discussions on several female playwrights writing during the Harlem Renaissance: Bonner, Burrill, Grimké, Johnson, and May Miller.

Burton, Jennifer. "Introduction." In *Zora Neale Hurston, Eulalie Spence, Marita Bonner, and Others; The Prize Plays and Other One-Acts Published in Periodicals.* Edited by Henry Louis Gates, Jr., xix-lx. New York: G.K. Hall, 1996.

Burton's solid introduction to the plays of early women playwrights provides background on Grimké and briefly explores each of her plays. The introduction is accompanied by extensive notes and a bibliography.

Greene, Michael, "Angelina Weld Grimké." *In Dictionary of Literary Biography:* Vol. 50. *Afro-American Writers from the Harlem Renaissance.* Edited by Trudier Harris, 149–155. Detroit: Gale Research, 1987.

Greene provides a basic introduction to the life and work of Grimké.

Peterson, Bernard L. *Early Black American Playwrights and Dramatic Writers: A Biographical Directory and Catalog of Plays, Films, and Broadcasting Scripts.* New York: Greenwood, 1990.

The entry on Grimké includes a brief biography, plot summaries, staging history, and a list of secondary sources.

Roses, Lorraine Elena, and Ruth Elizabeth Randolph. *Harlem Renaissance and Beyond: Literary Biographies of 100 Black Women Writers, 1900–1945.* Boston: G.K. Hall, 1990.

The entry on Grimké offers biographical informaton and a selected list of primary and secondary sources.

Rachel: A Play in Three Acts

(Myrtilla Miner School, Drama Committee of the NAACP, Washington, D.C., 1916; later performed in New York City and Cambridge, Massachusetts)

Playscripts

Black Theater U.S.A.: Forty-Five Plays by Black Americans, 1847–1974. Edited by James V. Hatch, and Ted Shine, 137–173. New York: The Free Press, 1974.

Black Theatre USA: Plays by African Americans, 1847 to Today. Rev. Ed. Edited by James V. Hatch and Ted Shine, 133–168. New York: The Free Press, 1996.

Rachel. Boston: Cornhill, 1921.

Rachel. Washington, D.C.: McGrath, 1969.

The Schomburg Library of Nineteenth Century Black Women Writers: Selected Works of Angelina Weld Grimké. Edited by Carolivia Herron, 123–209. Oxford University Press, 1991.

Summary of Play

Mrs. Loving reveals the truth to her children, Rachel and Tom, about the deaths of their father and stepbrother, who were lynched ten years ago to the day. Their father, the publisher of a small Southern Negro newspaper had publicly denounced the lynching of a black man by a mob of whites who knew that their victim was innocent. Mr. Loving had refused to heed a warning to retract his accusation. A dozen masked men then burst into the Loving house. Mr. Loving had been able to kill four of the intruders before the rest of the mob had dragged him and his son outside and hanged them. Mrs. Loving then moved with her two remaining children north. Four years pass after the revelation of the lynchings. Rachel's sheltered life begins to crumble when she experiences racism firsthand. Rachel, a graduate in domestic science, and Tom, trained as an electrical engineer, cannot find jobs because of their race. In addition, the neighborhood children and Rachel's adopted son, Jimmy, are traumatized by the prejudice they experience at school. Rachel is overwhelmed by the injustice of white oppression. She renounces her beau, thus rejecting motherhood.

Criticism

Abramson, Doris E. "Angelina Weld Grimké, Mary T. Burrill, Georgia Douglas Johnson, and Marita O. Bonner." *Sage* 2, no. 1 (Spring 1985): 9–13.

Abramson observes that Grimké's *Rachel* and Mary Burrill's *They That Sit in Darkness* are similiar in that they both "share a concern for children, the future of the race." Their differences lie in the choice each protagonist makes concerning childbirth. In *Rachel,* the protagonist chooses not to have children because of the horrific treatment they receive from whites. On the other hand, Burrill's Malinda and her husband, out of ignorance of birth control methods, have too many children to care for responsibly.

Anderson, Addell Austin. "Theatre Review." *Theatre Journal* 43 (Oct. 1991): 385–386.

Anderson reviews a production of *Rachel* mounted by the Department of Theatre and Drama at Spelman College, Atlanta. Director Tisch Jones had adapted the play to minimize its melodrama, sentimentality, and Victorianism. Jones also reduced some of the more lengthy monologues, cut several roles for children, and added some comic business between Rachel and her brother, Tom, in Act 1. Anderson remarks that this production of *Rachel* "proves that *Rachel* should no longer be dismissed as 'historically significant'" but unproducible for late-twentieth-century audiences. The drama depicts a part of the American experience that the stage too often neglects: "It conveys the pain of feeling less than human but also the undaunted determination of those who refuse to succumb to the debilitating effects of racism."

Black Female Playwrights: An Anthology of Plays Before 1950. Edited by Kathy A. Perkins. Bloomington: Indiana University Press, 1990.

Although Perkins does not include Grimké's *Rachel* in her anthology, she discusses the play and the public's reaction to its political nature.

Bond, Frederick W. *The Negro and the Drama,* 189–190. Washington, D.C.: Associated Publishers, 1940.

According to Bond, *Rachel* "lack[s] in the fundamental principles of drama [and the] piece is preposterous, and will hardly meet the approval of an audience."

Bradley, Gerald. "Goodbye Mister Bones: The Emergence of Negro Themes and Characters in American Drama." *Drama Critique* 7 (Spring 1964): 79–85.

Bradley indicates that Grimké wrote *Rachel* "for propaganda purposes" for the NAACP. He comments that while the play "is stilted and didactic, [it] has merit on the basis of its theme and characters."

Burke, Sally. *American Feminist Playwrights: A Critical History.* New York: Twayne, 1996.

Burke provides an introduction to Grimké's life and a brief discussion of *Rachel.*

Davis, Arthur P. *From the Dark Tower: Afro-American Writers, 1900–1960.* Washington, D.C.: Howard University Press 1974.

Davis considers *Rachel* the first successful stage drama to be written by an African-American.

Greene, Michael. "Angelina Weld Grimké." In *Dictionary of Literary Biography.* Vol. 50. *Afro-American Writers Before the Harlem Renaissance.* Edited by Trudier Harris, 149–155. Detroit: Gale Research, 1986.

Greene provides an introductory article surveying the life and work of Grimké. Accompanying the article are primary and secondary sources.

Grimké, Angelina. "*Rachel* the Play of the Month: The Reason and Synopsis by The Author." *Competitor* 1 (1920): 51–52. Reprinted in *Lost Plays of the Harlem Renaissance, 1920–1940.* Edited by James V. Hatch and Leo Hamalian, 424–426. Detroit: Wayne State University Press, 1996.

Grimké responds to complaints that *Rachel* "preaches race suicide." She intended this play to appeal not so much to blacks but to whites, especially women, because she sees them as "the worst enemies with which the colored race has to contend." She believes that if white women "could see, feel, understand just what effect their prejudice and the prejudice of their fathers, brothers, husbands, sons were having on the souls of the colored mothers everywhere, and upon the mothers that are to be, a great power to affect public opinion would be set free and the battle would be half won."

Hull, Gloria T. "Angelina Weld Grimké." In *Color, Sex, and Poetry: Three Women Writers of the Harlem Renaissance,* 107–155. Bloomington: Indiana University Press, 1987.

Hull provides the most substantial critique of *Rachel.* Incorporating key quotes from several reviews, Hull explores the mixed reaction to the play. While many reviewers saw the play as sincere and honest, others criticized it for being maudlin, overwrought, and preaching racial genocide. As to whether the play reached white women, the target audience of *Rachel,* Hull quotes the reactions of some white women as unconvinced by Grimké's message. Hull asserts that while the play is sentimental and the heroine saccharine, Grimké "evidences considerable skill in dramaturgy. . . . Particularly notable is her handling of exposition, elapsed time, and pacing." Hull also discusses *Mara,* an unpublished play similar in theme to *Rachel:* although the "plot sounds like Gothic melodrama . . . Mara holds attention better than *Rachel* does. [It] is fairly exciting and more imaginative . . . [and the] reader's patience and credulity are not taxed by an excess of preciousness and sentimentality."

Keyssar, Helene. "Rites and Responsibilities: The Drama of Black American Women." In *Feminine Focus: The New Women Playwrights.* Edited by Enoch Brater, 226–240. Cambridge: Oxford University Press, 1989.

Keyssar maintains that there is "potential power" in the plays of black women playwrights because of black women's duality of perception: They "see the world as an American *woman* and as a black *woman.*" Thus the duality of perception results in viewing experiences prismatically. For Rachel, her denial of motherhood is an act of abortion. Keyssar argues that it is "the only act that will authenticate [Rachel's] double existence as woman and black person. Any other act would, for her, be a false resolution of her hybrid self." Keyssar also assesses the works of Lorraine Hansberry *(Raisin in the Sun),* Adrienne Kennedy *(The Owl Answers),* Ntozake Shange *(Boogie Woogie Landscapes),* and Sonia Sanchez *(Sister Son/ji).*

McKay, Nellie. "'What Were They Saying?': Black Women Playwrights of the Harlem Renaissance." In *The Harlem Renaissance Re-examined.* Edited by Victor A. Kramer, 129–147. New York: AMS, 1987.

Rachel generated a debate among artists and intellectuals about the role of politics in art. McKay argues that black women playwrights seemed to agree with Grimké's notion that art cannot separate itself from identity. These dramatists made "no attempt to disguise their political motives and they spoke directly to the realistic problems that black people, especially black women, faced in their daily lives."

Miller, Jeanne-Marie A. "Angelina Weld Grimké: Playwright and Poet." *CLA Journal* 21, no. 4 (June 1978): 513–524.

Miller contends that Grimké countered the ubiquitous stage stereotypes of blacks—the contented slave and the traditional darky—by developing black characters from, as Grimké says, "the best type of colored people." Although the play is significant in that it dramatizes the debilitating effects of racism in America, it has its weaknesses. Miller points out that some of "the play's contrivances are too obvious, the dialogue in the long speeches too unrealistic, and Rachel's hypersensitivity seeming almost incredulous by today's standards." Miller compares *Rachel* to Grimké's unpublished play, *Mara.* The latter work, Miller contends "is a highly literary work, less overtly a protest play than *Rachel.* "Both plays have sensitive female protagonists, both of whom are named after biblical characters. But the most salient aspect of both plays is "Grimké's use of black genteel characters, whose refinement is in glaring contrast to the cruelties waged against them solely because of their race. Grimké uses them to make a bold statement about the condition of all blacks in American."

———. "Black Women Playwrights from Grimké to Shange: Selected Synopses of Their Works." In *But Some of Us Are Brave: Black Women's Studies.* Edited by Gloria T. Hull, P.B. Scott, and Barbara Smith, 280–290. Old Westbury, N.Y.: Feminist Press, 1982.

Miller surveys the work of several African-American women whose plays "offer a unique insight into the Black experience," including Angelina Weld Grimké, Marita Bonner, Georgia Douglas Johnson, Mary Burrill, Lorraine Hansberry, Alice Childress, Ntozake Shange, Adrienne Kennedy, Sonia Sanchez, J.E. Franklin, and Martie Charles.

"Rachel." The Grinnell Review (Jan. 1921): 334.

This unsigned review of the text of *Rachel* remarks that "[e]xaggeration spoils this play. Had Miss Grimké's [N]egroes been less shabby-genteel, their tragedy would have been more convincing. But that there is tragedy in the relations of black and white, in the hopeless future that is the burden of the black man, we are made to feel with sufficient force to be thoroughly uncomfortable. What is to be done? Miss Grimké's suggestions are only a partial solution of the problem."

Russell, Sandi. *Render Me My Song: African-American Women Writers from Slavery to the Present.* New York: St. Martin's,1990.

Russell provides brief introductions to the work of several black women playwrights: Angelina Weld Grimké, Zora Neale Hurston, Alice Childress, Lorraine Hansberry, and Ntozake Shange.

Stephens, Judith L. "Anti-Lynch Plays by African-American Women: Race, Gender, and Social Protest in American Drama." *African American Review* 26, no. 2 (Summer 1992): 329–339.

Stephens's purpose "is to establish a critical framework for the study of the anti-lynch play as a primary site of struggle against dominant racial and gender ideologies of late-nineteenth and early-twentieth-century America." Her critical approach is to employ both feminist theater and black feminist literary criticism, because the former traditionally has privileged gender over race and class. According to Stephens, "Anti-lynch plays are of particular value to [the struggle against oppression] because they are based in a social protest movement which revealed the role of white women in maintaining a system of racial oppression. The Anti-Lynch Movement also revealed how the exploitation of black men and women and white women were interdependent and vital to an ideology of white-male supremacy." Stephens's article covers Grimké's *Rachel,* Georgia Douglas Johnson's *A Sunday Morning in the South,* and Alice Childress's *Trouble in Mind.* See also Stephens's earlier article, "The Anti-Lynch Play: Toward an Interracial Feminist Dialogue in Theatre." *Journal of American Drama and Theatre* 2, no. 3 (1990): 59–69.

Storm, William. "Reactions of a Highly-Strung-Girl: Psychology and Dramatic Representation in Angelina W. Grimké's *Rachel.*" *African American Review* (Fall 1993): 461–470.

Most discussions of *Rachel* emphasize its historical significance rather than examining the work in terms of its intrinsic value as drama. Storm argues that the protagonist is "an extraordinarily complex . . . character. Rachel is a figure of considerable psychological intricacy and emotional volatility, and these are factors that continually complicate and enrich the larger drama and provide many of the play's interactions with an arresting, unusual, and highly charged dramatic tension."

Tate, Claudia. *Domestic Allegories of Political Desire: The Black Heroine's Text at the Turn of the Century,* 209–214. New York: Oxford University Press, 1992.

Tate asserts that Grimké's work signals a change of direction in U.S. literary history and African-American literary history: "Her works designate a point in U.S. literary culture where the growing social alienation that would later be identified as the modern condition intersects Victorian positivism, reflected in nineteenth-century sentimentality. In specifically black literary culture, Grimké's writings mark a place where the domestic plots of social optimism become outmoded, and explicit depictions of social alientation and racial protest commence to satisfy the expectations of twentieth-century readers. Thus the self-affirming, maternal discourses of political desire in the works of her black female predecessors seem transformed into blues epics in Grimké's works."

Young, Patricia. "Shackled: Angelina Weld Grimké." *Women and Language* 15 (Fall 1992):25–31.

In addition to addressing Grimké's purpose of debunking black stereotypes, racial injustice, and black misogyny, Young concentrates on the sociopolitical implications of Rachel's rejection of motherhood. Young reports that some theatergoers were "agitated" by what they saw as Grimké's promoting "genocide as the response to bigotry." Yet, clearly from Grimké's writings, she wrote to raise the white audience's awareness of racial prejudice. Young also amplifies Grimké's negative attitude toward marriage and motherhood in *Rachel* that parallels experiences in her private life.

Additional Performance Reviews

Fauset, Jessie Redmon. "Rachel." *The Crisis* 21 (1920):24

Graves, Ralph. "Review." *Washington Post* (March 19, 1917).

Chapter Five
Lorraine Hansberry

Brief Biography

Lorraine Vivian Hansberry (1930–1965) was the first African-American to have a play produced on Broadway. She was also the first black and the youngest dramatist to win the Best Play Award from the New York Drama Critics' Circle Award for *A Raisin in the Sun* (1959), which won over Eugene O'Neill's *A Touch of the Poet,* Archibald MacLeish's *JB,* and Tennessee Williams' *Sweet Bird of Youth.* Her Broadway hit endures today. The playscript is still in print, has been translated into several languages, and has had several revivals on stage and screen. The musical *Raisin* was based on the play and won a Tony in 1974.

Hansberry wrote several other plays, all of which reflect her versatility and humanity. Her second play, *The Sign in Sidney Brustein's Window* (1964), surprised many because its protagonist was a white, Jewish intellectual. Although Hansberry was very committed to the social, political, and economic liberation of black people, she did not restrict herself to the black cause. She categorized herself as a humanist and as such was opposed to oppression of any sort. Her plays were indictments of the greed and cruelty of American society, yet they engaged both white and black audiences, who could relate to the problems of the characters in her plays.

Although Hansberry's socioeconomic circumstances differed from that of *Raisin in the Sun's* Younger family (Hansberry's father was a successful businessman), art imitates life in at least one instance. In the play, Lena Younger wants to move her family to a better neighborhood, which happens to be white. Hansberry's father tried to do the same. When Hansberry was eight, she and her family moved to a white neighborhood. Their neighbors, however, did not welcome them. At one point, someone threw a brick through their window. The future playwright, her mother, and siblings had to face these hostile neighbors alone because her father spent a great deal of time in Washington with his case challenging segregated housing in Chicago. He fought his case all the way to the U.S. Supreme Court and won the right to live in an all-white neighborhood.

Hansberry attended mostly segregated public schools on the South Side of Chicago; although her parents were wealthy enough for private schools, they did not believe in private instruction. She went to the University of Wisconsin, quit after two years, and moved to New York in 1950. There she became exposed to theater. It entered her life, she later recalled, "like *k-pow!*"

In New York, Hansberry became politically active. This activism would later inform her plays. In 1952 she became associate editor of Paul Robeson's periodical *Freedom.* Her position brought her into contact with prominent black intellectuals such as W.E.B. Du Bois, Dr. Alphaus Hunton, and Louis Burnham. Hansberry actively protested the oppression of Africa, Asia, and Latin America and American interference in Indochina. In 1953 she resigned from *Freedom* so that she could devote more time to playwrighting.

In 1953 Hansberry married Robert Barron Nemiroff, a white university student of Jewish ancestry. The couple met while Hansberry was reporting on a protest against discrimination at New York University. Although they later divorced in1964, they continued to work together as artists and activists. Nemiroff became Hansberry's literary executor upon her death in 1965 of pancreatic cancer.

A Raisin in the Sun served as a catalyst for black theater artists. Many critics saw Hansberry's work as prophetic. This and other plays anticipated the issues that would surface in the 1960s during the civil rights movement and the black arts movement. As Amiri Baraka pointed out, Hansberry's vision about class and ideological struggles foreshadowed the same concerns as the civil rights movement.

Hansberry was concerned with the civil rights not only of blacks but also of women and homosexuals. The women characters in her plays gave voice to many feminist issues and challenged the traditional roles relegated to women in society and in the theater. Hansberry's lesbianism, according to Robert Nemiroff, "was not a peripheral . . . part of her life but contributed significantly . . . to the sensitivity and complexity of her view of human beings and of the world." Hansberry's feminism and her homosexuality deeply informed her artistic and political vision.

During the 1960s Hansberry fell out of favor with many black critics and white liberals who believed she had nothing relevant to say. Black nationalists especially saw her as selling out to white middle-class values. They disapproved of Hansberry's having the Younger family in *A Raisin in the Sun* move to a white neighborhood. She was not what they expected her to be—a black "separatist."

But this downward turn in Hansberry's artistic reputation was of short duration. Beginning in the early 1970s her work grew in stature. Musical versions of two of her plays *(Raisin* and *Les Blancs)* have been produced, as well as plays about her life *(To Be Young, Gifted, and Black* and *Love to All, Lorraine).* Revivals of Hansberry's plays continue along with scholarly discussions.

The strength of Hansberry's art lies in what Steven Carter describes as "the product of two warring, but ultimately harmonious, impulses: her desire for control and her desire for freedom. The need for control in . . . art gave her the ability to form clear ideas. . . . The yearning for freedom drove her to push against this control in favor of spontaneity, expressiveness and inventiveness."

Profiles and Interviews

Adams, Michael. "Lorraine Hansberry." *Dictionary of Literary Biography:* Vol.7. *Twentieth-Century American Dramatists.* Edited by John MacNicholas, 247–254. Detroit: Gale Research, 1981.

This introductory article includes an extensive biographical and critical survey of Hansberry's career as a writer. A primary and secondary bibliography of her works is included. See also Steven Carter's "Lorraine Hansberry. "*Dictionary of Literary Biography:* Vol. 38. *Afro-American Writers After 1955: Dramatists and Prose Writers.* Edited by Thadious M. Davis and Trudier Harris, 120–134. Detroit: Gale Research Company, 1985.

Baldwin, James. "Sweet Lorraine." *Esquire* 72 (Nov. 1969): 139–140.

Baldwin reminisces about Hansberry, whom he met during a production of *Giovanni's Room,* a dramatization of his novel. He comments that Hansberry refused to succumb to what happened to so many artists—isolating themselves from their community. Baldwin maintains that the black artist must remain true to himself and retain a connection with the community, "from which . . . all of the pressures of American life . . . conspire to remove [him]. . . . And when he is effectively removed, he falls silent—and the people have lost another hope." See also Baldwin's article "Lorraine Hansberry at the Summit." *Freedomways* 19 (4th Quarter 1979): 269–272.

Carter, Steven. "Lorraine Hansberry. "*Dictionary of Literary Biography:* Volume 38. Afro-American Writers after1955: Dramatists and Prose

Writers. Edited by Thadious M. Davis and Trudier Harris, 120–134. Detroit: Gale Research, 1985.

Carter, who has written extensively on Hansberry, provides an introductory article surveying her life and art. A primary and secondary bibliography of her works is included.

Contemporary Authors: A Bio-Bibliographical Guide. Vol. 109. Edited by Hal May, 175–177. Detroit: Gale Research, 1983.

The entry includes a biographical sketch, a list of Hansberry's plays, and a brief discussion of her works.

Gatewood, Tracey. "Lorraine Hansberry—Still a Name on Stage." *Baltimore Afro-American* (Feb. 3, 1996): B10.

Gatewood traces the life and work of Hansberry.

Giovanni, Nikki. "An Emotional View of Lorraine Hansberry." *Freedomways* 19 (4th Quarter 1979): 281–282.

According to Giovanni, Hansberry "possessed that quality of courage to say what had to be said to those who needed to hear it. . . . She made it possible for all of us to look a little deeper."

Hairstone, Loyle. "A Writer for the Generations." *N.Y. Amersterdam News* (Dec. 23, 1978): D7.

Hairston writes a glowing profile of Hansberry on the occasion of ABC's TV's documentary on Hansberry, "Like It Is."

Peterson, Bernard L. *Contemporary Black American Playwrights and Their Plays: A Biographical Directory and Dramatic Index.* Westport, Conn.: Greenwood, 1988.

Peterson provides a biographical sketch and a brief staging history of Hansberry's plays.

Poston, Ted. "We Have So Much to Say." *New York Post* (March 22, 1959): 2.

Poston profiles Hansberry, whom he calls "Broadway's latest Cinderella Girl." Hansberry talks about the birth of *A Raisin in the Sun* which, at one point, she "decided was the worst effort I'd ever made at anything." If a movie is optioned, she says she will write the screenplay. She asserts that "nobody's going to turn this thing into a minstrel show as far as I'm concerned. And if this blocks a sale, then it just won't be sold." Hansberry also mentions two works in progress. One is *Toussaint (A Work in Progress)* a book for an opera based on Toussaint L'Ouverture, the slave who freed Haiti from French rule. The other project is an adaptation of the Negro novelist Charles Chesnutt's *The Marrow of Tradition.*

———. "Lorraine Hansberry." In *Notable Women in the American Theatre: A Biographical Dictionary.* Edited by Alice M. Robinson, Vera Mowry Roberts, and Milly S. Barranger, 374–380. New York: Greenwood, 1989.

The first of its kind, this handbook focuses solely on the contributions of women in the theater. The entry on Lorraine Hansberry includes a biographical sketch, a general discussion of her major plays, and a selected list of primary and secondary sources.

"Talk of the Town: Playwright." *New Yorker* 35 (May 9, 1959): 33–35.

This interview of Hansberry highlights her life outside the theater. She comments, for example, that *Raisin's* Younger family does not represent her real-life family, which more closely approximates the Murchison family in the play ("We were more typical of the bourgeois Negro").

Terkel, Studs. "An Interview with Lorraine Hansberry." *WFMT Chicago Fine Arts Guide* 10 (April 1961):8–14. [Excerpts reprinted in *American Theatre* 1 (Nov. 1984): 5–8, 41.]

Hansberry touches upon *Raisin,* especially the character of Walter Lee. To Terkel's question "Is [*Raisin*] really a Negro play?" Hansberry remarks that good drama demands portraying the universal. But to do this, the playwright must "pay great attention to the specific. . . . Not only is this a Negro family . . . it is specifically [about a family from] South Side Chicago. . . . So it's definitely a Negro play before it's anything else."

Wilkerson, Margaret B. "The Dark Vision of Lorraine Hansberry: Excerpts from a Literary Biography." *Massachusetts Review* 28, no. 4 (Winter 1987): 642–650.

Wilkerson highlights Hansberry's plays from the perspective of how they reflect her as a woman of contradictions. Publicly Hansberry insisted on the meaningfulness of life, but privately she was haunted by loneliness and was despondent about the human condition. But, like Sidney Brustein, the protagonist of her second play, "by sheer force of will she imposed a reason for life on life, despite all the evidence to the contrary."

Additional Biographical Entries

Andrews, Laura. "Artists Celebrate Life of Lorraine Hansberry." *N.Y. Amsterdam News* (July 22, 1995): 34.

American Women Writers: A Critical Reference Guide from Colonial Times to the Present. Vol. 2. Edited by Lina Mainiero, 236–239. New York: Frederick Ungar, 1980.

Black Writers: A Selection of Sketches from Contemporary Authors. Edited by Linda Metzger, 245–247. New York: Gale Research 1989.

Contemporary American Dramatists. Edited by K.A. Berney, 247–249. London: St. James Press, 1994.

Current Biography Yearbook. Edited by Charles Moritz,165–166. New York: H.W. Wilson, 1960.

Encyclopedia of African-American Culture and History. Vol. 3. Edited by Jack Salzman et al. New York: Simon & Schuster/ Macmillan, 1996.

Encyclopedia of Black America. New York: McGraw-Hill, 1981.

Great Women Writers: The Lives and Words of 135 of the World's Most Important Women Writers, from Antiquity to the Present. Edited by Frank Magill, 199–202. New York: Henry Holt, 1994.

Great Writers of the English Language: Dramatists. Edited by James Vinson, 271–273. New York: St. Martin's, 1979.

McGraw-Hill Encyclopedia of World Drama. 2nd ed. Edited by Stanley Hochman, 444–445. New York: McGraw-Hill, 1984.

The Negro Almanac: The Afro-American, 984–985. New York: John Wiley & Sons.

Notable American Women; The Modern Period: A Biographical Dictionary. Edited by Edward T. James, 310–312. Cambridge, Mass.: Belknap, 1980.

Sears, Art Jr. "Lorraine Hansberry." Jet (Jan. 28, 1965): 20–22.

"Women in the News: Her Dream Came True." *New York Times* (April 9, 59): 37.

General Criticism

Adler, Thomas P. "Lorraine Hansberry: Exploring Dreams, Explosive Drama." In *American Drama, 1940–1960: A Critical History.* New York: Twayne, 1994.

Underlying Adler's discussion of Hansberry's plays (*A Raisin in the Sun, Les Blancs, The Drinking Gourd,* and *The Sign in Sidney Brustein's Window*) is his contention that Hansberry did not compromise her art for the sake of white audiences: "She not only adamantly refuses to soothe her largely white audience's guilt over their responsibility for past racial inequities but increasingly challenges them in three powerful plays to adopt, if need be, an openly revolutionary stance aimed at ending those injustices."

Ashley, Leonard R.N. "Lorraine Hansberry and the Great Black Way." In *Modern American Drama: The Female Canon.* Edited by June Schlueter, 151–160. Rutherford, N.J.: Fairleigh Dickinson University Press, 1990.

In his reevaluation of Hansberry's work, Ashley concludes that her "importance is minor but must not be ignored." *A Raisin in the Sun* is not a great play, but it "has an enduring place in American theater history." Hansberry's importance lies in her role as a dramatist who exposed audiences to the experiences of the black individual as artist as well as a member of American society. As a work of art, Ashley deplores *Raisin*'s conventionality, awkward plotting, and unreliable dialogue. But the play, Ashley concedes, "had an undeniable impact . . . [and made] a historic contribution." *The Sign in Sidney Brustein's Window,* according to Ashley, suffers from "too many ideas . . . [it] leaves black questions aside and jumps on the horse of social satire and rides off in several directions." Although the dialogue includes some "zingers," the play's antagonist, Sidney Brustein, lacks the complexity of *Raisin*'s Walter Lee. As for *Les Blancs,* Ashley agrees with those reviewers who believe that the play encourages violence against whites: "[The play] is gauche as much as leftist; it substitutes anger and artiness for articulateness and art." Ashley has not much good to say about *The Drinking Gourd*—Hansberry "had so little critical taste that she believed it was better [than Samuel Beckett's *Waiting for Godot*]."

Black Literature Criticism: Excerpts from Criticism of the Most Significant Works of Black Authors over the Past 200 Years. Vol. 2. Edited by James P. Draper, 950–974. Detroit: Gale Research, 1992.

The volume provides a biographical sketch as well as excerpts from essays and reviews.

Bond, Jean Carey. "Lorraine Hansberry: To Reclaim Her Legacy." *Freedomways* 19 (1979): 183–185.

Bond's editorial introduces *Freedomways'* special issue, "Lorraine Hansberry, Art of Thunder, Vision of Light," which comprises seventeen essays and one bibliography that focus on the life and canon of Hansberry. The purpose of the special issue, Bond explains, is twofold: to acquaint and reacquaint those readers who may be unfamiliar with the breadth of Hansberry's art and to establish that Hansberry's "artistry entitles her to inclusion among the best contemporary American writers."

Brown-Guillory, Elizabeth. *Their Place on the Stage: Black Women Playwrights in America.* Westport, Conn.: Greenwood, 1988.

Until Brown-Guillory's book, there had been no comprehensive study of black women dramatists. The author provides an in-depth analysis of the works of Lorraine Hansberry, Alice Childress, and Ntozake Shange, playwrights whose works "are crucial links in the development of black playwriting in America from the 1950's to the 1980's." In her examination of these playwrights, Brown-Guillory compares the works of these playwrights to the dramas of their male counterparts. She begins by presenting a historical overview of the "long and vibrant" theatrical tradition from which black female playwrights evolved, and devotes a chapter to the works of women dramatists identified with the Harlem Renaissance including May Miller, Angelina Weld Grimké, and Georgia Douglas Johnson.

Carter, Steven R. *Hansberry's Drama: Commitment and Complexity.* Urbana: University of Illinois, 1991.

Carter's is the first comprehensive study of Hansberry's published and unpublished work. Underlying the analyses of Hansberry's work is Carter's assertion that Hansberry's treatment of humanity within a diverse and complex society informed her artistic vision. He notes that her vision was unfashionable during her lifetime. Many writers of her era embraced an absurdist vision in which the world was devoid of a god, of absolute values, and of certainty. Although Hansberry agreed with the absurdists that there is no god or values existing outside humankind, Carter points out that she "boldly argued against them and at times against her own weaker feelings, that humans might just 'do what the apes never will—*impose* the reason for life on life.'" Rather than focus on the problem of why we are here, Hansberry preferred to concentrate on how to make the world a tolerable place to live. Although Hansberry's primary goal was the liberation of blacks, she also championed the rights of women and homosexuals. Again, she differed from many militant feminists in that she allowed "that some remarkable men would always spring to defend the rights of others." She also advocated the importance of women recognizing that in their oppression they are closely connected with other oppressed groups. She was deeply disturbed by the rampant sexism and homophobism that informed American society. She also felt that many plays were labeled propagandistic simply because they included unorthodox ideas. Carter praises Hansberry's universality, her ability to dramatize issues of concern to different cultural groups. Although she strongly identified with being a black American and a woman, she did not allow her identification to blind her to the multiplicity and complexity of humans and their motivations: "She desire[d] to transcend a host of arbitrary artistic and social limitations." In his analysis, Carter covers *A Raisin in the Sun* (including filmscripts and the musical), *The Sign in Sidney Brustein's Window, Les Blancs, The Drinking Gourd,* and *What Use Are Flowers?* See also Carter's articles "Commitment and Complexity: Lorraine Hansberry's Life in Action." *Melus* 7 (Fall 1980): 39–52 and "The John Brown Theatre: Lorraine Hansberry's Cultural Views and Dramatic Goals." *Freedomways* 19 (1979):186–191.

Cheney, Anne. *Lorraine Hansberry.* Boston: Twayne, 1984.

This is the first book-length discussion of Hansberry's life and work. The study is based in part on interviews with and unpublished material provided by Robert Nemiroff, Hansberry's former husband and executor of her estate. Cheney begins by chronicling Hansberry's early life. She points out that at a very early age, Hansberry was sensitive to the less fortunate, as illustrated in this recollection: When Lorraine Hansberry was five, her well-to-do parents gave her a white fur coat for Christmas. She wore the coat to school and the children there, most of whom were poor, "assailed her with fists, curses, and inkwells." Hansberry understood and empathized with their anger and resentment. She "respected their courage, their fight [and] admired these rebels . . . who refused to be embarrassed [by their] poverty." Cheney next focuses on Hansberry's work. She is strongest when providing the sociohistorical context for the plays. She fails, however, to provide critical analyses of *A Raisin in the Sun, The Sign in Sidney Brustein's Window, Les Blancs, The Drinking Gourd, What Use Are Flowers,* and *To Be Young, Gifted and Black.*

Contemporary Literary Criticism: Excerpts of Criticism from the Works of Today's Novelists, Poets, Playwrights and Other Creative Writers. Vol. 62.

Edited by Roger Matuz, 211–248. Detroit: Gale Research, 1991. See also Vol. 17 of *Contemporary Literary Criticism,* 187–193.

Davis, Arthur P. "Lorraine Hansberry." In *From the Dark Tower: Afro-American Writers, 1900 to 1960,* 203–207. Washington, D.C.: Howard University Press, 1974.

Davis provides a profile and assessment of *A Raisin in the Sun* and *The Sign in Sidney Brustein's Window.* He praises Hansberry for infusing humor in her plays and observes that many black writers since her time "have forgotten how to laugh." Davis notes that although Hansberry dramatized human folly and greed, she never relinquished her belief in the the possibilities of the human spirit.

Elder, Lonne. "Lorraine Hansberry: Social Consciousness and the Will." *Freedomways* 19 (1979): 213–218.

Elder asserts that, unlike the writings of Kafka and Nietzsche, who consider the internal will and social consciouness as one, Hansberry's works reflect that social consciousness and internal will regard each other as adversaries. Hansberry, Elder contends, held that "the creation of art is worthy and relevant only when the artist is seeking tangible resolves; that art must attempt the decoding of mysteries, not their embellishment." He says that Hansberry refused to restrict her art within the bounds of the movement; instead, she explored aesthetic expression outside the civil rights movement: "Hers was not an act of defiance but of willful preservation." Yet Hansberry was not blinded by the avant-garde, which she saw as self-serving and egocentric.

Friedman, Sharon. "Feminism as Theme in Twentieth-Century American Women's Drama." *American Studies* 25 (Spring 1984): 69–89.

Friedman explores the work of Lorraine Hansberry, Susan Glaspell, Rachel Crothers, and Lillian Hellman. The works of these dramatists, asserts Friedman, focus on the oppression of women in both public and private spheres and their tendency toward resistance. Hansberry's characterizations of black mothers in *A Raisin in the Sun* and *The Drinking Gourd* show that Hansberry had strong feminist concerns that were deeply embedded in her themes of racial and economic oppression. Hansberry, Friedman points out, rejected the stereotype of black women, especially mothers, as "castrating and conservative." The characters Lena *(A Raisin in the Sun)* and Rissa *(The Drinking Gourd),* for example, can be formidable, but they are also nurturing and revolutionary. In the final analysis, Hansberry's mothers "repudiate the negative images of black women as passive and/or destructive. . . .[They] contributed not only to the survival of their families and communities, but also to the active resistance often necessary to that survival."

———. "Lorraine Hansberry." In *Contemporary Authors Bibliographical Series: American Dramatists.* Vol. 3. Edited by Matthew C. Roudane, 69–89. Detroit: Gale Research 1989.

This bibliographical essay assesses the critical reputation of Hansberry's work. It includes a bibliography of primary and secondary sources.

Gomez, Jewelle L. "Lorraine Hansberry: Uncommon Warrior." In *Reading Black, Reading Feminist: A Critical Anthology.* Edited by Henry Louis Gates, Jr., 307–317. New York: Meridian, 1990.

Gomez observes that the critics of the 1960s were wrong in denouncing Hansberry as irrelevant because she was grounded in middle-class-values. Gomez seeks to "rediscover" the significance of Hansberry as dramatist and to uncover how her social and political activism influenced her plays. Hansberry believed that the essence of a work was in its universality. But to illuminate universal truths, she believed that one must dramatize the specific—"peeling back the generalities, whether those generalities were culture, ethnicity, gender or language." Gomez says that Hansberry "was convinced that beneath any combination of these elements was a distinct human being who . . . would make a valid statement about humankind." Hansberry's outspoken political views anticipated the civil rights movements of blacks, women, and gays. She believed that the solutions to the problems of one group were closely connected to the resolutions of problems for the other groups.

Hansberry, Lorraine. "This Complex of Womanhood." *Ebony* 15 (Aug. 1960): 40. [Reprinted in *Ebony* 18 (Sept 1963): 88.]

According to Hansberry, the modern Negro woman is a product of two romantic viewpoints. On the one hand, the Negro poet has created an "image of a figure of supreme tenderness and humanity and dignity." But there is another portrayal of the Negro woman, one who is an "uncooperative, overbearing, humiliating, deprecating" creature destined to harass the male. Although when considered separately, these images are romantic stereotypes, when combined, "they embrace some truths and present the complex of womanhood."

———. "The Negro Writer and His Roots: Toward a New Romanticism." *The Black Scholar* 12 (March./April. 1981): 2–12.

Hansberry outlines her aesthetic vision in this reprint of a speech delivered at the conference of the American Society of African Culture two weeks before the Broadway opening of *A Raisin in the Sun* (1959). Central to her vision is that social consciousness cannot be divorced from art: "The question is not whether one will make a social statement in one's work—but only *what* the statement will say, for if it says anything at all, it will be social." The view that art is and should be separate from society generates illusions that deeply affect black writers. One illusion is the claim among many artists that the individual is autonomous. Another illusion, Hansberry observes, is the assumption that America is represented by a homogenous middle class "whose values are thought to be not only the values of the nation but . . . of the whole world." She warns black writers not to get caught up in movements of the Beats and the Absurdists because they encourage a commitment to nothing. Instead, she argues, black artists must look outward as well as inward: "We have given the world many of its heroes . . . [who turned] inward to where a culture has never . . . adequately understood that the destiny of African Americans and Africans "are inextricably and magnificently bound up together forever." But writers must not enforce the romanticism of the black bourgeoisie, Hansberry maintains: "The evils of the ghetto, whatever they are, must emerge as evils—not as the romantic and exotic offshoots of a hilarious people who can simply endure anything." Hansberry concludes that she is deeply aware of the greedy and cruel nature of humans, but at the same time she believes that "[M]an is unique in the universe, the only creature who has in fact the power to transform the universe. . . . [M]an might just do what the apes never will—*impose* the reason for life on life." See also Hansberry's article on the Negro in the American theater, "Me Tink Me Hear Sounds in de night." *Theatre Arts* 44 (Oct. 1960): 9–11, 69–70.

———. Prospectus for the John Brown Memorial Theatre of Harlem. *The Black Scholar* (July/Aug. 1979): 14–15.

Hansberry envisions the John Brown Memorial Theatre of Harlem, which would be dedicated to "the aspirations and culture of the Afro-American people" and would nurture and develop artistic expression of black Americans. However, the theater would not exclude white culture; rather, it "will readily, freely and with the spirit of the creativity of all mankind also utilize all and any forces of the Western heritage . . . in the arts." Steven Carter, in his essay "The John Brown Theatre: Lorraine Hansberry's Cultural Views and Dramatics Goals," *Freedomways* 19 (4th Quarter 1979): 186–192, discusses Hansberry's naming a black theater after a white man. As Carter points out, Hansberry's act "emphasizes the consciously paradoxical nature of [her] world view and art."

Kaiser, Ernest, and Robert Nemiroff. "A Lorraine Hansberry Bibliography." *Freedomways* 19 (4th Quarter 1979): 285–304.

The first comprehensive bibliography of Hansberry's primary works and criticism.

Lester, Julius. "The Voice and Vision of Lorraine Hansberry: The Politics of Caring." In Lorraine *Hansberry: The Collected Last Plays.* Edited by Robert Nemiroff, 262–275. New York: New American Library, 1983.

This moving introduction to Hansberry's political and artistic vision includes a discussion of *Raisin* and *Sidney Brustein.*

A Library of Literary Criticism: Modern American Literature. Vol. 4, supplement to the 4th ed. Edited by Dorothy Nyren, 211–216. New York: Frederick Ungar, 1976.

This is a compendium of excerpts of performance reviews and criticism.

"A Lorraine Hansberry Rap." *Freedomways* 19 (1979): 226–233.

Lerone Bennett, Jr. (historian and editor of *Ebony*) and Margaret G. Burroughs (contributing editor of *Freedomways* and director of the DuSable Museum in Chicago) discuss the life and work of Lorraine Hansberry.

Malpede, Karen, ed. "Lorraine Hansberry." In *Women in Theatre: Compassion and Hope,* 163–176. New York: Drama Book Publishers, 1983.

In her introduction, Malpede notes that Hansberry had intended the characters of Sidney Brustein and Tshembe Matoseh to be women. Malpede asks, "Did she censor herself, knowing she would be censured? Or did the forms of a woman-centered drama still elude her because the feminist community was not yet strong enough to provide the actual examples required?" Following the brief introduction, Malpede includes the text of Hansberry's article, "An Author's Reflections: Willy Loman, Walter Younger, and He Who Must Live" from the *Village Voice* and two letters that reflect her feminist awareness, which was "an abiding concern of hers [but] was never fully realized in her stage work."

Mayfield, Julian. "Lorraine Hansberry: A Woman for All Seasons." *Freedomways* 19 (4th Quarter 1979): 263–268.

Mayfield, who, in the early 1950s, directed a variety show written by Hansberry, makes observations about the political side of her art. Despite her instant celebrity with *Raisin,* she retained her strong political convictions. For example, in 1961, Hansberry participated in a meeting of black intellectuals with Malcolm X, who at the time was shunned by many black celebrities until "he was safely dead." Hansberry exploited her celebrity "to advance her people." Mayfield recalls when the famous playwright defended a group of blacks who held a demonstration at the United Nations Security Council chambers to protest the assassination of Patrice Lumumba, prime minister of the Republic of the Congo. Hansberry also anticipated the 1960s slogan "Black is beautiful" when, in 1959, she expressed to journalist Mike Wallace in a TV interview, "What we want now is a recognition of the beauty of things African, the beauty of things black." But Mayfield points out that to truly understand Hansberry's vision, one must examine her art and politics within the context of her time. Her concern for the coming generation permeates her work. In his conclusion, Mayfield implies obliquely that Hansberry's death, as well as the deaths of several other young radicals during the early 1960s, could have been caused by the U.S. government, which views such people as "troublesome Afro-Americans and Africans who dared the powerful."

Miller, Jeanne-Marie. "Black Women Playwrights from Grimké to Shange: Selected Synopses of Their Works." In *But Some of Us Are Brave: Black Women's Studies.* Edited by Gloria T. Hull, P.B. Scott, and Barbara Smith, 280–290. Old Westbury, N.Y.: Feminist Press, 1982.

Miller surveys the work of several African-American women whose plays "offer a unique insight into the Black experience," including Angelina Weld Grimké, Marita Bonner, Georgia Douglas Johnson, Mary Burrill, Lorraine Hansberry, Alice Childress, Ntozake Shange, Adrienne Kennedy, Sonia Sanchez, J.E. Franklin, and Martie Charles.

Miller, Jordan Y. "Lorraine Hansberry." In *The Black American Writer: Poetry and Drama.* Vol. 2. Edited by C.W.E. Bigsby, 157–170. Deland, Fla.: Everett/Edwards, 1969.

Miller insists on excluding the context of race relations when analyzing Hansberry's plays: "We are going to avoid any temptation to place them in any niche of 'social significance.'" Miller argues that *A Raisin in the Sun* and *The Sign in Sidney Brustein's Window* are "superior" plays, despite the fact that they are written according to traditional dramatic conventions. Miller's method of discussing the plots, characters, and conflicts of the two plays isolated from social considerations runs counter to the approach of many other critics.

Molette, Barbara. "They Speak: Who Listens?" *Black World* 25 (April 1976): 28–34.

Molette believes that the reason why few African-American women playwrights get their plays produced is because they "are at the mercy of various media brokers," the producers and publishers (usually white males) who "will not present informative entertainment or the exposition of truths that might be of some use to an oppressed group of people in reducing their oppression." Molette argues that whites are uncomfortable with the realistic portrayal of blacks and the issues they engender. To substantiate her accusation, the author cites the example of a few black female playwrights including Lorraine Hansberry.

Rahman, Aishah. "To Be Black, Female, and a Playwright." *Freedomways* 19 (4th Quarter 1979): 256–60.

Rahman confronts the dilemmas facing black playwrights, especially African-American female dramatists, writing and producing for the predominately white American theater audience. Rahman suggests that black women playwrights face hostility from the commercial theater as well as from their male counterparts. As Rahman comments, "Black women playwrights are judged differently and with more hostility by both women and men than are black male playwrights." She cites Hansberry, the first black playwright to be produced on Broadway, to support her contention. Many in the black community criticized Hansberry's plays as being too bourgeois and too commercial and charged that being female made it easier for her to make it to Broadway because "women could get through the barrier more easily than black men." Rahman asserts that black and white male playwrights distort the images of black women. Rahman is "determined to pick up the standard of the Hansberry legacy by portraying black women in real terms, not as the perverted characters of someone's nightmare." Rahman also discusses the work of Adrienne Kennedy and Sonia Sanchez.

Rich, Adrienne. "The Problem with Lorraine Hansberry." *Freedomways* 19 (1979): 247–255.

Poet and feminist, Rich insists that Hansberry "is a problem [for her] because she is black, female and dead." First, Rich questions that Hansberry's life and work are seen primarily through the lens of her former husband and literary executor, Robert Nemiroff. For example, *To Be Young, Gifted and Black* is not an autobiographical theater piece written by Hansberry. Instead, it is based on her writings and was produced posthumously by Nemiroff and others. Furthermore, because Nemiroff synthesized scenes and added dialogue "to bridge gaps," Rich points out that she does not know what is Hansberry's and what is Nemiroff's. She complains that researchers should have open access to Hansberry's papers so that they might draw their own conclusions. Therefore, for Rich, "To read Lorraine Hansberry, to understand the meaning of her work, means for me of necessity to question all filters, all 'translations,' to view the work in the context of what it means to be both black and female in a world where each is . . . an erased identity."

Riley, Clayton. "Lorraine Hansberry: A Melody in a Different Key." *Freedomways* 19 (4th Quarter 1979):205–212.

Underlying Riley's cursory overview of *A Raisin in the Sun, Les Blancs, The Sign in Sidney Brustein's Window,* and *A Drinking Gourd* is his observation that Hansberry understands that racial conflict is an artificial element of society "into which the real, fundamental conflicts that characterize our species are channeled."

Russell, Sandi. *Render Me My Song: African-American Women Writers from Slavery to the Present.* New York: St. Martin's,1990.

Russell provides introductions to the work of several black women playwrights: Angelina Weld Grimké, Zora Neale Hurston, Alice Childress, Lorraine Hansberry, and Ntozake Shange.

Walker, Jesse. "Meet Miss Hansberry." *N.Y. Amsterdam News* (March 14, 1959).

Walker points out that Hansberry ignores textbook theories of drama; she has developed her own set of rules of what drama should be. Her models are Sean O'Casey and Arthur Miller.

Whitlow, Roger. *Black American Literature: A Critical History,* 141–145. Totowa, N.J.: Rowman & Allanheld, 1974.

Whitlow surveys Hansberry's life and two of her works: *A Raisin in the Sun* and *The Sign in Sidney Brustein's Window.* Despite the implication in the book's title, Whitlow's discussion contains very little analysis of Hansberry.

Wilkerson, Margaret B. "Introduction." In *Lorraine Hansberry: The Collected Last Plays.* Edited by Robert Nemiroff, 3–23. New York: New American Library, 1983.

Wilkerson provides introductory comments on Hansberry's life and work. She bases her introduction on her articles: "The Sighted Eyes and Feeling Heart of Lorraine Hansberry (*Black American Literature Forum,* 1983. See *A Raisin in the Sun,* Criticism and Performance Reviews) and "Lorraine Hansberry: The Complete Feminist" (*Freedomways,* 1979. See *A Raisin in the Sun,* Criticism and Performance Reviews).

A Drinking Gourd

(A dramatization commissioned in 1959 by NBC-TV that was never aired because it was considered too controversial)

Playscripts

Black Theater U.S.A.: Forty-Five Plays by Black Americans, 1847–1974. Edited by James V. Hatch and Ted Shine, 713–736. New York: The Free Press, 1974.

Les Blancs: The Collected Last Plays of Lorraine Hansberry. Edited by Robert Nemiroff. New York: Random House, 1972.

Lorraine Hansberry: The Collected Last Plays. Edited by Robert Nemiroff, 143–220. New York: New American Library, 1983.

Summary of Play

The play opens with Hannibal, a nineteen-year-old slave, telling Sarah about his desire to escape to freedom, as his brother did before him. Back at the "Big House," the master, Hiram Sweet, his son, Everett, and their guest, Dr. Macon Bullett, argue about the impending war with the North. Each has his own opinion: Young and cocky Everett just knows Southerners will whip the North in six months, Dr. Bullett assumes that the Yankee businessmen want to control Congress, and Hiram Sweet believes the South will lose. Shortly after this scene, Hiram suffers a heart attack and his son assumes control of the plantation, although his father remains its titular head. Everett hires a poor white, Zeb Dudley, to be overseer. Meanwhile, Rissa, one of the four original slaves bought by Hiram Sweet, tells her son Hannibal that she wants him to work at the "Big House," so that he will be safe. Hannibal is repelled by her wish. He admits to Rissa that he is learning to read, a dangerous act, because literacy for slaves is forbidden by law. The younger son of the master, Tommy Sweet, is Hannibal's teacher. Later, Hannibal is hassled by the ruthless Dudley. Hannibal runs away and meets Tommy, and they resume Hannibal's studies. However, Everett and Dudley catch them and Everett orders Dudley to blind Hannibal. Hiram, shocked by the blinding of Hannibal, goes to Rissa and tells her he knew nothing of it. Rissa replies, "Why, ain't you marster? How can a man be marster of some men and not at all of others?" Crushed by Rissa's scorn, Hiram leaves her but collapses outside on her porch. Rissa does nothing but listen to his dying cries for help. Later, as the blinded Hannibal and Sarah prepare to leave the plantation, Rissa gives them Hiram's cherished gun.

For a discussion of why *The Drinking Gourd* was never aired by NBC, see Robert Nemiroff's "A Critical Background: *The Drinking Gourd.*" In *Lorraine Hansberry: The Collected Last Plays.* New York: New American Library, 1983.

Criticism

Brown-Guillory, Elizabeth. "Black Women Playwrights: Exorcising Myths." *Phylon* 68 (Fall 1987): 230–238.

Brown-Guillory focuses on Lorraine Hansberry, Alice Childress, and Ntozake Shange, who "present a vital slice of [black] life." They offer realistic images of the black experience that differ markedly from the perceptions of male writers, both black and white. In effect, the images of these female dramatists smash the misconceptions of "the contented slave," "tragic mulatto," "the comic Negro," "the exotic primitive," and "the spiritual singing, toe-tapping faithful servant." According to Brown-Guillory, Hansberry, Childress, and Shange use three images repeatedly in their work: "the black male in search of his manhood," the black male as "the walking wounded," and, "the evolving black woman." See also discussions of *The Drinking Gourd* in Brown-Guillory's *Their Place on the Stage: Black Women Playwrights in America.* Westport, Conn.: Greenwood, 1988 and her article, "Lorraine Hansberry: The Politics of the Politics Surrounding *The Drinking Gourd.*" *Griot* 4 (Winter-Summer 1985):18–28, in which she explores why *The Drinking Gourd* has yet to be produced in its entirety.

Farrison, W. Edward. "Lorraine Hansberry's Last Dramas." *CLA Journal* 16, no. 2 (Dec. 1972): 188–197.

This article includes a discussion of *The Drinking Gourd,* along with *Les Blancs* and *What Use Are Flowers?* Farrison considers *The Drinking Gourd* superior to *Les Blancs.*

Nemiroff, Robert. "A Critical Background: *The Drinking Gourd.*" In *Lorraine Hansberry: The Collected Last Plays.* Edited by Robert Nemiroff. New York: New American Library, 1983.

Nemiroff recounts the fate of *The Drinking Gourd* and explains why NBC-TV failed to broadcast the drama. First, Hansberry's drama treated all characters, both black and white, fairly. The audience, for example, empathizes with the black man blinded because he was educated but is also made to empathize with the white man who blinded him. As Nemiroff points out, "it is one thing for the black writer to view the *black* as victim, but to also view the *white* as victim is to step entirely outside the racial categories upon which the society stands." Such an act deprives whites of "their claim to uniqueness," while giving blacks freedom to consider both races as equal—both of whom are victimized by society. The second reason Nemiroff cites as to why this play never aired is grounded in the subversive character of Rissa. She appears to be similar to other strong black matriarchs in literature, but in the end she ignores the needs of her white master in order to help her son. Nemiroff writes, "In effect, she murders [the white man]—and what is more, steals his guns and places them in the black hands of her children." For once, the black matriarch acts according to the consciousness of the black artist, not the white.

Powell, Bertie J. "The Black Experience in Margaret Walker's *Jubilee* and Lorraine Hansberry's *The Drinking Gourd.*" *CLA Journal* 21, no. 2 (Dec. 1977): 304–311.

Powell discusses how Walker and Hansberry depict the black experience during slavery. While both works provide "vivid and stirring accounts," Hansberry's play "illustrates in some detail the more humane attributes of individual White characters, while [*Jubilee*] alludes to this aspect only briefly."

Les Blancs

(Longacre Theatre, New York, 1970)

Playscripts

The Collected Last Plays. Edited by Robert Nemiroff [with an introduction Margaret B. Wilkerson]. New York: Vintage Books, 1994.

Les Blancs: The Collected Last Plays of Lorraine Hansberry. Edited by Robert Nemiroff [with introduction by Julius Lester]. New York: Random House, 1972.

Les Blancs: A Drama in Two Acts [final text]. Adapted by Robert Nemiroff. New York: Samuel French, 1972.

Lorraine Hansberry: The Collected Last Plays. Edited by Robert Nemiroff, 125–139. New York: New American Library, 1983.

Lorraine Hansberry's Les Blancs: A Drama in Two Acts. [final text]. Adapted by Robert Nemiroff. New York: Samuel French, 1972.

Summary of Play

Les Blancs, according to Robert Nemiroff, is the first play written by a black American writer that deals with African independence. Hansberry apparently wrote the play in response to Jean Genet's treatment of blacks as noble exotics in *Les Negres (The Blacks).* In1963 part of an early version of the work was staged by the Actors Studio Writers' Workshop by Arthur Penn. Hansberry continued to work on the draft until her death. Robert Nemiroff, acting as Hansberry's literary agent, finalized the draft in 1966.

Tshembe, a young African, leaves his European wife and child at home in England to attend the funeral of his father in a fictional country in Africa. Upon his return to his homeland, he finds his countrymen in rebellion against their oppressors, the European colonials. He and his two brothers, Abioseh and Eric, each respond to the conflict of colonialism in different ways. Tshembe, a burned out nationalist, wishes to rise above the conflict; his brother Abioseh chooses to help his people through his position as a Catholic priest; their younger half-brother Eric advocates the violent overthrow of the white settlers' control of the African people. Although comfortably ensconced in the white man's ways, Tshembe is deeply connected to his tribal roots and upon his return to Africa finds it difficult to remain an observer amid the turmoil within his country.

Criticism and Performance Reviews

Aufderheide, Pat. "*Les Blancs* Rekindles Racial Controversies." *In These Times* (March 9–15, 1988): 18.

The racial issues raised in this play are just as relevant as they were during the time of the play's first performance in 1970. According to

Aufderheide, "This revival at the Arena Stage in Washington, D.C., occurs in a high tide of open racism, at a peak moment of media conglomeration, at a low ebb for inspiring and empowering political leadership." The reviewer draws parallels to *Hamlet.* As in Shakespeare's drama, the action revolves around the protagonist Tshembe's indecisiveness. No sentimental heroes and villains here; each character, no matter how unlikeable, has his own "intelligible logic" to his motives. Although he praises the play, Aufderheide finds it weak in the second act and its ending—"The play hiccups at the end, with a series of abrupt resolutions."

Barnes, Clive. "Theater: *Les Blancs.*" *New York Times* (Nov. 16, 1970).

According to Barnes, the play's superficial dramatizing of ideas reduces it to political propaganda. The ideas expressed are familiar and simplistic. The characters "are debased to labeled puppets mouthing thoughts, hopes and fears that lack the surprise and vitality of life." Barnes suspects that Hansberry and her adapter, Robert Nemiroff, were not so much concerned about depicting the volatile situation in Africa as presenting it as an allegory of the racial situation in America. Hence, the stilted dialogue and unfocused arguments: "It is obvious that they are trying to tell us something about America—and I think they would have done better to have told it to us straight."

Clurman, Harold. "Theatre." *The Nation* (Nov. 30, 1970): 573.

Clurman defends the play against many "professional theatre-tasters," who claim that the play is propaganda promoting a "simplistic argument." Their attitude, Clurman contends, "is a rationalization for social embarrassment." Rather, the play is an honest attempt at revealing the tragic implications of race relations and the "complexity of motivation and effect" when countries are colonized by Europeans. Offering no resolution, Hansberry forcefully clarifies the problems inherent in imperialism.

———. "Theatre." *The Nation* (Dec. 7, 1970): 606.

Responding to criticism of his previous review (Harold Clurman,"Theatre." *The Nation,* Nov. 30, 1970. See *Les Blancs,* Criticism and Performance Reviews) by "friends [who] have taken [him] to task for having reacted favorably to a play they thought . . . 'propaganda' on behalf of blacks opposed to whites," Clurman declares that Hansberry "was not a 'black panther,' but an intelligent, compassionate human being." The play is not about blacks hating whites but dramatizes the fact that "humankind has always made its progress through a mess of bloody injustice and inevitable cruelty. There can be no 'nice' war, however 'justified' it may be." As the protagonist Tshembe points out to Morris, the American journalist, white supremacy is a "device—no more, no less. It explains nothing at all." White racists use their supremacy as an excuse to rob and oppress blacks. Clurman argues that to "wave aside *Les Blancs* . . . is an evasion which I am inclined to ascribe to bad faith."

Erstein, Hap. "*Les Blancs* at Arena: Perceptive Black Drama." *Washington Times* (Feb. 12, 1988): E3.

Erstein hails the revival of *Les Blancs* at the Arena Stage in Washington, D.C., despite its long-windedness and untidiness, as "electrifying . . . the drama proves extremely stageworthy, retaining its power—or perhaps gaining some—in the intervening years." Erstein likens the play to Bernard Shaw's work in that the characters debate one another, each representing a different perspective on colonialism. But while Shaw's characters confront one another with cool civility, Hansberry's face each other with "heat."

Fuchs, Elinor. "Rethinking Lorraine Hansberry." *Village Voice* (March 15, 1988): 93, 98, 105.

Fuchs praises *Les Blancs,* saying that it reflects Hansberry's abilities as "a brilliant geopolitical intelligence, a powerful moral imagination, and an emerging command of the great traditions of Western theater." Fuchs also takes issue with critic David Richards's negative review. She accuses him of missing the point of the play when he infers that the central characters in the play are the white settlers rather than Tshembe and his brothers.

Gant, Liz. *"Les Blancs." Black World* 20 (April 1971): 46–47.

Gant considers *Les Blancs* one of Hansberry's best plays because, as in *A Raisin in the Sun,* Hansberry deals with "real Black issues." However, Gant maintains that this play "has been made victim of a rip-off on the Broadway scene." According to Gant, the play "has been killed on Broadway" because of preproduction rumors to the effect that her former husband, Robert Nemiroff, wrote most of the final script. This rumor, Gant observes, is contradicted by the production's playbill, which informed the audience that Hansberry wrote several drafts of the play over several years and was "polishing" the play at the time of her death.

Gill, Brendan. "The Theatre." *The New Yorker* (Nov. 21, 1970): 104.

Gill complains that the play is dated and didactic: "We are being lectured to and made to see things in the light that Teacher wishes us to see them in and not otherwise."

Gottfried, Martin. "Theatre." *Women's Wear Daily* (Nov. 16, 1970). Reprinted in *New York Theatre Critics' Reviews* (1970):152–155.

Gottfried considers the play didactic. Characters merely exist as spokespersons for ideas—"created as points of view rather than as people." Robert Nemiroff, whom Gottfried accuses of building a reputation on Hansberry's work, "has done little to 'adapt' whatever of this play she left."

Gruesser, John. *"Lies That Kill: Lorraine Hansberry's Answer to Heart of Darkness in Les Blancs." American Drama* (Spring 1992): 1–14.

Gruesser bases his analysis of *Les Blancs* on the premise that Hansberry wrote the play to change the predominate images of Africa: "[B]y rewriting Joseph Conrad's *Heart of Darkness,* [the critic attempts to demonstrate] that in *Les Blancs* Hansberry tries to pioneer a non-Africanist means of depicting Africa, something rarely accomplished by an outsider, whether Euro-American or African-American." Having an educated African as the protagonist and attributing colonialism and Africanist agendas as causing the violence and decay in Africa, Hansberry began correcting distorted images of Africa and Africans and in so doing inspired a host of outsider writers to do the same.

Kelly, Kevin. "Stage Review: *Les Blancs.*" *Boston Globe* (Jan. 19, 1989): Arts: 80.

"Simply a bad play," reviewer Kelly observes of *Les Blancs,* as produced by the Huntington Theater company at Boston University. He commends Hansberry for her subject matter, but, complains that "the art behind [the play] is insupportable." The play is an unfocused string of speeches mouthed by stereotyped characters—"polemics delivered halfway between arias and political hard-sell." The production itself is "interesting," with some "gee-whiz" staging by Harold Scott. The production was based on the uncut version adapted by Hansberry's former husband, Robert Nemiroff.

Kerr, Walter. *"Les Blancs." New York Times* (Nov. 29, 1970): 3. [Reprinted in *New York Theatre Critics' Reviews* (1970):152–155.]

Kerr warns potential audiences not to dismiss this play as simply a tribute to a gifted playwright who died before she was able to fully mature as an artist. Especially impressive is the play's language, which "achieves an internal pressure, a demand that you listen to it." Kerr praises James Earl Jones as Tshembe, who "seizes the [language], toys with it, spits it back at the other players." The other actors are "immaculate," even those whose characters lack development, such as Cameron Mitchell's Charlie Morris, whose sole role is to "set up pomposities for Mr. Jones to puncture."

Killens, John Oliver. "Lorraine Hansberry: On Time!" *Freedomways* 19 (4th Quarter 1979): 273–276.

Novelist Killens recognizes Hansberry as a "one-woman literary warrior for change." But her plays are not agit-prop. Her "flesh and blood characters," especially those in *A Raisin in the Sun* and *Les Blancs,* dramatize the importance of revolution and change. Killens asserts that Hansberry was "a Pan-Africanist with a socialist perspective." She believed passionately in the freedom of blacks as well as the "demise of capitalism." Hansberry's strength was her insight into the contradictions of the human condition.

Kraus, Ted. "Theatre East." *Players* 46 (Feb./March 1971): 122.

Kraus praises the play's potential but complains that it never "progressed beyond its primary stating of universal racial conflicts."

Kroll, Jack. "Between Two Worlds." *Newsweek* 76 (Nov. 30, 1970): 98.

Kroll sums up the play as dramatizing Hansberry's inner conflict as a black writer. He observes that the playwright is "caught between the humanism that was natural to her and the violent militancy that she saw as inevitable and even right for black people." The play is "highly schematic." Kroll predicts that had Hansberry survived, she might have been able to "compress this explosive and difficult subject into a play that would work on its own terms as drama."

Nemiroff, Robert. "A Critical Background: *Les Blancs.*" In *Lorraine Hansberry: The Collected Last Plays.* Edited by Robert Nemiroff, 27–35. New York: New American Library, 1983.

Nemiroff recounts how from an early age Hansberry immersed herself in African history and culture. She once wrote that the "destiny and aspirations" of Africans and American blacks are "inextricably and magnificently bound up together forever." *Les Blancs,* Nemiroff contends, was a "visceral response" to Jean Genet's *Les Negres (The Blacks).* Hansberry felt that Genet's play failed to probe "the real confrontation" between white colonials and Africans because the play is "haunted by guilt . . . and too steeped in the romance of racial exoticism." Hansberry felt it was not enough for whites simply to purge themselves by condemning and then absolving themselves because "we are spared . . . the ultimate anguish—of *man's* oppression of man." *Les Blancs* "explores to what degree color was — and was not—the root cause of the conflict" between colonialism and race.

Ness, David E. "Lorraine Hansberry's *Les Blancs:* The Victory of the Man Who Must." *Freedomways* 13 (4th Quarter 1973): 294–306.

Ness observes that Hansberry's plays, especially *Les Blancs,* reflect the deep concern Hansberry had with her dedication to the black struggle for equality. As an activist in politics and the theater, she questioned her fidelity to the cause. Ness quotes Hansberry, "Do I remain a revolutionary? Intellectually —without a doubt. But am I prepared to give my body or even my comforts? This is what I puzzle about." Protagonist Tshembe Matoseh's dilemma is similar. For years he has fought passionately for Africa's independence from the white colonialists, yet after many struggles, he believes he has "lost heart." Yet by the end of the play, Tshembe does not sell out to the Europeans, but "make[s] his peace with the forces that live and grow by destroying his people."

New York Theatre Critics' Reviews (1970):152–155.

This is a collection of reprinted reviews from several New York newspapers.

Richards, David. "Barren *Blancs;* Bombast and Contrivance at Arena." *Washington Post* (Feb. 12, 1988): Style: B1.

Richards's assessment of the production of *Les Blancs* at the Arena Stage is that the unfinished play "should have been left in the trunk." Clearly, he complains, the play is in need of "refinements." Although Hansberry wrote some "masterful" lines, much of the play "consists . . . of undramatized rhetoric and argument, punctuated by occasional bursts of offstage action." As a result, "the play is as dry as a treatise." For a rebuttal to this review see "Lorraine Hansberry's Contributions." *Washington Post* (Feb. 27, 1988): A22.

Rudin, Seymour. "Theatre Chronicle: Fall 1970." *Massachusetts Review* (Winter 1971): 150–161.

Although *Les Blancs* reminds us of Hansberry's talent, Rudin maintains that the play is problematic due to "its sketchiness, its awkwardness, its sometimes trenchant but too often cliché-ridden dialogue" and its dated treatment of racial conflict.

Sainer, Arthur. "Is Terror the Way?" *Village Voice* (Nov. 16, 1970): 58.

Sainer concludes that the "best thing about this play is the intelligence of Lorraine Hansberry, the passion and courage." Hansberry refrains from moral absolutes except for the "necessity to become free." However, Sainer finds the play "overly worked-on." The play is all gloss with very little life. The only character who "suggests the ravages of being alive at this time" is the blind woman, who "reaches beyond production values and toward Miss Hansberry's humanity and terror."

Silver, Lee. "*Les Blancs* Fine Drama." *New York Daily News* (Nov. 16, 1970): 55. [Reprinted in *New York Theatre Critics' Reviews* (1970):152–155.]

Silver hails *Les Blancs* as a "most absorbing drama" and says that it is refreshing to see characters who are able to move the audience with who they are and what they have to say.

"Theater." *Playboy* 18 (April 1971): 36–37.

This piece on the contemporary black theater movement uses Hansberry's *Les Blancs* to show that while some critics are sympathetic to the objectives of black theater, others are disturbed. For example, some critics were "appalled" by *Les Blancs*, which they viewed as promoting genocide.

Watts, Richard. "Conflict in Black Africa." *New York Post* (Dec. 5, 1970): 18.

Watts insists that *Les Blancs* "is a timely and powerful work and one of the most important [of] this season." Despite Hansberry's angry position, Watts observes that "she was not out to get 'whitey' but to understand him." He finds the character of the American correspondent as being the most sympathetic of the male characters. The journalist's goodness and his earnestness in attempting to befriend Tshembe are not patronizing. However, the most complex character is the African leader, Tshembe, "wonderfully" played by James Earl Jones. Watts concludes his review by remarking that *Les Blancs* "is truthful as well as deeply haunting." See also Watts's article: "Grim Fruits of Colonialism." *New York Post* (Nov. 16, 1970). [Reprinted in *New York Theatre Critics' Reviews* (1970):152–155.]

Weales, Gerald. "The Stage." *Commonweal* 93 (Jan. 22, 1971): 397.

In this review, Weales finds that the most interesting thing about *Les Blancs* is James Earl Jones's performance as Tshembe, noting that he "plays the part with a strong sense of the character's ambivalence toward this situation and the resulting mockery of himself as well as others."

A Raisin in the Sun

(Ethel Barrymore Theatre, New York, 1959)

Summary of Play

As the play opens, the Younger family, living in a run-down, vermin-infested tenement in Chicago, awaits the arrival of Lena Younger's insurance check of $10,000, a bequest from Lena's deceased husband, Big Walter. The family quarrel among themselves as to how the money should be spent. Lena wants to use it to escape to a better life in the suburbs and to pay for her daughter Beneatha's medical school expenses. But Walter Lee, Lena's son, wants the money to invest in a liquor store so that he can free himself from chauffeuring white men around for a living. However, the insurance money cannot satisfy the desires of both mother and son. Lena makes it clear to Walter Lee that she will not give him the money to buy a liquor store, a venture she finds morally offensive. Walter Lee becomes incensed and leaves the apartment. Thinking she knows what's best for her family, Lena puts a down payment on a house in an all-white suburb. Gradually, however, she realizes that Walter Lee must have something of his own. She entrusts the remainder of the money to Walter Lee, telling him to do what he thinks best with it but reminding him that part of the money must go toward Beneatha's schooling. Consequently, Walter Lee gives the money, including Beneatha's portion, to one of his partners, who flees town. Blinded by guilt, Walter Lee considers recouping the loss of the money by accepting a "bribe," an offer made by the suburban neighborhood association, to buy back the Youngers' new house at a profit to them. But Walter Lee refuses the bribe, and the family moves into the new neighborhood.

Playscripts

Afro-American Literature: Drama. Edited by William Adams, Peter Conn, and Barry Slepian, 1–100. Boston: Houghton Mifflin, 1970.

Black Theater: A 20th-Century Collection of the Work of Its Best Playwrights. Edited by Lindsay Patterson. New York: Dodd, Mead, 1971.

Black Theater U.S.A: Plays by African Americans, 1847 to Today. Rev. ed.

Edited by James V. Hatch and Ted Shine, 512–554. New York: Free Press, 1996.

"The Complete Text of *A Raisin in the Sun.*" *Theatre Arts* 44 (Oct. 1960): 28–58.

Contemporary Black Drama; from A Raisin in the Sun to No Place To Be Somebody. Edited by Clinton F. Oliver. New York: Scribner, 1974.

Four Contemporary Plays. Edited by Bennett Cerf. New York: Vintage, 1961.

Norton Anthology of African American Literature. Edited by Henry Louis Gates and Nellie McKay, 1725–1790. New York: W.W. Norton, 1997.

Plays of Our Time. Edited by Bennett Cerf, 544–630. New York: Random House, 1967.

A Raisin in the Sun. New York: Modern Library, 1995.

A Raisin in the Sun and *The Sign in Sidney Brustein's Window* [with critical essays by Amiri Baraka et al.]. Edited by Robert Nemiroff. New York: Vintage Books, 1995.

A Raisin in the Sun [with an introduction by Robert Nemiroff]. New York: Vintage Books, 1994.

A Raisin in the Sun [30th anniversary edition]. New York: Samuel French, 1988. Includes script revisions.

A Raisin in the Sun [with a new introduction by Robert Nemiroff]. New York: Penguin Group, 1988.

A Raisin in the Sun. London: Methuen, 1960.

A Raisin in the Sun: A Drama in Three Acts. A Raisin in the Sun and *The Sign in Sidney Brustein's Window* [new foreword by Robert Nemiroff and critical essays by Amiri Baraka, Frank Rich, and John Brain]. Edited by Robert Nemiroff. New York: New American Library, 1987.

A Raisin in the Sun: A Drama in Three Acts. New York: Random House, 1959.

A Raisin in the Sun: A Drama in Three Acts. New York: Samuel French, 1959.

Six American Plays. Edited by Bennett Cerf. New York: Modern Library, 1961.

Criticism and Performance Reviews

Abramson, Doris E. *Negro Playwrights in the American Theatre, 1925–1959*. New York: Columbia University Press, 1969.

The structure of *A Raisin in the Sun* is a "clash of dreams," between old and young, men and women, black and white. Abramson asserts that despite Hansberry's statement to the contrary, this play "*is* a Negro play." Abramson makes some salient general comments about the play and sums up the reviews of several of the New York critics.

Adams, George R. "Black Militant Drama." *American Imago* 28 (Summer 1971): 107–128.

Adams argues that the emotional intensity with which an audience responds to a play corresponds to the spectators' "psychic structure." In short, "the more a given play is a landscape of our mind, the more important and threatening it will seem . . ." To test this thesis, Adams applies the three Freudian divisions of the psyche (ego, id, and superego) to three well known plays: Lorraine Hansberry's *A Raisin in the Sun* (ego), Amiri Baraka's *Dutchman* (id), and James Baldwin's *Blues for Mr. Charlie* (superego). Adams classifies *Raisin* as an "ego-play" because, of the three plays, it enjoys the widest acceptance by society. In addition, the play dramatizes the growth of the ego—"how a black family comes to the right relationship with 'reality.'" Walter and his family mature within the parameters of the dominant society's value system. In order to survive, the play seems to be saying, the mature ego must adjust to "genuine" white values.

Adler, Thomas P. *Mirror on the Stage: The Pulitzer Plays as an Approach to American Drama*. West Lafayette, Ind.: Purdue University Press, 1987.

Although *Raisin* did not receive a Pulitzer Prize, Adler includes a brief discussion of the play.

Alvarez, A. "That Evening Sun." *New Statesman* (Aug. 15, 1959): 190–191.

Alvarez reports on the London production of *A Raisin in the Sun,* directed by Lloyd Richards at the Adelphi. Although Hansberry's play closely approximates a "tearjerker," "it makes an extraordinarily compelling evening's theatre." Like the Celts, Hansberry has a highly developed sense of rhetorical drama, but unlike her Irish and Welsh counterparts, Hansberry has something of import to say: "Her rhetoric is not just colourful; it has a natural dignity, which presumably has something to do with the fact that the rhythms and diction of passionate Negro speech come straight from the Bible."

Anderson, Mary Louise. "Black Matriarchy: Portrayal of Women in Three Plays." *Negro American Literature Forum* 10 (Spring 1976): 93–95.

Anderson examines the role of the black matriarch, which "white society has forced" on the black woman, in three plays: Lorraine Hansberry's *A Raisin in the Sun,* James Baldwin's *The Amen Corner,* and Alice Childress's *Wine in the Wilderness.* Anderson describes the stereotyped black matriarch as deeply religious, as one who identifies strongly with her role as mother, nurturer, and protector, and who teaches her children to accept the condemnation of whites. Furthermore, the black matriarch is often portrayed as being responsible for the black man's inability to exercise his masculinity. In *Raisin,* Lena Younger resembles the black matriarch figure and her daughter-in-law Ruth "struggles with the matriarch role." Lena attempts to infuse her deeply felt religious beliefs in her children. Lena would sacrifice anything for her family, who will always come first. By blocking her son's purchase of a liquor store, she emasculates him and "keep[s] him from asserting himself as protector of the family." Ruth often sides with Lena and shares in Walter's emasculation by not trying to fulfill his needs as a man.

Arnow, Robert. "Juicy Raisin." *Jewish Currents* 18 (Sept. 1959): 38–39.

Arnow comments that *Raisin* has a particular poignancy for Jewish audiences: "The still restricted, but infinitely freer, Jew cannot afford to disregard the Negro in his time of trial without moral hurt to himself as well as risking the loss of a powerful ally."

Aston, Frank. "*Raisin in the Sun* Is a Moving Tale." *New York World-Telegram and The Sun* (March 12, 1959). [Reprinted in *New York Theatre Critics' Reviews* (1959): 344–347.]

Aston's review echoes the sentiments of most of the New York reviewers. He praises the play for its humor and pathos, yet fails to see its complexity, by describing it as a "simple tale."

Atkinson, Brooks. "The Theatre: *A Raisin in the Sun.*" *New York Times* (March 12, 1959): 27. [Reprinted in *New York Theatre Critics' Reviews* (1959): 344–347 and *On Stage: Selected Theatre Reviews from the* New York Times, *1920–1970.* New York: Arno Press: 1973.]

According to Atkinson, *Raisin*'s honesty lies in its portrayal of the conflicts of a present-day Negro family. The play's candor "is likely to destroy the complacency of anyone who sees it." If there are any "crudities in the craftsmanship," they are minimized by the honesty of the writing and stage work. Atkinson observes that both *Raisin* and Chekhov's *The Cherry Orchard* dramatize characters manipulated by their surroundings. Atkinson praises this "first-rate" play yet, like his New York counterpart, minimizes the play's complexity by discussing the characters in one-dimensional terms: for example, Lena is a noble but "simple character," and Diana Sands's portrayal of the "overintellectualized daughter" is "amusing." See also Atkinson's article "*A Raisin in the Sun*; Vivid Drama About a Poor Negro Family." *New York Times* (March 29, 1959): sec. 2:1.

Baraka, Amiri. "*A Raisin in the Sun*'s Enduring Passion." *Washington Post* (Nov. 16, 1986): sec. F: 1–3.

Upon the occasion of the revival of *Raisin* at the Kennedy Center in 1986, poet and playwright Baraka reflects on the continued relevance of the play, which was first performed in New York in 1959. He acknowledges that in 1959 many, including himself, viewed the play as conservative because its focus on middle-class concerns. However, "we missed the essence of the work . . . Hansberry had created a family engaged in the same class and ideological struggles as existed in the [civil rights] movement—and within individuals." Baraka argues that neither his play *Dutchman* or James Baldwin's *Blues for Mr. Charlie* "is as much a statement from the majority of blacks as is *Raisin.*" Those middle class issues Hansberry raises "actually reflect the essence of black will to defeat segregation, discrimination and oppression."

Barthelemy, Anthony. "Mother, Sister, Wife: A Dramatic Perspective." *Southern Review* 21, no. 3 (Summer 1985): 770–789.

Barthelemy considers how *A Raisin in the Sun* is a feminist revision of Theodore Ward's *Big White Fog* (1938) and how Joseph Walker's *The River Niger* (1973) counters Hansberry's feminist vision with a traditional patriarchal agenda. When examined as a group, the plays reveal how playwrights affect one another's work as well how character and plot are influenced by the playwrights' political vision. The plots of *A Raisin in the Sun* and *Big White Fog* are similar. Both deal with families living in Chicago and the lead males of both plays struggle to achieve in a society rife with racism and oppression. However, the plays diverge in their portrayal of women. Ward's female characters for the most part are negative, especially the character of Martha Brooks, who measures individuals according to the color of their skin. Antithetical to Brooks is Hansberry's Lena Younger, who measures character based on love and understanding. In *The River Niger*, Walker's portrayal of women "challenges and faults Hansberry's representation of black men and women . . . machismo is accompanied by its near-cousin, misogyny." Barthelemy also points out that although the last scenes of Ward and Hansberry's plays deal with the removal of the families' furnishings, the resolution of each play is very different. While Victor in *The River Niger* is shot by a bailiff for resisting eviction by attempting to move his family's furniture back into their house, the furniture of *Raisin*'s Younger family is removed from their shabby ghetto home to a newly purchased home in the white suburbs, representing the Younger's entry into the American bourgeoisie.

Benston, Kimberley W. Baraka: *The Renegade and the Mask*, 227. New Haven, Conn.: Yale University Press, 1976.

Benston contrasts Hansberry's matriarchal figure Lena with Baraka's Mother in his play *Madheart*. According to Benston, Baraka's Mother "encourages her child not so much to endure as to succeed at all costs and, further, teaches that 'success' means substitution of white crudity and gaudy riches for black values." Baraka makes fun of the formidable single black mother keeping her family together "through pure toughness and unyielding hope."

Bonin, Jane. *Major Themes in Prize-Winning American Drama*. Metuchen, N.J.: Scarecrow Press, 1975.

Bonin attempts to explore the values and attitudes of mainstream Americans by examining twentieth-century plays that have won the Pulitzer, Obie, the Drama Critics' Circle Award, or the Tony. She limits her study to what she considers "man's most . . . universal concerns: his relationships to his family, his vocation, his society, and his God." Bonin uses *Raisin* to demonstrate that the American dream has been for the most part "the white man's dream." But the unrealistic quest for the dream can also be "the white man's disease," for it overshadows the pride and dignity of the family unit.

Brien, Alan. "Theatre: Suspected Persons." *The Spectator* 58 (Aug. 14, 1959): 189, 191.

According to Brien, in *Raisin*, Hansberry "buries" the dilemma of whether to assimilate or withstand the white man's culture. Furthermore, he argues, the play is not specifically about Negroes—other oppressed groups such as Jews, homosexuals, and communists could easily be substituted: "The Negroes on stage are stage Negroes . . . [D]espite the genuineness of the actors their colour still seems to have been applied with a paint stick. . . . [This play] is the prototype television play about little people facing a crisis which threatens to crack the family group like a dropped tea cup."

Brooks, Mary Ellen. "Reactionary Trends in Recent Black Drama." *Literature and Ideology* 10 (1970): 41–48.

Brooks provides a rhapsodic critique of several "reactionary" playwrights, including Lorraine Hansberry, whose plays advocate collaborating with the bourgeoisie instead of promoting revolutionary change against the "imperialist" United States. Underlying their plays is the reactionary notion that "human nature . . . transcends class interests." Although both are diminished by the relationship, the slave ultimately "destroys the power of the slave master." Brooks asserts that *A Raisin in the Sun* dramatizes blacks "on the make." The Younger family for a time struggle with defiance within a racist society, but ultimately they sink back into subservience.

Brown, Lloyd W. "Lorraine Hansberry as Ironist: A Reappraisal *of A Raisin in the Sun*." *Journal of Black Studies* 4, no. 3 (March 1974): 237–247.

Brown observes that Hansberry has "been caught up in the continuing conflict between the ethnic criteria of social protesters and the pro-integrationist's ethos of love and reconciliation." On the one hand, critic Harold Cruse deplores Hansberry's pro-bourgeois stand. But other critics, such as C.W.E. Bigsby (Confrontation and Commitment: A Study of Contemporary Drama 1959–1966. Columbia: University of Missouri Press, 1967) and Richard A. Duprey ("Today's Dramatists." *American Theatre. Stratford-Upon-Avon Studies* 10 (1967): 209–224) praise Hansberry's transcendence of racial politics with compassion and understanding. And Jordan Miller (5.52) contends that *Raisin* should be judged solely by its text, not its sociopolitical statements. According to Brown, these critics represent a recurrent problem in black literary criticism: isolating structure and technique from socio-political factors. By titling the play after a negative connotation in Langston Hughes' poem of what happens to a "dream deferred," Hansberry's irony is evident. Brown argues that Hansberry accepts the ideal of the American dream but at the same time she accepts its dark realities for poor black people, like Walter Younger "whose dreams, or hopes, have dried up": "The point is not that Lorraine Hansberry rejects integration or the economic and moral promise of the American dream, but that she remains loyal to this dream ideal while looking, realistically, at its corruption in the United States."

Bruckner, D.J.R. "Stage: At Roundabout, *A Raisin in the Sun." New York Times* (Aug. 15, 1986): C3.

Bruckner reviews a revival of *Raisin* at the Roundabout Theater Company in New York City. He observes that Hansberry's powerful dramatization of the issues of race conflict, class, and personal identity overshadows "the many flaws in the play." Part of the problem, Bruckner contends, is that director Harold Scott "approaches the play with a little too much reverence." Scott's interpretation accentuates the powerful dialogue over emotional impact, thus creating a distance from the theatergoers. The reviewer highlights Starletta Dupois' portrayal of Ruth Younger. In most productions Ruth "remains a kind of blotting paper for the emotional outpourings of the others," but Dupois's rendition of Ruth is very full-bodied and "compelling." Sylvianne Gold of the *Wall Street Journal* also reviewed this production (5.14).

Carter, Steven R. "Images of Men in Lorraine Hansberry's Writing." *Black American Literature Forum* 19 (Winter 1985): 160–162.

Hansberry informs both her male and female characters with her feminist vision. She did not portray strong female characters at the expense of males, playing sympathetic women against one-dimensional male villains and abusers. Male spectators can relate to her full-bodied male characters, yet, according to Carter, Hansberry "carefully emphasized the ways in which these sympathetic creations are caught in the web of sympathetic conditioning in male supremacy and the resulting harm that they do to women and themselves." Hansberry's males are often heroic in their efforts to deal with personal, social, and economic pressures but often in the process they oppress the women in their lives. For example, in *A Raisin in the Sun*, Walter's treatment of his mother, wife, and sister fluctuates depending on his financial situation. When he lacks money, his hostility toward them intensifies, yet when he is flush with money, he "behaves more gently and responsively" to them. Furthermore, although in different ways, Beneatha's suitors, George Murchison and Joseph Asagai, attempt to limit Beneatha. Asagai has the potential to "free himself" from his chauvinism so that their relationship can grow.

Chapman, John. "*A Raisin in the Sun:* A Glowingly Lovely and Touching Little Play." *New York Daily News* (March 12, 1959). [Reprinted in in *New York Theatre Critics' Reviews* (1959): 344–347.]

A must read for those who wish to examine an example of how many contemporary critics' misunderstood the play, overlooked its complexity, and patronized Hansberry's craftsmanship and artistry. According to Chapman, *Raisin* (in the 1959 production at the Ethel Barrymore Theatre), being a "slight and simple" story, is a not a "big play and probably not even an important one," but it is "affectionately human, funny and touching." He further explains that "its great appeal lies in its affection and understanding, rather than in the mechanics of telling a story." Chapman's misinterpretation of the play is especially obvious in his superficial analysis of the play's resolution, which he describes as "heartening."

Christiansen, Richard. "Goodman Taps Fine Wine with Raisin." *Chicago Tribune* (Oct. 4, 1983): sec. 2: 8.

Christiansen praises the revival of *Raisin,* as directed by Tom Bullard, at the Goodman Theater in Chicago. The play "still works": "It rings with ironies that give it added meaning, added sorrow and perhaps even added hope."

Clurman, Harold. "Theater." *Nation* 188 (April 4, 1959): 301–302.

Clurman observes that although *Raisin* has some traits of neo-realism, its "inspiration is . . . less ambitious and more plainly specific than that of neo-realist writers." The play's only weakness in an otherwise "extraordinarily gratifying" evening is that the ending is a bit sentimental. The characters "become somewhat picturesquely heroic."

Coleman, Robert. "*Raisin in Sun* Superior Play." *Daily Mirror* (Mar. 12, 1959). [Reprinted in *New York Theatre Critics' Reviews* (1959): 344–347.]

Coleman highly praises this "smash hit." He hails Hansberry as "the most gifted dramatist to reach the Rialto in several semesters."

Collins, William B. "Drama Guild Revives *A Raisin in the Sun.*" *Philadelphia Inquirer* (Dec. 5, 1985): C1, C9.

Collins contends that *A Raisin in the Sun,* a revival presented by the Philadelphia Drama Guild, "cannot be viewed as a sociological relic." According to him, the issues the play deals with are as alive today as they were a quarter of a century ago when the play was first performed.

Cook, William. "Mom, Dad and God: Values in Black Theater." In *The Theater of Black Americans*. Vol.1. Edited by Errol Hill, 168–184. Englewood Cliffs, N.J.: Prentice-Hall, 1980.

Cook analyzes *Raisin* to assess how the values of the matrifocal family and church influence the protagonist. Lena does not impose her will on her children but rather tries to infuse the values of their father—"to mold them into the kind of people he would have them be." She also wants them to draw on religion, which has given her the strength she has needed to overcome so much. When her son, Walter, finally comes into his manhood, "[t]he transformation of the boy Walter into the man is complete, the restoration of the father as source of pride is accomplished, the integration of religious values with secular concerns has triumphed and Lena, high priestess and exegete, can say amen and rest."

Cooper, David D. *"A Raisin in the Sun." Explicator* 52, no.1 (1993): 59–61.

Cooper explicates *Raisin* within the context of *The Moral Life of Children* by Robert Coles.

Cruse, Harold R. "Lorraine Hansberry." In *Crisis of the Negro Intellectual,* 267–284. New York: Quill, 1984.

Cruse hails *Raisin* as the "most cleverly written piece of glorified soap opera I, personally, have ever seen on a stage." He criticizes Hansberry for writing a play that reinforces the movement to integrate the Negro not only into the American mainstream artistic community but also into the American middle-class value system. Hansberry's Younger family does not represent the Negro working-class family but a lower-middle-class or middle-class family. Thus the Youngers are much more palatable to the white middle class. Cruse contends that the Youngers cannot possibly represent the Negro working class because the latter does not have access to "the economic keys" available to the Youngers. For example, Cruse asks how a poor family could afford a $10,000 insurance policy, support a daughter going to college, and have the connections and credit to buy a liquor store. According to Cruse, Hansberry's integrationist views blind her to the necessity of examining the "internal facts of Negro ethnic life. . . . Negro playwrights have never gone past their own subjectivity to explore the severe stress and strain of class conflict within the Negro groups." He maintains that middle-class Negro playwrights, in their zeal to integrate with the white middle class, will never create plays that "portray some unpleasant truths about their own class."

Davis, Ossie. "The Significance of Lorraine Hansberry." *Freedomways* 5 (Summer 1965): 396–402.

Davis argues that *A Raisin in the Sun* is deemed a very good play by critics and audiences for the wrong reasons. "She got success, but that in her success she was cheated, both as a writer and as a Negro." One reason for its wide acceptance is that many audiences found that the Younger family resembled a typical American family, *"color-ain't-got-nothing-to-do-with-it."* This assumption was embodied in the character of Lena, the matriarch of the family. Audiences felt comfortable with Lena; "they could surrender themselves to her so completely, could find somebody they could trust absolutely up there on that stage." This sentimental attitude toward Lena was not, Davis argues, the focus of the play. The play was about Walter Lee's attempt at the American dream. Although the liquor store he desired would "enable him to exploit the misery of his fellow slum dwellers," it was his dream. Walter Lee symbolized frustrated black youth, surrounded by wealth and opportunity, yet continually "slapped down" when they tried to "reach up and grab, like everybody else." But rather than exploding from frustration, Walter is rescued by Hansberry, who allows him to flee, with Mama, to the suburbs. But, questions Davis, "Has not Walter merely swapped one impossible dream for another?"

"Domestic Drama from the Top Drawer." Theatre Arts (July 1959): 58–61.

This is a pictorial essay of the 1959 Broadway production of *A Raisin in the Sun* at the Ethel Barrymore Theatre.

Driver, Tom F. "Theater: *A Raisin in the Sun*." *The New Republic* 140 (April 13, 1959): 21.

Driver concludes that as drama, *Raisin* is "old-fashioned. . . . [M]uch of its success is due to our sentimentality over the 'Negro question.'"

Fabre, Genevieve. *Drumbeats, Masks and Metaphor: Contemporary Afro-American Theatre.* Cambridge, Mass.: Harvard University Press, 1983.

Fabre suggests that *Raisin* is dishonest. Through its happy ending, the play asserts that integrating into a white neighborhood is salvation. The Youngers "deserve" to move into the white suburbs because they have adopted the values of the middle class that they hope to join. Fabre argues that *Raisin* is an important play in the way Hansberry dramatizes the conflicts between a man and a woman. For example, while Ruth is portrayed as strong and honest, she also "keeps her man from dreaming and realizing his dreams." Fabre asserts that "this role will be more clearly defined as castrator, and the woman will appear quite often as the major obstacle to the man's affirmation of virility."

Fletcher, Leah. "Black Theatre Alive and Struggling Hard." *Bay State Banner* (March 20, 1975): 16.

The Boston Black Repertory Company chose *Raisin* as its first major production. The reason, according to director Harold Stewart, is that he considers Hansberry's play an "institution . . . it is one of the best plays ever written, black or white." This play "will be read, performed, talked about and above all it will live on."

France, Arthur. "*A Raisin* Revisited: A Re-evaluation of *A Raisin in the Sun* as Tragedy." *Freedomways* 5 (Summer 1965): 403–410.

France explicates the play on the assumption that it is a tragedy according to the Aristotelian tradition.

"From *Raisin* to the Present." *American Theatre* 1 (Nov. 1984): 9–11.

Selected artists and writers reflect on how Lorraine Hansberry and her plays have affected them and black theater. Included are Woodie King, Jr., James Baldwin, Ishmael Reed, Gregory Mosher, Margaret B. Wilkerson, John O'Neal, Steven Woolf, Hal Scott, and Michele Shay.

Gill, Glenda. "Techniques of Teaching Lorraine Hansberry: Liberation from Boredom." *Negro American Literature Forum* 8 (1974): 226–228.

Gill begins by providing a rationale as to why teachers should mainstream black authors in American literature courses. For some teachers, the task is "complex [and] uncomfortable" because of the resistance they experience from some parents and students. Gill shares her successful lesson plan of teaching *A Raisin in the Sun* as part of her sophomore drama course.

Gold, Sylviane. "Timeless Play About Black Experience in White America." *Wall Street Journal* (Sept. 2, 1986): sec. 1: 24.

Gold praises this "solid revival" of *Raisin* at the Roundabout Theatre in New York City. Unlike Bruckner (5.31), who saw Ruth as the most compelling character, Gold considers Olivia Cole's character of Lena as the "liveliest of all." Gold sees Starletta DuPois's Ruth as "exaggerated naturalism."

Gottlieb, Daniel W. "*A Raisin in the Sun* Premieres at Shubert." *Hartford Times* (Jan. 22, 1959).

Gottlieb hails *Raisin* as a "landmark in modern drama," one that "neither dissects the human race in pseudo-Freudian style nor stomps on it unmercifully."

Greenfield, Thomas Allen. *Work and the Work Ethic in American Drama, 1920–1970.* Columbia: University of Missouri Press, 1982.

Greenfield observes that *Raisin* is an important play because it explores the complex issues of blacks working in urban, white America, such as the differences in attitudes between rural blacks and blacks living in cities and between educated and uneducated blacks. Hansberry also "presents a credible picture" of the crisis of the black man's self-identity. But Greenfield insists that the "play cheats itself." That is, the play does not address the question of how blacks cope "economically or psychologically with their own job failure." From an economic perspective, Greenfield asserts that "Hansberry's answer is wholly unsatisfactory." Although his dignity is restored at the end of the play, for example, Walter is still a chauffeur with the additional financial burden of a new house. Greenfield notes that the play "seems to sugarcoat the very serious problems it raises by turning into an uplifting drama of racial pride after presenting the central conflicts in economic and work-related terms."

"Hail *A Raisin in the Sun* as Broadway Dramatic Hit." *Jet* (March 26, 1959): 60–62.

The reviewer describes the response of theatergoers to the opening night performance of *A Raisin in the Sun.* The performers received a seven-minute standing ovation and nine curtain calls. Sidney Poitier, as Walter Lee, "hoisted" playwright Hansberry from the orchestra pit to the stage to receive her applause. According to the reviewer, the play is significant for its exposure of "a piece of everyday life which is only incidentally about Negroes, more precisely about people."

Haley, Alex. "The Once and Future Vision of Lorraine Hansberry." *Freedomways* 19 (4th Quarter 1979): 277–280.

Haley, author of *The Autobiography of Malcolm X* and *Roots,* highlights the contributions of Lorraine Hansberry. Her plays reveal her ability to foresee the social protests that ignited the civil rights movement of the 1960s. Her uniqueness lies in her "populariz[ing]" of the relationship between blacks residing in America and blacks indigenous to Africa. For example, Beneatha's Nigerian suitor in *A Raisin in the Sun,* "dispel[ed] the myth of the 'cannibal' African with a bone in his hair." Also, many audiences saw for the first time on stage a woman clothed in African dress and coifed in an Afro. Despite Hansberry's strong social and political beliefs, she steered clear of typecasting her villains—"she treated all of her characters equally." Carl Lindner, in *Raisin,* is not a stereotypical racist, but a man conditioned by society to be racist. Likewise, Hansberry's heroes were flawed; they were at times cruel and weak. Her refusal to stereotype reflects her "understanding of the struggles that engulf and frustrate individuals—and which drive humanity."

Hansberry, Lorraine. "Willie Loman, Walter Younger, And He Who Must Live." *Village Voice* (Aug. 12, 1959): 7–8. [Reprinted in *The* Village Voice *Reader: A Mixed Bag from the Greenwich Village Newspaper*. Edited by Daniel Wolf and Edwin Fanche. Garden City, N.Y.: Doubleday, 1962.]

Hansberry discusses the parallels between Arthur Miller's Willy Loman in *Death of a Salesman* and Walter Lee Younger in *A Raisin in the Sun.* Although Willy Loman was instantly recognizable to audiences because they were familiar with his background, Walter Younger, "jumped out . . . from a play about a largely unknown world." Yet both men were Americans, entrapped by American cultural values. Willy and Walter sense that something impedes their progress of getting ahead. Yet, Hansberry observes, neither "question[s] the nature of this desired ascendancy." Walter survives because he is able to "draw on the strength of an incredible people who, historically, have simply refused to give up."

Harrison, Paul Carter. *The Drama of Nommo.* New York: Grove Press, 1972.

Harrison argues that "despite Hansberry's obvious misrepresentation of the black family's aspirations in a socio-realistic play which, at best, gives only a linear description of the forces of oppression, she demonstrates a profound understanding of how a family is spiritually cemented. With naturalistic detail, she orders the principle Kintu-money into its proper relationship to the family's oppression. And when money exerts its force, threatening to split up the family, she has the mother Nommo the male principle forward into its rightful, symbolic position in the family by giving her son, Walter Lee, the money . . . the spiritual legacy of the dead father."

Hays, Peter L. "*Raisin in the Sun* and *Juno and the Paycock.*" *Phylon* 33 (Summer 1972): 175–176.

Hays draws parallels between *Raisin* and Irish playwright Sean O'Casey's *Juno and the Paycock.* Both plays take place in the city and during a time of social rebellion; both have families as protagonists; in both works, women support their families emotionally and financially; both have intellectually curious daughters conflicted between two suitors; and, finally, in both plays the families depend on a financial legacy to pull them out of poverty but the legacy fails to materialize. However, the endings are quite different —O'Casey's tragically and Hansberry's with hope. O'Casey's protagonist Jack Boyle slides into alcoholism when the money is lost to him. On the other hand, Hansberry's Walter Lee finds himself restored as patriarch of the Younger family.

Hewes, Henry. "A Plant Grows in Chicago." *Saturday Review* 42 (April 4, 1959): 28.

Hewes proclaims that finally "we have . . . a play that deals with real people." Although the Younger family must deal with racial issues, this fact "seems less important than that they are people with exactly the same problems everyone else has."

Isaacs, Harold R. "Five Writers and Their Ancestors, Part II." *Phylon* (1960): 243–336.

Isaacs discusses how Hansberry, Langston Hughes, Richard Wright, James Baldwin, and Ralph Ellison confront their African ancestors in their writing. Isaacs suggests a parallel between Hughes's and Hansberry's treatment of Africa. Both have a romantic vision of reuniting the black American and the black African. But Hansberry's vision is "shaped by new times, new outlooks." She does not yearn for "lost primitivism, nor does she beat it out on synthetic tomtoms." Africa, for Hansberry, does not mean the only choice for black Americans to relieve themselves of their despair. Rather, Africa has "become a choice between new freedoms now in the grasp of black men, both African and American."

———. "Lorraine Hansberry." In *The New World of Negro Americans*, 277–287. New York: John Day, 1963.

Isaacs includes Hansberry in a section of his book that deals with how Negro writers have come to terms with their African heritage. The significance of *A Raisin in the Sun* is not only in its depiction of a Negro family confronting white America but also making visible the idea of Africa to American audiences, who heretofore saw them as "spear throwing savages." According to Isaac, Hansberry considers herself a "a strong Negro nationalist" She believed that a some point all peoples would merge but until that time "oppressed peoples must express themselves" through their unique identities.

Kerr, Walter. *"A Raisin in the Sun." New York Times* (March 12, 1959): 27. Reprinted in *New York Theatre Critics' Reviews* (1959): 344–347.

Kerr hails Hansberry's first play as "impressive" and "beautifully acted." Unlike some of the other reviewers, Kerr analyzes the complexity of the characters, especially Ruth: "Wan, winsome, holding back the tartness that is always ready at the edge of her tongue, this wraithlike figure slowly comes into focus as the bond between embattled souls who cannot help betraying one another." Kerr feels that the second act is relentless in its desperation—"Blow follows blow, snarl follows snarl, and we are threatened with a monotone of defeat." The "caustic comedy" that added relief to earlier scenes is "mysteriously missing." See also Kerr's article "Theatre: *A Raisin in the Sun.*" *New York Herald Tribune* (March 22, 1959): Lively Arts:1–2.

Keyssar, Helene. *Feminist Theatre: An Introduction to Plays of Contemporary British and American Women.* London: Macmillan, 1984.

Keyssar contends that Ruth and Beneatha represent the most interesting women to appear in traditional American drama: "These roles are important within the context of feminist drama because they represent how women are abused by male protagonists." Initially, Hansberry seems to establish empathy for Walter when Ruth appears disinterested in his aspirations to being an owner of a liquor store ("Man say to his woman, I got me a dream. . . . His woman say, eat your eggs and go to work"). Not only is Ruth disinterested, but she is a conspirator in the "creation of the impotent black male." Yet Hansberry dramatizes a less appealing side of Walter—his narcissism, which contributes, in part, to Ruth's considering aborting their baby. Walter's sister clearly wants more out of life than being somebody's wife, but she has difficulty convincing the men that surround her, including her two suitors. Keyssar observes that *Raisin* "raises the curtain on the complex interaction between racism and sexism but lowers it quickly, as if to warn the audience that such chaos lies on this terrain that more clearing of the land must occur before such territory can be encompassed on stage." See also Keyssar's *The Curtain and the Veil: Strategies in Black Drama.* New York: Burt Franklin, 1982; "Black Drama: Reflections on Class and Class Consciousness," *Prospects: A Journal of American Studies* 3 (1977): 263–288; and "Rites and Responsibilities: The Drama of Black American Women." In *Feminine Focus: The New Women Playwrights.* Edited by Enoch Brater, 226–240. Cambridge: Oxford University Press, 1989.

King, Woodie Jr. "Legacy of *A Raisin in the Sun*: Hansberry's Children." In *Black Theatre: Present Condition*, 94–96. National Black Theatre Touring Circuit, 1981.

King describes the deep effect *Raisin* has had on black artists. "The power of the play had made us all aware of our uniqueness as Blacks and has encouraged us to pursue our dreams. Indeed, the play had confirmed that our dreams were possible."

———. "Lorraine Hansberry's Children: Black Artists and *A Raisin in the Sun*." *Freedomways* 19 (4th Quarter1979): 219–221.

According to King, many of the important black artists in theater have been greatly influenced by the work and vision of Lorraine Hansberry: "The power of [*A Raisin in the Sun*] had made us all aware of our uniqueness as Blacks and had encouraged us to pursue our dreams."

Laufe, Abe. *Anatomy of a Hit: Long-Run Plays on Broadway from 1900 to the Present Day*. New York: Hawthorn Books, 1966.

Laufe examines the conditions that make for long-running plays. *Raisin* enjoyed a long run because Hansberry avoided making the play polemical or overly critical of whites. The treatment of blacks and whites is balanced. Although Hansberry advocates better conditions for blacks, "she does not present it militantly."

Lewis, Theophilus. "Social Protest in *A Raisin in the Sun*." *The Catholic World* 190 (Oct. 1959): 31–35.

According to Lewis, *Raisin* is a "great play." A summary of its plot does not come close to the emotional complexity of the play—"few will come away from a performance unmoved by its total impact." The emotional tautness emanates from "Negroes under pressure." Hansberry seems to be saying that "Negroes have to be tough to survive." The play appeals to Lewis on two other levels. First, he praises the play for lacking a Freudian agenda—"no characters . . . motivated by hidden compulsions or childhood trauma." Second, unlike many writers of social drama, Hansberry does not attempt to mount a crusade or dramatize reform; rather she "holds the mirror . . . allowing her audience to supply the interpretation."

———. "Theatre." *America* 101 (May 2, 1959): 286–287.

Lewis applauds Hansberry for crafting a "social drama" that avoids "the pulpit [the] social reformer, and the working politician." The conflict, suspense, and humor emerge from the conflicted relationships of a Negro family "under pressure." Lewis agrees with Walter Kerr's assertion that the "obvious flaws" of the play are overshadowed by "understanding, by sensitive direction and by superlative acting."

Littlejohn, David. "Negro Writers Today: The Playwrights." In *Black on White: A Critical Survey of Writing by American Negroes,* 66–79. New York: Grossman, 1966.

Littlejohn identifies Hansberry as one of several black playwrights of note, along with Ossie Davis, James Baldwin, and LeRoi Jones. In his discussion of *Raisin,* Littlejohn concludes that the play is "too straightforward, in the end, too loving and simple and direct to wound effectively, though it may teach something of the inner pressure of Negro life." Although some scenes are intense, the play ends well and, thus the white audience "may be left safely content. "

"London Critics Cool to *Raisin in the Sun.*" *New York Times* (Aug. 5, 1959): 32.

The *Times* reports that although the audience responded warmly to *Raisin* (Adelphi Theatre, London), the critics were "cool." Alan Dent of *The News Chronicle* and W.A. Darlington of *The Daily Telegraph* found the play slow, although they praised its story and acting.

Malcolm, D. "Theatre." *The New Yorker* 35 (March 21, 1959): 100–102.

Malcolm lauds the play for its "relaxed freewheeling interplay of a magnificent team of Negro actors, " who "drew [him] unresisting into a world of their making, their suffering, their thinking, and their rejoicing." He remarks, however, that sentimentality limits the character of Lena and wishes that Hansberry had not idealized "such a stolid old conservative."

McClain, John. "Gives a 'Wonderful Emotional Evening.'" *New York Journal American* (March 12, 1959): 18. Reprinted in *New York Theatre Critics' Reviews* (1959): 344–347.

McClain's review is one of the few reviews of the 1959 Broadway performance that discusses the play within the context of the black experience. He finds the play impressive for its veracity—"[T]here are no 'Uncle Toms,' [no] humility, [and no] abnormal exploitation of the current racial problems." McClain argues that Sidney Poitier as Walter Lee, "has several moments of extravagant emotion which could be less extravagant" and that the character is "often nebulous." Furthermore, although Lloyd Richards "directed well," he did so at times "with a bit too much emphasis."

McKelly, James C. "Hymns of Sedition: Portraits of the Artist in Contemporary African-American Drama." *Arizona Quarterly,* 48, no. 1 (Spring 1992): 87–107.

McKelly uses *A Raisin in the Sun* as a catalyst to discuss the black artist caught in a balancing act between being true to an artistic vision while at the same time responding to the social and political experience of African-Americans. Whites embraced Hansberry's play because the play supported the basic values of the American work ethic—"that American democratic capitalism can be the vehicle of African-American political and economic ascent." Thus whites did not feel threatened. Even the modern Beneatha, a thinly disguised self-portrait of an artist, is caught between Asagai, the Nigerian representing traditional African values, and George Murchison, the "scion of the new black bourgeoisie." By the end of the play, she still has not chosen between the two, but she is confident that the American system "though resistant, will eventually accommodate her desire to achieve the self-expression for which she longs." But Hansberry's view of the artist changed in subsequent years. She recognized "that the black artist is as much inclined to an art of insurrection as to an art of the beautiful; [there is a] fundamental tension between art and politics which is the black artist's responsibility, or curse."

Miller, Jordan Y. "Lorraine Hansberry." In *The Black American Writer.* Vol. 2. Edited by C.W.E. Bigsby, 157–170. Deland, Fla: Everett/Edwards, 1969.

Miller provides an overview of Hansberyr's work and aesthetic vision within the contest of the times in which she wrote.

Mitchell, Loften. *Black Drama: The Story of the American Negro in the Theatre.* New York: Hawthorn Books, 1967.

Loften discusses the controversy that surrounded the original production of *Raisin.* Blacks resented whites who claimed they could identify with the Younger family. Some alleged that the play did well because "it was really a Jewish play." And still others became angry at those critics who praised Hansberry for writing a "balanced" play devoid of anger. Loften observes that *Raisin* "crystallized the era Negro playwrights began to call the 'nots'. . . . [T]he black playwrights were being praised for *not* making white people uncomfortable in the theatre."

———. "I Work Here to Please You." In *The Black Aesthetic.* Edited by Gayle Addison, 291–304. Garden City, N.Y.: Doubleday, 1971.

Loften points out that, despite the good reviews, *Raisin* suffered from many misinterpretations by critics. For example, he claims that some reviewers hailed this play as a "Negro *Cherry Orchard*" or "Negro *Awake and Sing*." Categorizing seems to be germane only to black work—one never sees critics praising Chekhov's *The Sea Gull* as a "Russian *Wild Duck*." Mitchell observes this is a penchant on the part of critics to indicate their desire "to reduce the Black Aesthetic to an imitative level, to deny it its originality."

Molette, Carlton W. and Barbara J. *Black Theatre: Premise and Presentation,* 119–121. Bristol, Ind.: Wyndham Hall Press, 1986.

The authors argue that of all the characters in *Raisin,* Walter Lee is the only one whose transformation is the result of self-realization. Yet most white critics do not consider Walter Lee as the central character, much less the hero of the play. Many of these critics are predisposed to believe the notion that black families are controlled by the matriarch. But the authors assert that what critics do not realize is that Walter Lee is following the African tradition of seeking advice from his elder. Although he does not have to act on her advice, he must listen to it: "Somehow, the respect Lena receives from Walter . . . as mother and elder is misconstrued by [w]hites to be matriarchal rule."

New York Theatre Critics' Reviews. (1959): 344–347.

This is a collection of reprints of major New York newspaper reviews of *A Raisin in the Sun.*

Norment, Lynn. "Raisin Celebrates Its 25th Anniversary." *Ebony* 39 (March 1984): 57–60.

Norment profiles Hansberry and discusses *Raisin,* which, in commemoration of its influence on drama, was to be performed at the Goodman Theatre in Chicago and at the Yale Repertory Theater. Norment comments that *Raisin* foreshadows the women's movement of the 1960s in that "it touches upon the importance of the Black woman's moral support of her husband and her contribution to the family's financial welfare."

Parks, Sheri. "In My Mother's House: Black Feminist Aesthetics, Television, and *A Raisin in the Sun.*" In *Theatre and Feminist Aesthetics.* Edited by Karen Laughlin and Catherine Schuler, 200–228. Madison, N.J.: Fairleigh Dickinson University Press, 1995.

Acknowledging that many feminists reject the notion of television as a "medium of feminist aesthetics" because they assume that the medium is antifeminist, Parks demonstrates how the television version of *A Raisin in the Sun* (1989) "lends more evidence that the form of television has the potential to communicate successfully the themes, issues, and communication strategies which Hansberry originally wrote into her script and to deliver them in to the homes of ordinary black women."

Phillips, Elizabeth. "Command of Human Destiny as Exemplified in Two Plays: Lillian Hellman's *The Little Foxes* and Lorraine Hansberry's *A Raisin in the Sun.*" *Interpretations* 4 (1972): 29–39.

Phillips observes that both plays assert that "man may command his own destiny." She also discusses several other parallels between the two plays. Both plays, for example, center on families whose heritage is deeply rooted in the South. Hansberry and Hellman both deal with the dire consequences resulting from greed, bigotry, and self-centeredness. Phillips examines both plays in terms of the values that are revered in each, then analyzes them to determine the true from the false values. For example, the importance of manhood is dramatized in both plays. In *Foxes,* Horace's sense of himself as a man is nearly destroyed by his wife, Regina. However, he regains his manhood after he blocks her attempt to exploit the town. In *Raisin* Walter Lee nearly sacrifices his manhood when he is tempted to sell out to Lindner and the white neighborhood association he represents. But Walter Lee reaffirms his maleness when he spurns their financial offer.

Potter, Vilma R. "New Politics, New Mothers." *CLA Journal* 16, no. 2 (Dec. 1972): 247–255.

Potter asserts that from *A Raisin in the Sun* to Ben Caldwell's *Family Portrait or My Son, the Black Nationalist,* black playwrights "have shifted the focus of characterization to present an imitation of things as they were or are . . . to an imitation of things as they are thought to be, for the express purpose, as Aristotle perceives it, to secure a greater good or avert a greater evil." Lena, the matriarch of *Raisin*'s Younger family, is a notable personage—strong with deep religious convictions, hardworking, generous, and protective of her family. Potter sees Lena as affirming the white audience's own commitment to these values.

"*A Raisin in the Sun.*" *Theatre Arts* (May 1959): 22–23.

Hansberry's play demonstrates that the "Negro has come a long way in the American theatre." The characters in *Raisin* are devoid of the stereotypes long typified in drama. The "happy" ending reflects "the age of improving but still imperfect race relations."

Richards, Lloyd. "An Unlikely History." *American Theatre* 1 (Nov. 1984): 8.

Richards, the original director of *Raisin,* recounts how the play came close to not being performed. At the time, there were no major granting agencies to fund a play written by an unknown (Hansberry), directed by an unknown (Richards), and produced by someone (Philip Rose) who had produced only records. According to Richards, the play had more investors than any other Broadway production—"little people who believed in an idea, the naive first-time investor who had not yet been educated to understand what was impossible." *Raisin* was finally performed to rave reviews in New Haven and Philadelphia.

Robertson, Nan. "Dramatist Against Odds." *New York Times* (Mar. 8, 1959): sec. 2: 3.

Robertson recounts how Hansberry overcame the obstacles to persuade the producers to back *Raisin.* She deplores the poor response of backers to plays written by Negroes. These backers read her play and exclaimed, "It's beautiful! Too bad it isn't a musical. White audiences aren't interested in a Negro play." But Hansberry insisted that *Raisin* "wasn't a 'Negro play'. . . . It was a play about honest-to-God, believable, many-sided people who happened to be Negroes." According to Robert Nemiroff, Hansberry sent a letter, which was never published, to the *Times* denying parts of this interview.

Sacks, Glendyr. *"A Raisin in the Sun."* In *Contemporary American Dramatists.* Edited by K.A. Berney, 711–712. London: St. James Press, 1994.

Sacks presents a basic explication of the play.

Scanlon, Tom. *Family, Drama, and American Dreams,* 196–201. Westport, Conn.: Greenwood, 1978.

Scanlon argues that *a Raisin* remains the best of the recent black family dramas.

Scharine, Richard G. *From Class to Caste in American Drama: Political and Social Themes Since the 1930s.* New York: Greenwood, 1991.

Scharine considers *Raisin* "the best protest play ever written because of its ability to turn an audience's perception of 'them' into a mutual 'we.'"

Seaton, Sandra. "*A Raisin in the Sun*: A Study in Afro-American Culture." *Midwestern Miscellany* 20 (1992): 40–49.

Seaton refutes the criticism of Harold Cruse, who believes that *Raisin* ignores the complexities of black life, and C.W.E. Bigsby, who condemns the play for its parochial attitude toward the race issue. Both criticize the play's ending but for different reasons. Cruse sees the ending as the family's selling out to white middle-class values, and Bigsby sees the end as "something of a specious *deus ex machina.*" Seaton avers that Cruse would like Hansberry to write characters and situations that reflect the sociological record, but Hansberry's purpose is not to minimize differences to make political statements but to "create characters whose complexities are both true to life and true to the demands of art." The strength of *Raisin* lies in its "subtle probing of the conflicts within the black culture."

Shinn, Thelma J. "Living the Answer: The Emergence of African American Feminist Drama." *Studies in the Humanities* 17 (Dec. 1990): 149–159.

Examining the works of Hansberry, Childress, Kennedy, and Shange, Shinn traces the shift of focus from the stories of men to those of women, with a concomitant shift from traditional dramatic conventions to postmodernist theater forms. While all four playwrights deal with race relations, gender is foregrounded in the works of Childress, Kennedy, and Shange. The plays discussed include *A Raisin in the Sun, Wine in the Wilderness, Funnyhouse of a Negro, Cities in Bezique,* and *for colored girls. . . .*

Siegel, Ed. "A Riveting *Raisin in the Sun.*" *Boston Globe* (May 26, 1995): Living: 81.

Siegel reviews the twenty-fifth anniversary restaging of *Raisin* produced by the Huntington Theatre Company of Boston University. This production reincorporated the cuts Hansberry made, according to Siegel, to satisfy the white audiences of the 1959 production. Siegel says that "[t]here were limits [to what white audiences] . . . wanted to hear about black life." The power of the uncut version is the balance between art and ideas: "The ideas are in the conflicts so smoothly laid out by Hansberry. . . . [The art] lies in how Hansberry handles those conflicts: with a profound respect that shows us the world through each of the Youngers' eyes." The ideas and conflicts are explosive, but "the play retains its power from how softly her authorial presence treads." Hassan El-Amin's interpretation of Walter Lee differs from that of Danny Glover's (1988 PBS television production) in that he brings "an everyman and everyclass quality" rather than "eject[ing] the underclass lava" as Glover does. Siegel points out two disappointing aspects of the play. First, this production leaves out the scene in which Beneatha changes her hairdo to an Afro. Second, El-Amin's "less-volcanic" portrayal of Walter works everywhere except in the scene where he has hit bottom after learning that he has lost the insurance money. His despair is not quite believable.

Talbot, William. "Every Negro in His Place: The Scene On and Off Broadway." *Drama Critique* 7 (Spring 1964): 92–98.

Talbot, an editor for Samuel French, professor, and writer, assesses *A Raisin in the Sun* by focusing on the position of blacks in the theater arts. Talbot asserts that although heretofore the theater has "disparaged the Negro more often than it has raised him to eminence," he foresees that the dramatic media will provide "the subtlest and most powerful influence in dignifying the American Negro." Talbot sees *Raisin,* as having "some protest in it," but the drama is primarily about a family, its hopes and dreams, and its relationships.

Tallmer, Jerry. "Theatre Uptown: Welcome, Miss Hansberry." *Village Voice* (March 18, 1959): 7.

Tallmer believes that the New York critics are "overguarded" in their praise of *Raisin*. This play is "quietly revolutionary." Hansberry "has done nothing less than to pick her people up and shove them dramatically—as *people,* not as A People—into the middle of the twentieth century."

"Theater." *Catholic World* 189 (May 1959): 159.

This review summarizes the plot and concludes that the play is honest, "splendidly acted [and] deserves a warm welcome."

"Theater: *A Raisin in the Sun." Time* 73 (March 23, 1959): 58–59.

The reviewer hails Hansberry as a "fine, fresh playwriting talent" and praises her play for its "intelligence, honesty, and humor. " According to the reviewer, the play's major strength is its "saving absence of racial partisanship." The play might have dwindled into sentimentality had it not been for its keen insight into its milieu, the flavorful speech, and "its infectious sense of fun so caustic."

"Theater: With a Wallop." *Newsweek* 53 (March 23, 1959): 76.

The reviewer salutes *Raisin* as "one of the most stirring and revealing productions of the year" and predicts that it will be nominated for a best play of the year award. See also *Newsweek* (April 20, 1959): 75.

Tynan, Kenneth. "*A Raisin the Sun.*" *The New Yorker* (March 21, 1959): 97–100. [Reprinted in *Curtains: Selections from the Drama Criticism and Related Writings,* 307–309. New York: Atheneum, 1961.]

Tynan observes that the "supreme virtue" of *A Raisin in the Sun* "is its proud, joyous proximity to its source, which is life as the dramatist has lived it." The characters drew him "unresisting into a world of their making, their suffering, their thinking, and their rejoicing." Tynan's only real complaint regarding the play is the sentimentality of Lena Younger—"I wish the dramatist had refrained from idealizing such a stolid old conservative."

Ward, Douglas Turner. "Lorraine Hansberry and the Passion of Walter Lee." *Freedomways* 19 (4th Quarter 1979): 223–25.

Ward, himself a playwright, actor, and former artistic director of the Negro Ensemble Company of New York, asserts that most interpretations of *Raisin* are "tendentiously simplistic." Critics emphasize Walter's redemption when he refuses to "sell out" the dignity of black people. Such emphasis assumes a character who, prior to his salvation, throws tantrums when his dreams of material gain are thwarted and was "only redeemed in the end by his opting to grow up." The emphasis, according to Ward, should instead be on Walter's prophetic quality. Walter represented the state of the black man, present and future: "His restless impatience, his discontent with the way things are, his acute perception of societal disparities, his fury at status inequities, his refusal to accept his 'place' . . . gives the play prophetic significance." The unsettling questions Walter raises in the play undoubtedly threatened many in the 1959 audiences. The play seemed to be asking them, "Where would all this raging frustration lead?"

Washington, J. Charles. "*A Raisin in the Sun* Revisited." *Black American Literature Forum* 22, no. 1 (Spring 1988):110–124.

Critics and theater audiences view Walter as somewhat diminished by Lena's moral strength because they judge his actions according to a moral code more appropriate for Lena than Walter. Judging Walter according to his mother's moral and spiritual code is a mistake, according to Washington, because it upsets the "proper balance between Lena and Walter." Washington argues that Walter's moral strength is "as great as, if not greater than, his mother's." They must be considered dual protagonists; if not, the dramatic and emotional tension of the play is weakened. Unlike his mother,

Walter sees the American dream in terms of economics, not in terms of surviving in a racist society with a modicum of dignity. For Walter, money is the way to overcome racial inferiority. However, Walter's desire for wealth is not for personal material gain but to improve the living conditions of his family: "The selflessness and nobility of this dream are what give Walter's character its dignity and spiritual dimension." Although Walter fails at achieving the American dream, he transcends that tragedy as he represents the trials and tribulations of Black Americans.

Watts, Richard. "Two on the Aisle: Honest Drama of A Negro Family" *New York Post* (March 12, 1959). [Reprinted in *New York Theatre Critics' Reviews.* (1959): 344–347.]

Watts praises Hansberry's play for its honesty and lack of sentimentality in depicting the conflicts of a black family living in a white man's world. Hansberry demonstrates a "fine sense of character, a gift of wry humor, the ability to give a scene emotional impact, and a capacity to see the weaknesses and pettiness of people without losing her respect for them as puzzled human beings."

Weales, Gerald. "Thoughts on *A Raisin in the Sun.*" *Commentary* 27 (June 1959): 527–530.

Despite its flaws, Weales considers *Raisin* a "good play." Its power is grounded in the character of Walter Lee, who, according to Weales, "transcends his being a Negro." The play would have been simply "editorial" if Hansberry had limited the conflict to a racial one. However, Walter Lee is swayed, like Willy Loman, by the American myth. By making this the central conflict, Hansberry "has come as close as possible to what she intended—a play about Negroes which is not simply a Negro play." Of the play's weaknesses, Weales asserts that its naturalism makes it "old-fashioned": "Practically no serious playwright, in or out of America, works in such a determinedly naturalistic from."

Wilkerson, Margaret. "Lorraine Hansberry: The Complete Feminist." *Freedomways* 19 (4th Quarter 1979): 235–245.

The tension of being black and female forms Hansberry's worldview and aesthetic vision. According to Wilkerson, she keeps both her blackness and femaleness in balance; however, she does not manipulate the issues facing black males to feed her feminist vision. Rather than divorcing ideology from the protagonists' environment, Hansberry "refuses to diminish the pain, suffering or truths of any one group in order to benefit another." Like the black feminist Ida B. Wells, Hansberry rejects the idea of reserving a woman "to a place" but "emphasize[s] . . . the importance of her full participation in the life and struggles of the race." Hansberry never wrote a "feminist play," but the women characters of *Raisin* are deeply involved in the play's plot. For example, the character of Lena at first appears to be a portrayal of the stereotypical black matriarch. Yet, as the play progresses, Lena's motives are not to dominate her family but rather that "she believes [her actions] are right for her children."

———. "*A Raisin in the Sun*: Anniversary of an American Classic." *Theatre Journal* 38, no. 4 (Dec. 1986): 441–452. [Reprinted in *Performing Feminisms: Feminist Critical Theory and Theatre.* Edited by Sue-Ellen Case, 119–130. Baltimore: Johns Hopkins University Press, 1990.]

In the three decades since its groundbreaking premiere, *Raisin* has continued to attract theatergoers. Wilkerson traces the sociopolitical forces surrounding the initial production of the play, looks at the critics' reactions, and concludes with a discussion of the political and cultural factors that have ensured the play's continued relevance to audiences.

———. "The Sighted Eyes and Feeling Heart of Lorraine Hansberry." *Black American Literature Forum* 17 (Spring 1983): 8–13.

Wilkerson argues that Hansberry's work prophesied the black arts movement of the 1960s and that she was "one of its major literary catalysts." Walter, for example, represents the "symbolic father of the aggressive, articulate black characters" created in the 1960s. Although Walter is a victim of a racist society, he is a descendant of proud ancestors who struggles to overcome those who would oppress him. At first, Walter believes that money will free him and his family and provide respect and dignity, but in the end, when he refuses the offer of his white neighbors to buy him out, he has "begun to shed the materialism of the majority culture [and] leads the march to a different drum." Brief discussions of *The Drinking Gourd* and *Les Blancs* are included.

Willis, Robert J. "Anger and the Contemporary Black Theatre." *Negro American Literature Forum* 8 (1974): 213–215.

Although the anger in Hansberry's *Raisin* is "somewhat tempered" compared to later playwrights, such as Baraka and Baldwin, Hansberry was a visionary who "pointed the way to a new direction, a newness in content and attitude, and a purpose for Black theatre."

Zolotow, Sam. "*A Raisin in Sun* Basks in Praise; 7 Critics Welcome Play by Miss Hansberry." *New York Times* (March 13, 1959): 25.

Zolotow reports that *Raisin* rivals Tennessee Williams's *Sweet Bird of Youth* for accolades from the major New York theater critics. However, *Raisin* has a "more rugged road to travel" than Williams play because its cast and director are less well known. Although the trial productions of *Raisin* in New Haven, Philadelphia, and Chicago were well received, "there was no immediate box office stampede." However, this situation changed quickly. One of the play's sponsors, Philip Rose, attributed the spurt of interest to the fact that "the audience gets color-blind and they no longer see Negroes on the stage."

Additional Performance Reviews

Beckerman, Jim. "We Remember Mama in This *Raisin*." *The Record* (New Brunswick) (Jan. 20, 1995): Lifestyle:11

Coleman, Robert. "*Raisin in Sun* Superior Play." *New York Daily Mirror* (March 16, 1959). [Reprinted in *New York Theatre Critics' Reviews (1959)*: 344–347.]

The Commonweal (April 17, 1959): 81–82. (ill)

Herman, Jan. "*Raisin in Sun* Enlightens But Loses Subtle Shadings." *Los Angeles Times* (Feb. 2, 1994): sec. Calendar:1.

Hubbard, George R. "Theater Review: *A Raisin in the Sun*." *Courier-Journal* (Louisville) (Oct. 21, 1989): Scene: 19S.

"Rich, Relevant *Raisin*." *Seattle Times* (Oct. 28, 1994): H25.

"Theater." *Playboy* 18 (April 1971): 36–37.

The Sign in Sidney Brustein's Window
(Longacre Theater, New York, 1964)

Playscripts

A Raisin in the Sun and *The Sign in Sidney Brustein's Window* [with critical essays by Amiri Baraka et al.]. Edited by Robert Nemiroff. New York: Vintage Books, 1995.

A Raisin in the Sun and *The Sign in Sidney Brustein's Window* [new foreword by

Robert Nemiroff and critical essays by Amiri Baraka, Frank Rich, and John Brain.] Edited by Robert Nemiroff. New York: New American Library, 1987.

The Sign in Sidney Brustein's Window. Rev. Stage Ed. New York: Samuel French, 1986.

The Sign in Sidney Brustein's Window: A Drama in Three Acts. New York: Random House, 1965.

The Sign in Sidney Brustein's Window: A Drama in Three Acts. New York: Samuel French, 1965.

Three Negro Plays [with an introduction by C.W.E. Bigsby]. Harmondsworth: Penguin, 1969.

Summary of Plot

Spending a great deal of his past trying to save the world and living according to absolute truths, Sidney Brustein, at the opening of the first scene, is a burned-out idealist. He has survived several causes and "feels cynical, scarred, and combat-weary." He defends his position as a "wounded reformer" to two of his friends, who try to persuade him to advocate a reform political campaign in his fledgling newspaper. Yet, as the story progresses, a series of characters systematically break down Sidney's "smug sense of superiority." His wife, Iris, a frustrated actress, becomes increasingly alienated from Sidney because of his self-absorption and sense of superiority. Iris's sister, Mavis, also pierces Sidney's intellectual superiority. Sidney is shocked to learn that Mavis, whom he always saw as "square," has suffered quietly for years in a hollow marriage to protect her child and the image of a respectable marriage. She points out to him that "[t]here are no squares, Sidney. Believe me when I tell you, everybody is his own hipster." He is further appalled when his friend Alton Scales, an African-American, announces that he is breaking his engagement to Sidney's other sister-in-law, Gloria, because he has discovered that she is a prostitute. Sidney believed his leftist friend could not be affected by such middle-class biases. When Gloria hears of her fiancé's rejection, she commits suicide. The final blow to Sidney's illusory world is the fact that the "reform" candidate, whom he actively supported, won the election; but the candidate turns out to be a false prophet, part of the established political machine. Sidney realizes he has been used. But instead of recoiling, his growing awareness enables him to mature as he begins to see the world as it is, not as it should be.

Criticism and Performance Reviews

Bain, Myrna. "Theater." *National Review* (March 23, 1965): 249.

Bain insists that the publicity surrounding *The Sign in Sidney Brustein's Window* "was generated to help a play that should have closed on opening night." Since the play lacked a plot, Bain contends that Sidney is reduced to "long-winded exercise[s] in how great it is to be committed to 'serious' issues." Hansberry "had hoped no doubt to immortalize all the Sidneys of the world; instead she succeeded only in embalming them." Bain accuses Hansberry as well as LeRoi Jones, whose *The Slave* and *The Toilet* she also reviews, of "lightly rehash[ing] the contents of the thirties proletarian theater."

Barnes, Clive. "Stage: *Sidney Brustein.*" *New York Times* (Jan. 27, 1972): 44.

Although far from "perfect," and not very "profound," Barnes considers *Sidney Brustein* "provocative." Hansberry is a "master at the dramatic confrontation—savage and surprising impact of people upon one another." Despite the interesting characters, the parts are superior to the whole. Barnes also finds fault with the music and "folksy chorus," which impede the action. Such an ineffective device is unfortunate, Barnes maintains, because the "staging is smooth . . . [and] the acting is good."

Braine, John. "Theatre Uptown." *Village Voice* (Nov. 26, 1964): 17, 21.

Unlike most of the New York critics, Braine, a British author and critic, thinks the play is "great." He believes that these critics, because of their stiff deadlines, failed to recognize the greatness of the play: " I am convinced that sooner or later . . . the public's judgment will prove better." See also Braine's essay, "An Appreciation: Sidney Brustein—A Great Play—No Other Word Is Possible." In *A Raisin in the Sun: A Drama in Three Acts. A Raisin in the Sun* and *The Sign in Sidney Brustein's Window* [new foreword by Robert Nemiroff and critical essays by Amiri Baraka, Frank Rich, and John Brain.] Edited by Robert Nemiroff, 155–159. New York: New American Library, 1987.

Carter, Steven R. "Inter-ethnic Issues in Lorraine Hansberry's *The Sign in Sidney Brustein's Window.*" *Explorations in Ethnic Studies* 11 (July 1988): 1–13.

Hansberry's second play, *The Sign in Sidney Brustein*'s *Window*, prompted some to accuse her of abandoning the "cause" of blacks and "trying too hard to win acclaim as a 'universal writer.'" Carter disagrees, asserting that Hansberry continued her exploration of oppression and this society's attempt to wipe out resistance "through the concept of the 'melting pot.'" Hansberry's complex vision encompassed a society that respected differences in race and cultural background. For Hansberry, "a multiethnic society has far more to offer than any homogeneous society." But Hansberry was no Pollyanna; she realized that overcoming intolerance to attain a functional, culturally diverse society is a painful struggle. It is no accident that the protagonist, Sidney, is Jewish. He represents the "Jews' historical resilience in oppression and adversity and . . . the sensitivity, courage and insight that they derived from this." Sidney embodies Hansberry's close identity with the Jewish intellectual movement, as well as her recognition of the historical bond between Jews and blacks in America. But Hansberry also recognized that even so-called enlightened people can have their flaws. Although others respect Sidney for his sensitivity and straightforwardness, "he too can be vicious and unreasonable and highly unjust." For example, Sidney behaves insensitively toward his sister-in-law Mavis, the gay playwright David Ragin, and his wife, Iris. Following this essay is a brief critique by Helen MacLam.

Gassner, John. "Lorraine Hansberry: The *Sign in Sidney Brustein's Window.*" In *Dramatic Soundings: Evaluations and Retractions Culled from 30 Years of Dramatic Criticism,* 579–580. New York: Crown, Publishers,1968.

Like many other critics, Gassner criticizes Hansberry's play for creating a play "without quite precipitating one." Gassner praises Hansberry for not falling victim to the racial stereotypes of the 1960s, but he wishes she would have practiced the same avoidance when it came to her portrayal of the homosexual dramatist, which Gassner "found both tasteless and unfair."

Gill, Brendan. "All Thumbs." *The New Yorker* (Feb. 5, 1972): 69.

Gill complains that this version of *Sidney Brustein* is no improvement over the first production in 1964, which was "a poor play." The adaptation by Robert Nemiroff, who according to Gill, "has made a . . . career since [Hansberry's] death out of tinkering with her literary works," attempted to update the play by applying "cosmetic scatological invective" and "some mindless incidental songs."

Hansberry, Lorraine. "Village Intellect Revealed." *New York Times* (Oct. 11, 1964): sec., 2: 1, 3.

Hansberry contends that the character of the title role in *Sidney Brustein* debunks the stereotypical intellectual seen so much on stage and in film. Theatergoers rarely see a "corduroy-wearing, chukka-booted, Bergman film-loving, non-cold-water-flat-living, New School lecture-attending, Washington Square concert-going, middle- class and usually Jewish argument-loving Greenwich Village intellectual." She also complains that people have asked why she did not continue writing about the "the Negro question." Hansberry responds that she never has written about "the Negro question." *Raisin* confronted the avariciousness of American society in which the characters happened to be black. However, as Hansberry points out, the characters of her plays are both black and white: "I write plays about various matters which have both Negro and white characters in them, and there is really nothing else that I can think of to say about the matter."

Hewes, Henry. "Broadway Postscript." *Saturday Review* (Oct. 31, 1964): 31.

Hewes wishes that this rather rambling work had focused on one play "rather than offering us at least half a dozen." But he praises Hansberry for "her honesty, her accuracy of observation, and her superior dialogue."

Holtan, Orley I. "*Sidney Brustein* and the Plight of the American Intellectual." *Players* 46 (June/July 1971): 222–225.

Holtan seems to agree with those critics who believe that *Sidney* is a "far more mature work" than *A Raisin in the Sun,* despite the fact that Hansberry raises several issues in the play that never quite "coalesce." Holtan proceeds to explicate the play's meaning in a general way.

Killens, John Oliver. "Broadway in Black and White." *African Forum* 1, no. 3 (1965): 66–68.

Despite the complaints of several critics, Killens considers *Sidney Brustein* "brilliant." He derides these critics' complaint that the play attempts too many ideas: "Broadway critics have become accustomed to a diet of small-scoped, small-minded plays," in which the dialogue is much ado about nothing. According to Killens, Hansberry's untimely death deprived the black people of an "eloquent voice in their struggle to make a change in the country's emphasis."

Lewis, Theophilus. "Theatre: *The Sign in Sidney Brustein's Window.*" *America* 11 (Dec. 5, 1964): 758–759.

Although Lewis believes the plot often "gets lost" within a host of "skillfully etched scenes," he maintains that "Hansberry has given us a delectable chiaroscuro of life in the Village."

McCar, John. "Hansberry's Potpourri." *The New Yorker* (Oct. 24, 1964): 93.

McCar provides a negative critique of *Sidney Brustein.* He deems the play to be "overwrought," and finds that the script prevents the characters from being "reflective."

Mitchell, Loften. *Black Drama: The Story of the American Negro in the Theatre.* New York: Hawthorn Books, 1967.

Loften argues that *Sidney Brustein* is a "far more mature play on many levels" than *A Raisin in the Sun.* Although several issues Hansberry introduced did not coalesce, "she spoke of commitment, directly, sincerely and in theatrical terms." Loften also poignantly describes his last meeting with Hansberry before her death.

Ness, David E. "*The Sign in Sidney Brustein's Window*: A Black Playwright Looks at White America." *Freedomways* 11 (1971): 359–366.

Ness disagrees with many critics who contend that the structure is too loose and cluttered with characters with too many problems. But Ness argues that the disparate conflicts of the characters are grounded in their vulnerability to the political and economic power structure. One by one, their vulnerabilities converge on Sidney, who, in turn, "is forced by circumstances to examine the nature of his world, a collection of problems that are *of a piece.*" In the beginning Sidney is a white, middle-class, liberal intellectual; by the end of the play, he is an "American radical." His radicalism results not from accident but necessity. As his enlightenment of the real world intensifies, "Sidney's political commitment is forced into something strong." Ness observes that the theme of "what it takes to make a man committed to a cause" resonates throughout Hansberry's plays, such as *A Raisin in the Sun, The Drinking Gourd,* and *Les Blancs.*

Redding, Saunders. "In Search of Reality." *The Crisis* (March 1966): 175–176.

Redding comments that *Sidney Brustein* "is a good play. . . . It just misses being great"; unfortunately, he does not elaborate on this observation.

Schiff, Ellen. "The Jew and Other Outsiders." In *From Stereotype to Metaphor: The Jew in Contemporary Drama.* Edited by Ellen Schiff, 156–160. Albany: State University of New York Press, 1982.

Schiff includes a brief discussion of Sidney Brustein in her study of the images of the Jewish character on stage since World War II. Schiff views Brustein, an American Jew, as "personify[ing] an alien factor that has earned a degree of acceptance in society." He perceives social prejudices, such as racism and homophobia, as "bothersome clichés" and prefers to devote his life to "other pressing concerns." Brustein, Schiff observes, exemplifies "distinctly Jewish traits." For example, Brustein "loves life with the love of an idealist who prides himself on being true to his moral principles." He refuses to be depressed by bad luck. And, finally, he is an "incurable insurgent." Sidney Brustein embodies the "Jewish experience as archetypal, [which] furnishes the subtext" of the play.

Sheed, Wilfrid. "The Stage." *The Commonweal* (Nov. 6, 1964): 197–198.

The play dramatizes several plots, each of which would make a good play "if the other plots would leave it alone. Several of the scenes would be powerful if they weren't switched off too quickly in the interests of pace and zest." The scenes involving Alice Ghostley as Mavis and Ben Aliza as the black man who intends to marry a white prostitute have "the makings of real drama. . . . If either of those big scenes had been allowed to grow into a play, the play would have been a good one." Sheed also suggests that Hansberry follow through with the parody she hints at with quotes from Thoreau and Kafka.

"The Sign in Sidney Brustein's Window." National Review (March 23, 1965): 250.

In this very brief review, the reviewer complains that *Sidney Brustein* "should have closed on opening night." Moreover, Hansberry's play is not much more than a "rehash of the contents of the thirties proletarian theater."

Taubman, Howard. "Allowing for Flaws: Tolerance in Musicals Greater Than Plays." *New York Times* (Nov. 1, 1964): sec. 2: 1.

Despite its flaws, Taubman praises *The Sign in Sidney Brustein's Window* for its "passion, intelligence, and point of view." He notes that the most intense scenes are those that involve the "Negro questions."

———. "Theater." *New York Times* (Oct. 16, 1964): 32.

According to Taubman, there are some "good things scattered" throughout *The Sign in Sidney Brustein's Window,* but the the play lacks "concision and cohesion."

"Theater: Borrowed Bitchery." *Newsweek* 64 (Oct. 26, 1964): 101.

The reviewer did not like this play. Hansberry, it seems, has written an "incredibly awkward drama . . . [in which] character talks to character like droning telephone poles." The play consists of several individualized plots, which serve to dramatize her "venomous anger [at] homosexuals, liberals, abstract artists, nonrealistic playwrights, white people unwilling to commit suicide, Albert Camus, Jean Paul Sartre, Samuel Beckett, William Golding, and, especially, poor, plundered Edward Albee." The reviewer concludes by accusing Hansberry of "shifting her suffering to the backs of others, in using every easy trick to destroy what threatens her [and that] she has betrayed not only the function of art, but social responsibility, political possibility, her own cause and, most racially, herself."

"The Theater: Guilt Collectors." *Time* 84 (Oct. 23, 1964): 67.

In this review, *Sidney Brustein* is criticized for being "too loaded, overwritten and overwrought." The play lacks the directness of *A Raisin in the Sun,* having "too many minds of its own. . . . The play has diversity without direction." Despite these flaws, the critic praises the performances of Alice Ghostley as Iris, "an inflated marshmallow of a woman," and Ben Aliza, the black suitor of Iris's younger sister. However, eloquent as these scenes are, the reviewer finds that Hansberry's intelligent dialogue and sharp insight into the human condition are weakened by the lack of dramatic direction—"the play as a whole has the hazy look of a smudge fire."

"Theatre." *The Nation* 199 (Nov. 9, 1964): 340.

The reviewer believes that the play is too "sincere"; it tries "to say everything." The play becomes sluggish because of too much philosophizing. Hansberry attempts to dramatize the ills of urban life among the intellectuals and subsequently provides a "cure" through compassion for others. Ultimately, though, "nothing is dramatized . . . self-explanation takes the place of revelation." The reviewer notes, however, that one character that "comes to life" is Iris as played by Alice Ghostley. Despite Peter Kass's "emotionally vehement direction," the play's structure is "rickety," and much of the dialogue "function[s] not as substantial characterization but as wisecracks and facile editorializing."

Thurston, Chuck. "There's a Message Here, in All the Talk." *Detroit Free Press* (April 28, 1976): 12–A.

Thurston bemoans this production of *Sidney Brustein* as performed by Detroit's Group Theatre as slow, ("lengthy discussions [that] continue far into the night") and dated, ("The play needs severe trimming to suit today's mood").

Walker, Jesse H. "Miss Hansberry's New Play for Intellectuals." *N.Y. Amsterdam News* (Oct. 24, 1964).

Although the reviewer finds the play at times directionless and boring, *Sidney Brustein* "has its moments of passion, pathos, humor and some fine characterizations."

Additional Performance Reviews

Los Angeles Times (July 18, 1991): Calendar: 9

Sun-Sentinel (Fort Lauderdale) (April 4, 1995): Lifestyle: 3E.

Toussaint (A Work in Progress)

(An excerpt, directed by Lloyd Richards, was taped for the National Educational Television Broadcasting System [now PBS] for the program "Playwright at Work," on May 21, 1961.)

Playscripts

Wilkerson, Margaret B. ed. *Toussaint (A Work in Progress).* In *9 Plays by Black Women,* 51–66. New American Library, 1986.

Summary of Plot

The scene opens on the brink of the Haitian Revolution in the 1780s, as Bayon De Bergier, a manager of a sugar plantation on Santo Domingo, entreats his wife to help him entertain yet another representative of the absentee owner. But Bayon's Creole wife, Lucie De Bergier, refuses because she is bored with the talk of these men and their wives. She also resents Bayon's relationships with black mistresses and their illegitimate offspring. Underlying these tensions is Lucie's awareness that her husband is bitter because he had to marry beneath him. While Lucie and Bayon argue, they hear the cry of a slave being whipped by Bayon's steward, Toussaint. Lucie observes that Toussaint does not seem to take pleasure in whipping the slaves and seems to realize that Toussaint is the one really managing the plantation. As Steven R. Carter points out ("Lorraine Hansberry's Toussaint." *Black American Literature Forum,* 1989. Reprinted in *Hansberry's Drama,* 1991. See *Toussaint,* Criticism), Hansberry reveals in subsequent drafts that Toussaint is indeed not the contented steward

Bayon thinks he is but rather is training the slaves to obey him so that one day they will be in a position to overthrow the planters.

In Margaret Wilkerson's introduction to this unfinished play, Hansberry comments that since her teen years she has been impressed by the Haitian liberator Toussaint L'Ouverture. Yet many of the dramatic and fictional accounts offended Hansberry because their stereotypical views of Caribbean peoples misrepresented the "entire significance and genuine romance of the . . . magnificent essence of the Haitian Revolution and its heroes." Hansberry was fascinated by how the poor, illiterate, and divided people of Haiti overthrew France, a major world power. As Hansberry says in a note prefacing the play, "[The Haitians] waged a war and won it. They created a nation out of a savagely dazzling colonial jewel in the mighty French empire."

As Steven Carter notes, much of *Toussaint,* which Hansberry began in 1958, is comprised mostly of notes and roughly drawn scenes—only one scene is complete enough to be performed. Clearly, Carter observes, in its earlier stages, Hansberry meant the play to be a musical, referring to the piece as an "opera." However, the one polished scene performed for the National Education Television Broadcasting System (now PBS) in 1961 has only background music. For a more detailed discussion of Hansberry's intentions regarding the form of *Toussaint,* see Steven R. Carter's article, "Lorraine Hansberry's *Toussaint.*"

Criticism

Carter, Steven R. "Lorraine Hansberry's *Toussaint.*" *Black American Literature Forum* 23, no. 1 (Spring 1989): 139–148. [Reprinted in Carter, Steven R. *Hansberry's Drama: Commitment and Complexity.* Urbana: University of Illinois, 1991.]

Carter explains the background of Hansberry's incomplete play and explicates the most polished scene, which was produced for the National Educational Televsion Broadcasting System in 1961. He praises this scene as doing more than most full-length plays and literary works in "teach[ing] more . . . about slavery, colonialism, and pre-Revolutionary Haiti."

What Use Are Flowers? A Fable in One Act

(National Black Arts Festival, Atlanta, 1994)

Playscripts

The Best Short Plays of 1973. Edited by Stanley Richards, 100–130. Radnor, Pa: Chilton, 1973.

Les Blancs: The Collected Last Plays of Lorraine Hansberry. Edited by Robert Nemiroff. New York: Random House, 1972.

Lorraine Hansberry: The Collected Last Plays. Edited by Robert Nemiroff, 125–139. New York: New American Library, 1983.

Works in Progress/No. 5. Edited by Martha Saxton, 11–51. New York: Literary Guild, 1972.

Summary of Plot

After twenty years, a seventy-eight-year-old English professor turned hermit emerges from his place of refuge to find the earth devastated by a great holocaust. He happens upon a group of children, one girl and the rest boys, who apparently know nothing of the ways of civilized life: They eat raw meat, do not know what fire is, and cannot speak a language. The hermit attempts to teach the children about "the remnants of civilization" that he had earlier renounced. He shows them how to make a wheel. He dies. The children fight over the wheel and destroy it. The story ends with the children discussing how to repair the wheel.

Hansberry commented in a letter to Mme. Chen Jui-Lan of Peking University that the hermit "does not entirely succeed and we are left at the end, hopefully, with some appreciation of the fact of the cumulative processes which created modern man and his greatness and how we ought not go around blowing it up."

Criticism and Performance Reviews

Iverem, Esther. "One Final Play Depicts a World Full of Fear; Atlanta Premiere for Work by Lorraine Hansberry." *Newsday* (Aug. 1, 1994): sec. 2: B7.

Iverem discusses the premiere of Hansberry's last play, *What Use Are Flowers?,* which was produced as part of the National Black Arts Festival in Atlanta. Although Hansberry had completed the text of the play before her death, she had not been able to include the stage directions. Her estate hired Harold Scott, who knew Hansberry and had performed in a 1970s version of *Les Blancs* and directed a production of *A Raisin in the Sun* . Scott wrote the stage directions and deemphasized the "Eurocentric slant" of Hansberry's text. For example, to Scott, Hansberry's original hermit seemed too much of an "Anglican English teacher." Scott revised the hermit to be African-American. The director also added W.E.B. Du Bois to the hermit's list of great thinkers, which included Copernicus and Einstein; included some African songs in the hermit's repertoire of music that he teaches the children; and incorporated more girls into the band of children.

Nemiroff, Robert. "A Critical Background: *What Use Are Flowers?*" In *Lorraine Hansberry: The Collected Last Plays.* Edited by Robert Nemiroff, 223–226. New York: New American Library, 1983.

According to Nemiroff, Hansberry wrote this play in response not to William Golding's *Lord of the Flies* but to Samuel Beckett's *Waiting for Godot.* She attempted to address issues that Godot raised in his play about "life and death, survival and absurdity." According to Nemiroff, Hansberry originally wrote this play for television. Apparently she changed her mind after her experience with *The Drinking Gourd* and rewrote it for the stage. She set aside the play temporarily when she was unable to reconcile to her satisfaction problems inherent when switching from film to stage. Nemiroff reports that Hansberry had wanted to create a fantasy in which the hermit's monologues are juxtaposed with the dancing of the wild children. She died before she could realize her ideas.

Additional Performance Reviews

Hulbert, Dan. "Arts Entertainment News Backstage." *Atlanta Journal and Constitution* (July 13, 1994): sec. B:11.

Plays Based on Lorraine Hansberry's Life and Work

Love to All, Lorraine

(Actors Theatre, 1995)

Reviews

Bruckner, D.J.R. "*Jubilee!* Black Theater Festival. *New York Times* (May 30, 1985): C22.

Egerton, Judith. "Theater Review: *Love to All, Lorraine.*" *Courier-Journal* (Sept. 20, 1995): Features: 3C.

Lovingly Yours, Langston and Lorraine

(Ensemble Theatre, 1994)

Reviews

"Ensemble Theatre's *Lovingly Yours, Langston and Lorraine.*" *Call and Post* (Cleveland) (Feb. 17, 1994): 9.

Raisin

(Musical based on Hansberry's *A Raisin in the Sun:* 46th Street Theater, 1973; won the Antoinette Perry Award (Tony) for best musical of 1974)

Playscript

Woldin, Judd. *Raisin.* Libretto. Based on Lorraine Hansberry's *A Raisin in the Sun.* Book by Robert Nemiroff and Charlotte Zaltzberg. Music Judd Woldin. Lyrics by Robert Brittan. New York: Samuel French, 1978.

Reviews

Bates, Delores A. "A Comment on Culture." *Freedomways* 14 (1st quarter 1974): 53–58.

"Broadway Musical *Raisin* Comes to Oakland's Paramount Theatre." *The California Voice* (April 2, 1995): 8

Giddings, Paula. "*Raisin* Revisited." *Encore American & Worldwide News* (July 7, 1975): 29–31.

Gill, Brendan. "A Black Rose." *New Yorker* (Oct. 29, 1973):107

Gottfried, Martin. *"Raisin." Women's Wear Daily* (Oct. 19, 1973).

Jones, Clarence. "The Black Artistic Legacy." *N.Y. Amsterdam News* (June 9, 1973): A4

Kalem, T.E. "The Faith that Faded." *Time* (Oct. 29, 1973): 99.

Kroll, Jack. "Angry Dreams." *Newsweek* (Oct. 29, 1973): 67.

New York Theatre Critics' Reviews (1973): 218–222

"*Raisin,* River Niger Sweep B'way Tonys." *N.Y. Amsterdam News* (Apr. 27, 1974): A-1, A-3;

Washington Afro-American (March 11, 1995): B7

Watt, Douglas. "*Raisin,* a Black Period Musical, Brings Back *Raisin in the Sun.*" *Daily News* (New York) (Oct. 19, 1973). [Reprinted in *New York Theatre Critics' Reviews* (1973): 218–222.]

Watts, Richard. "Black Family in Chicago." *New York Post* (Oct. 19, 1973). Reprinted in *New York Theatre Critics' Reviews* (1973): 218-222.

Wilson, Edwin. "Putting Miss Hansberry's Play to Music." *Wall Street Journal* (Oct. 22, 1973): 6.

(1973):218–222; Winer, Linda. "The Boom in Black Theater." *Chicago Tribune* (May 30, 1976): sec. 6: 3.

To Be Young, Gifted, Black
(adaptation by Robert Nemiroff, Cherry Lane Theatre, 1969)

Playscripts

To Be Young, Gifted, and Black. New York: New American Library, 1969.

To Be Young, Gifted and Black: A Portrait of Lorraine Hansberry in Her Own Words. New York: Samuel French, 1971.

Reviews

Berson, Misha. "*Young, Gifted,* Still Relevant." *Seattle Times* (Feb. 4, 1994): Tempo: D16.

Duberman, Martin. "Black Theater." *Partisan Review* 36, no. 3 (1969): 488–490.

Gresham, Jewell Handy. "Lorraine Hansberry as Prose Stylist. *Freedomways* 19 (1979): 192–204

Hentoff, Nat. "They Fought—They Fought!" *New York Times* (May 25, 1969): sec. 2: 1, 18.

"Mixed Blood Theatre Co. Opens Summer Session." *Minneapolis Spokesman* (June 30, 1977): 6.

Steele, Mike. "Mixed Blood Theater Opens with *To Be Young, Gifted, Black. Minneapolis Tribune* (July 9, 1977): 78.

"Tribute to Hansberry." *Seattle Skanner* (Feb. 9, 1994): 8.

Chapter Six
Zora Neale Hurston

Chapter Six
Zora Neale Hurston

Brief Biography

The reputation of Zora Neale Hurston (1901–1960) rests primarily on her work as a fiction writer, in particular her novel *Their Eyes Were Watching God* (1937), and as a folklorist. However, she also wrote several plays and musical revues. In 1925 her first play, *Color Struck,* won second prize in a contest sponsored by *Opportunity: A Journal of Negro Life.* Hurston also cowrote with Langston Hughes the play *Mule Bone.* Their collaboration resulted in a lifelong quarrel that prevented the production of the play for nearly sixty years. The world premiere of the play was not until 1991, when it was produced on Broadway. Hurston's presence is immediately felt in *Mule Bone*; its language and dialogue reflect the intensive work she did in collecting folklore among the black communities of the South. As Warren J. Carson points out, Hurston's work "reinforce[s] her insistence that black drama should be a sincere, realistic reflection of black life."

According to Lillie P. Howard, from the 1930s until her death, Hurston "was the most prolific and accomplished black woman writer in America." She was unique among her generation because she considered her blackness as special. She refused to see herself as a victim: "I am not tragically colored. There is no great sorrow dammed up in my soul. . . . I do not belong to the sobbing school of Negrohood who hold that nature somehow has given them a lowdown dirty deal whose feelings are all hurt about it." She did not deny the existence of racism or react angrily to it. Instead she claimed she was "merely astonished. . . . How can any deny themselves the pleasure of my company! It's beyond me."

Hurston was born in 1901 in the small, all-black town of Eatonville, Florida. She said that the only white people she encountered in her early years were those traveling to and from Orlando. For Hurston, the "white people differed from colored . . . only in that they rode through town and never lived there. They liked to hear me 'speak pieces' and sing."

Playwright May Miller encouraged Hurston to attend Howard University, where she studied with Georgia Douglas Johnson and Alain Locke. In 1928 she graduated from Barnard College and continued her graduate work with the anthropologist Franz Boas at Columbia University.

Along with writing short stories, novels, plays, musical revues, and collections of folklore, Hurston worked as a drama instructor, joined the WPA Federal Theater Project, was awarded a Guggenheim fellowship, and married twice. She died of a stroke on January 28, 1960.

Profiles and General Criticism

Burton, Jennifer. "Introduction." In *Zora Neale Hurston, Eulalie Spence, Marita Bonner, and Others; The Prize Plays and Other One-Acts Published in Periodicals.* Edited by Henry Louis Gates, Jr., xix-lx. New York: G.K. Hall, 1996.

Burton provides a brief introduction to Hurston.

Carson, Warren J. "Hurston as Dramatist: The Florida Connection." In *Zora in Florida.* Edited by Steve Glassman and Kathryn Lee Seidel, 121–129. Orlando: University of Central Florida, 1991.

Carson's essay represents the very few lengthy discussions of Hurston's dramatic canon. He focuses on her career as a dramatist and concludes with the Florida aspects of her plays. Carson remarks that "Hurston was primarily concerned with authenticity in drama, a concern no doubt made more urgent by her training as an anthropologist." White authors, Hurston felt, failed to portray black life as blacks lived it.

Hemenway, Robert E. *Zora Neale Hurston: A Literary Biography.* Urbana: University of Illinois Press, 1977.

This definitive biography of Hurston provides some information on Hurston's dramatic endeavors. Hemenway sheds light on the dispute between Langston Hughes and Hurston over their collaborative *Mule Bone.*

Howard, Lillie P. "Zora Neale Hurston." In *Dictionary of Literary Biography:* Vol. 51. *Afro-American Writers from the Harlem Renaissance to 1940.* Edited by Trudier Harris, 133–145. Detroit: Gale Research, 1987.

Howard provides a good introduction to Hurston's life and works and, unlike most discussions of Hurston, devotes some attention to

Hurston's dramatic works. See also Howard's earlier *Zora Neale Hurston.* Boston: Twayne, 1980.

Peterson, Bernard L. *Early Black American Playwrights and Dramatic Wrtiers; A Biographical Directory and Catalog of Plays, Films, and Broadcasting Scripts.* New York: Greenwood, 1990.

The entry on Hurston includes a brief biography, plot summaries, staging history, and a list of secondary sources.

Rampersad, Arnold. *The Life of Langston Hughes:* Vol. 1. *1902–1941: I, Too, Sing America.* New York: Oxford University Press, 1986.

The biographer recounts the relationship between Hughes and Hurston, especially the dispute between the two over the play *Mule Bone.*

Roses, Lorraine Elena, and Ruth Elizabeth Randolph. *Harlem Renaissance and Beyond: Literary Biographies of 100 Black Women Writers, 1900–1945.* Boston: G.K. Hall, 1990.

The entry on Hurston provides biographical information and a selected list of primary and secondary sources.

Shafer, Yvonne. "Marita Bonner." In *American Women Playwrights, 1900–1950,* 403–408. New York: Peter Lang, 1995.

Shafer offers a basic introduction to Hurston and her work. Included are brief synopses and analyses of Hurston's plays.

Mule Bone: A Comedy of Negro Life in Three Acts

(Written in 1931 with Langston Hughes, world premiere, Ethel Barrymore Theater, New York, 1991)

Playscripts

Mule Bone: A Comedy of Negro Life. Edited by George Houston Bass and Henry Louis Gates, Jr., 1991.

"Mule Bone: A Comedy of Negro Life [exerpt only]." *Drama Critique* (Spring 1964): 103–107.

Summary of Play

Based on an idea from Hurston's short story "The Bone of Contention," this comic epic takes place in the 1920s in a black community of Florida. Two men, Jim and Dave, fight over the town beauty, Daisy. Jim hits Dave "up side the head" with a mule's thigh bone. In the subsequent trial, each is represented by a man of the cloth, Jim by a Methodist minister and Dave by a Baptist, who attempt to outshout one another in arguing whether or not a mule bone can be considered a weapon. Jim is exiled from the community.

The play generated much controversy. Due to a "mysterious" quarrel between Hughes and Hurston during their collaboration, the play was not produced or published during the lifetimes of Hughes and Hurston. Nearly sixty years later, a reading of the play ignited a debate over its depiction of blacks. For discussions related to its controversial nature, see Hughes's account of the quarrel in his autobiography *The Big Sea.* (New York: Hill and Wang, 1940). See also Henry Louis Gates, Jr.,. "Why the Mule Debate Goes On." *New York Times* (Feb. 10, 1991): sec.: 2: 5 and an interview with Hughes' biographer Arnold Rampersad in Short, Randall. "Black Theater's What-Might-Have-Been." *Newsday* (Jan. 31, 1991): Viewpoints: 109.

Performance Reviews

Beaufort, John. "*Mule Bone* Debuts After 60 Years." *Christian Science Monitor* (Feb. 26, 1991): Arts: 13. [Reprinted in *New York Theatre Critics' Reviews* (1991): 390–395.]

According to Beaufort, the comedy "occupies a unique place in the history of African-American theater."

Barnes, Clive. "*Mule Bone* Connected to Funny Bone. *New York Post* (Feb. 15, 1991). [Reprinted in *New York Theatre Critics' Reviews* (1991): 390–395.]

The critic hails *Mule Bone* as a "magnificent ensemble piece" for its rich dialect and vivid language. Barnes discounts fears that *Mule Bone* would reinforce the stereotypes typical of minstrel shows. On the contrary, this piece "suggests an artistic reality as palpable as that evoked by O'Casey or Chekhov, and, both revealingly and rewardingly, a black America as different from white America as, say, Ellington is from Gershwin."

New York Theatre Critics' Reviews (1991): 390–395.

This collection includes reprints of reviews from major New York newspapers.

Rich, Frank. "A Difficult Birth for *Mule Bone.*" *New York Times* (February 15, 1991): C1. [Reprinted in *New York Theatre Critics' Reviews* (1991): 390–395.]

Rich asserts that *Mule Bone* "has a candied Disneyesque tone, more folksy than folk." He concludes the review by observing that the play is "a false start that remains one of the American theater's more tantalizing might-have-beens."

Watt, Doug. "Second Thoughts on First Nights." *New York Daily News* (Feb. 22, 1991). [Reprinted in *New York Theatre Critics' Reviews* (1991): 390–395.]

Watt argues that *Mule Bone* "is little more than a theatrical curio, whose history is more interesting than the play itself." The music enhances the piece but, it is "really just padding for a simple fable."

Wilson, Edwin. "Fireworks and Folklore." *Wall Street Journal* (Feb. 27, 1991): A9. [Reprinted in *New York Theatre Critics' Reviews* (1991): 390–395.]

According to Wilson, the production has little passion compared to the text.

Winer, Linda. A Precious Peek at a Lively Legend." *Newsday* (Feb. 15, 1991): sec. 2: 97.

Mule Bone "has missed its real time and now feels more like a vivid work of archaeology than a universal work of theater." Winer finds that the work lacks a strong plot and "dramatic momentum." See also Aileen Jacobson. "Lost and Found." *Newsday* (Feb. 12, 1991): sec. 2: 52.

Additional Performance Reviews

Pacheco, Patrick. "A Discovery Worth the Wait?" *Los Angeles Times* (Feb. 24, 1991): Calendar: 4.

Ulansky, Gene. "The *Mule Bone* of Contention. *San Francisco Chronicle* (March 10, 1991): Saturday Review: 5.

Additional Plays

Color Struck

(Second prize *Opportunity* magazine contest, 1925; honorable mention, *Opportunity* contest for revised version, 1926.)

Playscripts

Black Female Playwrights: An Anthology of Plays Before 1950. Edited by Kathy A. Perkins, 89–102. Bloomington: Indiana University Press, 1990.

Fire!!, (Nov. 1926): 7–14.

Zora Neale Hurston, Eulalie Spence, Marita Bonner, and Others: The Prize Plays and Other One-Acts Published in Periodicals. Edited by Henry Louis Gates, Jr., 79–95. New York: G.K. Hall, 1996.

The Court Room

(From *Fast and Furious*, a Broadway musical revue, coauthored with Forbes Randolph, Jackie "Moms" Mabley, Lottie Meaney, and John Wells, 1931)

The Fiery Chariot; A One-Act Play

(Unpublished, see article Newson, Adie. "The Fiery Chariot." *The Zora Neale Hurston Forum* 1 (Fall 1986): 32–37.)

The First One

(Honorable mention, *Opportunity* magazine contest, 1926)

Playscripts

Black Female Playwrights; An Anthology of Plays Before 1950. Edited by Kathy A. Perkins, 80–88. Bloomington: Indiana University Press, 1990.

Black Theatre USA: Plays by African Americans, 1847 to Today. Rev. Ed. Edited by James V. Hatch and Ted Shine, 327–333. New York: The Free Press, 1996.

Ebony and Topaz: A Collectanea. Edited by Charles S. Johnson, 53–57. New York: Books for Libraries Press, 1971 (originally published in 1927).

The Roots of African American Drama. Edited by Leo Hamalian and James V. Hatch, 186–190. Detroit: Wayne State University, 1991.

Zora Neale Hurston, Eulalie Spence, Marita Bonner, and Others; The Prize Plays and Other One-Acts Published in Periodicals. Edited by Henry Louis Gates, Jr., 96–106. New York: G.K. Hall,1996.

The Great Day

(Musical revue, 1931–1934; subsequently revised as *From Sun to Sun*, later *Singing Steel*)

Polk County: A Comedy of Negro Life on a Sawmill Camp, with Authentic Negro Music, in Three Acts
(Co-authored with Dorothy Waring; unproduced)

Spears
(Honorable mention, *Opportunity* magazine contest, 1925)

Chapter Seven
Georgia Douglas Johnson

Brief Biography

Critics agree that, until recently, Georgia Douglas Johnson's (1880–1966) contributions to African-American literature have been largely ignored by theater practitioners and scholars. Only in the past several years, as Winona Fletcher has noted, Johnson has been "grant[ed] . . . a place among the best writers of the early twentieth century." The poet and playwright Georgia Douglas Johnson was born in Marietta, Georgia, and received an excellent education. She graduated from Atlanta University's normal school and studied music at the Oberlin Conservatory in Ohio and Cleveland College of Music. In 1903 she met her husband, Henry Lincoln Johnson, while teaching music in Atlanta. The couple moved to Washington, D.C., where Henry practiced law and was appointed to a federal government position by President William Howard Taft.

Following her husband's death in 1925, Johnson worked full time for the U.S. Department of Labor but continued to write poetry and plays. She also established the "S" Street Salon, a weekly meeting of the major writers and thinkers of the Harlem Rensaissance: Langston Hughes, Countee Cullen, Alain Locke, W.E.B. Du Bois, Marita Bonner, May Miller, Angelina Weld Grimké, Zora Neale Hurston, and Alice Dunbar-Nelson.

According to Sally Burke, Johnson chose to write dramas, after several years of writing poetry, because of the potential of this "living avenue" to be an important vehicle for effecting social progress." Johnson was deeply concerned about issues affecting women and blacks, ranging from lynching to black empowerment. Like other black women playwrights who were Johnson's contempories, she had trouble getting her plays produced. She submitted several to the Federal Theatre Project, which encouraged plays of social protest, but all were rejected.

Johnson wrote no more plays after the 1930s and devoted herself to writing poetry. As Winona Fletcher notes, Johnson became "disheartened by the reception of her efforts to bring serious matters of black life to the American stage."

Profiles and General Criticism

Abramson, Doris E. "Angelina Weld Grimké, Mary T. Burrill, Georgia Douglas Johnson, and Marita O. Bonner." *Sage* 2, no. 1 (Spring 1985): 9–13.

Abramson briefly discusses Johnson and her play *Plumes.*

Black Female Playwrights: An Anthology of Plays Before 1950. Edited by Kathy A. Perkins, 19–23. Bloomington: Indiana University Press, 1990.

Perkins provides a basic introduction to the dramas of Johnson, whom she refers to as "an inspiration and role model for the many black women writers who emerged during the 1920s."

Brown-Guillory, Elizabeth. *Their Place on the Stage: Black Women Playwrights in America.* New York: Praeger, 1990.

While focusing on later black women dramatists, Brown-Guillory includes discussions on several female playwrights active during the Harlem Renaissance: Bonner, Burrill, Grimké, Johnson, and May Miller.

Burke, Sally. *American Feminist Playwrights: A Critical History.* New York: Twayne, 1996.

Burke provides an introduction to Johnson's life and a brief discussion of her plays.

Fletcher, Winona L. "From Genteel Poet to Revolutionary Playwright: Georgia Douglas Johnson. " *Theatre Annual* 40 (1985): 40–64.

Fletcher's analyses of Johnson's works, most of which were social protest plays that were rejected by the Federal Theatre Project, demonstrate "why Mrs. Johnson, and black playwrights in general, failed in the American Theatre of the thirties—and any time when their serious dramas expose the evils of a racist society." The plays include *Blue-Eyed Black Boy, Safe, A Sunday Morning in the South, Ellen and William Craft* and *Frederick Douglass.* See also Fletcher's introductory article in *Notable Women in the American Theatre: A Biographical Dictionary.* Edited by Alice M. Robinson, Vera Mowry Roberts, and Milly S. Barranger, 473–477. New York: Greenwood, 1989, and *Dictionary of Literary Biography:* Vol. 51. *Afro-American Writers from the Harlem Renaissance to 1940.* Edited by Trudier Harris, 153–164. Detroit: Gale Research, 1987.

Hull, Gloria T. "Georgia Douglas Johnson." In *Color, Sex, and Poetry: Three Women Writers of the Harlem Renaissance*, 155–211. Bloomington: Indiana University Press, 1987.

Hull provides one of the most extensive discussions of Johnson's drama. She concludes that although Johnson is primarily known as a poet, were circumstances different she might just as well have been known as a dramatist. While there may be a degree of mediocrity in her plots, Hull asserts that Johnson "succeeded at . . . dramaturgy: undeniably, she knew how to write one-act plays."

McKay, Nellie. " 'What Were They Saying?': Black Women Playwrights of the Harlem Renaissance." In *The Harlem Rennaissance Re-examined*. Edited by Victor A. Kramer, 129–147. New York: AMS, 1987.

McKay offers a brief discussion of Johnson's plays.

Miller, Jeanne-Marie. "Black Women Playwrights from Grimké to Shange: Selected Synopses of Their Works." In *But Some of Us Are Brave: Black Women's Studies*. Edited by Gloria T. Hull, P.B. Scott, and Barbara Smith, 280–290. Old Westbury, N.Y.: Feminist Press, 1982.

Miller surveys the work of several African-American women whose plays "offer a unique insight into the Black experience," including Angelina Weld Grimké, Marita Bonner, Georgia Douglas Johnson, Mary Burrill, Lorraine Hansberry, Alice Childress, Ntozake Shange, Adrienne Kennedy, Sonia Sanchez, J.E. Franklin, and Martie Charles.

———. "Georgia Douglas Johnson and May Miller: Forgotten Playwrights of the New Negro Renaissance." *CLA Journal* 33, (June 1990): 349–366.

Miller recognizes Johnson and Miller as two forgotten playwrights who contributed significantly to the drama of the New Negro Renaissance. She considers the plays of these women to be "among the best written by black playwrights during the 1920s and the early 1930s, and their works serve as an important transition between the older extant black-authored plays—such as William Wells Brown's *The Escape* and Angelina Weld Grimké's *Rachel* (1916)—and the later works of black playwrights." The lynching plays, Miller observes, anticipate the later plays of social protest such as Theodore Ward's *Big White Fog* and Loften Mitchell's *A Land Beyond the River*. Miller includes discussions of the following plays: Johnson's *Plumes, The Starting Point, Blue Blood, Blue-Eyed Black Boy, A*

Sunday Morning in the South, William and Ellen Craft, and *Frederick Douglass* and Miller's *The Bog Guide, Graven Images, Moving Caravans, Christophe's Daughters, The Cuss'd Thing, Scratches,* and *Nails and Thorns.*

Peterson, Bernard L. *Early Black American Playwrights and Dramatic Writers: A Biographical Directory and Catalog of Plays, Films, and Broadcasting Scripts.* New York: Greenwood, 1990.

The entry on Johnson includes a brief biography, plot summaries, staging history, and a list of secondary sources.

Roses, Lorraine Elena, and Ruth Elizabeth Randolph. *Harlem Renaissance and Beyond: Literary Biographies of 100 Black Women Writers, 1900–1945.* Boston: G.K. Hall, 1990.

The entry on Johnson includes biographical information and a selected list of primary and secondary sources.

Shafer, Yvonne. "Georgia Douglas Johnson." In *American Women Playwrights, 1900–1950,* 229–240. New York: Peter Lang, 1995.

Shafer provides a basic introduction to Johnson and her work. Also included are synopses and analyses of Johnson's plays.

Sullivan, Megan. "Folk Plays, Home Girls, and Back Talk: Georgia Douglas Johnson and Women of the Harlem Renaissance." *CLA Journal* 38, no. 4 (June 1995): 404–419.

Sullivan employs Johnson's plays to explore the relationship between speech and performance: "the discourse—*or talk*—behind [black dialects]. This discourse reveals the ways in which women challenge hegemonic definitions of culture and rely on the solidarity of female friendships."

Blue Blood

(Krigwa Players, 1926; honorable mention, *Opportunity* contest, 1926)

Playscripts

Black Female Playwrights: An Anthology of Plays Before 1950. Edited by Kathy A. Perkins, 38–46. Bloomington: Indiana University Press, 1990.

Fifty More Contemporary One-Act Plays. Edited by Frank Shay, 297–304. New York: Appleton, 1928.

Selected Works of Georgia Douglas Johnson, 307–317. New York: G.K. Hall, 1997.

Wines in the Wilderness: Plays by African American Women from the Harlem Renaissance to the Present. Edited by Elizabeth Brown-Guillory, 17–25. New York: Greenwood, 1990.

Summary of Play

The action takes place shortly after the Civil War in Mrs. Bush's kitchen on the day of her daughter's marriage to John Temple. Mrs. Temple arrives to help with the preparations. Both women begin to brag about their children, especially about how close they are to white, referring to the lightness of their skin color. Mrs. Bush reveals that May's father is Captain Winfield. Mrs. Temple blanches at the revelation. She informs Mrs. Bush that May cannot marry her son because she was raped by May's father, the captain. Her son John was the result of the sexual assault. Both mothers tell the news to May and Randolph Strong. Knowing that John Temple, upon learning the truth, will kill his white father, they decide to hide the information. May will jilt John for Randolph and the two will run away to be married.

Plumes

(First prize, *Opportunity* magazine contest, 1927, Harlem Experimental Theatre, 1927)

Playscripts

Anthology of American Negro Literature. Edited by V.F. Calverton, 147–171. New York: Modern Library, 1929.

Black Female Playwrights: An Anthology of Plays Before 1950. Edited by Kathy A. Perkins, 24–30. Bloomington: Indiana University Press, 1990.

A Century of Plays. Edited by Rachel France. New York: Richards Rosen Press, 1979.

New Negro Renaissance: An Anthology. Edited by Arthur P. Davis and Michael W. Peplow, 314–322. New York: Holt, Rinehart and Winston, 1975.

Plays of Negro Life: A Source-Book of Native American Drama. Edited by Alain Locke, 287–299. New York: Harper & Brothers, 1927.

Plays by American Women, 1900–1930. Edited by Judith E. Barlow, 163–170. New York: Applause, 1985.

"Plumes." *Opportunity* (July 1927): 200–201, 217–218.

Plumes: A Play in One Act. New York: Samuel French, 1927.

Selected Works of Georgia Douglas Johnson, 319–331. New York: G.K. Hall, 1997.

Summary of Play

Charity Brown, who has already lost two loved ones, must make a decision as to whether to spend her meager savings on an operation for her very ill daughter, Emmerline, that might not help her, or on a proper funeral for Emmerline. Although she loves her daughter, Charity's superstitious beliefs and distrust of doctors persuade her that Emmerline is doomed to die. As Charity vacillates in her decison, Emmerline dies.

Safe

(Written in 1929)

Playscripts

Selected Works of Georgia Douglas Johnson, 377–384. New York: G.K. Hall, 1997.

Wines in the Wilderness: Plays by African American Women from the Harlem Renaissance to the Present. Edited by Elizabeth Brown-Guillory, 26–32. New York: Greenwood, 1990.

Summary of Play

In 1893 Liza Pettigrew, who is pregnant, witnesses the lynching of a young black man. Liza is overcome with grief and fear at the realization of how perilous life is for black men in America. Liza soon gives birth. When she learns that it is a boy, she strangles him, muttering, "Now he's safe—safe from the lynchers! Safe!"

Additional Plays

Blue-Eyed Black Boy

(Written in 1939)

Playscripts
Black Female Playwrights: An Anthology of Plays Before 1950. Edited by Kathy A. Perkins, 47–52. Bloomington: Indiana University Press, 1990.

Wines in the Wilderness: Plays by African American Women from the Harlem Renaissance to the Present. Edited by Elizabeth Brown-Guillory, 33–38. New York: Greenwood, 1990.

Frederick Douglass
(Written in 1935)

Playscript
Negro History in Thirteen Plays. Edited by Willis Richardson and May Miller, 143–163. Washington, D.C.: Associated Publishers, 1935.

Reviews
Bond, Frederick. *The Negro and the Drama*, 188–189. Washington, D.C.: Associated Publishers, 1940.

Tate, Claudia. "Introduction." *Selected Works of Georgia Douglas Johnson*, 333–352. New York: G.K. Hall, 1997.

Paupaulekejo: A Three-Act Play
(n.d., written under the pseudonym, John Tremaine)

Playscript
Selected Works of Georgia Douglas Johnson, 402–411. New York: G.K. Hall, 1997.

Starting Point
(n.d.)

Playscript
Selected Works of Georgia Douglas Johnson, 394–402. New York: G.K. Hall, 1997.

A Sunday Morning in the South
(Written in 1925)

Playscripts

Black Theater U.S.A.: Forty-Five Plays by Black Americans, 1847–1974. Edited by James V. Hatch and Ted Shine, 211–217. New York: The Free Press, 1974.

Black Theatre USA: Plays by African Americans, 1847 to Today. Rev. Ed. Edited by James V. Hatch and Ted Shine, 231–237. New York: The Free Press, 1996.

Black Female Playwrights; An Anthology of Plays Before 1950. Edited by Kathy A. Perkins, 31–38. Bloomington: Indiana University Press, 1990.

Selected Works of Georgia Douglas Johnson, 385–393. New York: G.K. Hall, 1997.

For a critique, see Judith Stevens, "Anti-Lynch Plays by African-American Women." *African American Review*, 1992. See Chapter Three, *Trouble in Mind,* Criticism and Performance Reviews.

William and Ellen Craft

(Written in 1935)

Playscript

Negro History in Thirteen Plays. Edited by Willis Richardson and May Miller, 164–186. Washington, D.C.: Associated Publishers, 1935.

Selected Works of Georgia Douglas Johnson, 353–376. New York: G.K. Hall, 1997.

Chapter Eight
Adrienne Kennedy

Brief Biography

Adrienne Kennedy (1931–) is best known for her surreal, expressionistic drama and lyrical dialogue. Forsaking traditional plot, her plays focus on isolated women tortured by multiple identities, whose existence is structured around a complex system of symbols and arcane and enigmatic images. Kennedy uses disturbing imagery (e.g., siblings that are part rat, a schooleacher in the form of a white dog, and a hunchbacked Jesus) to dramatize her protagonists' clash with self, family, and culture. Expressionism, for Kennedy, is a much more powerful medium than realism because it transcends the limitations imposed by psychological, physical, and cultural elements. Myth, enigmatic imagery, and poetic language is for Kennedy the most forceful and eloquent method of externalizing the intricacies of race that have been internalized by the self. Kennedy's plays interweave the personal and the social, referents of which emanate from her personal experiences, dreams, and from unconscious self. She has said that writing enables her to work through her own "psychological confusion."

Born on September 13, 1931, Kennedy spent a "comfortable" childhood in Cleveland in a middle-class integrated neighborhood; her friends and classmates were blacks, Jews, Poles, and Italians. As a child, Kennedy's parents introduced her to the progressive aspects of black culture. Kennedy remembers how her parents worked and socialized with people devoted to the "Negro Cause." Kennedy recalls that she admired her parents' glamorous friends, who "drank highballs . . . read *Crisis* magazine . . . were members of the NAACP and the Urban League, were members of the Alphas, Kappas . . . played bridge, poker, tonk . . . worshipped Paul Robeson, W.E.B. Du Bois, [and] Joe Louis." Her father introduced her to strong black women, including Billie Holiday, Mary Bethune, and Marian Anderson, and to the work of Paul Lawrence Dunbar.

The playwright's cultural experiences were enriched by her regular trips to Montezuma, Georgia, to visit relatives. As Kennedy comments in her memoir, *People Who Led to My Plays* (1987), "My mother often said that most of the white people of Montezuma's families came from England. I realized dimly that this meant some of our ancestors too had come from England, since, like most 'Negro' families in the town, we had white relations as well as 'Negro.' I became very interested in 'England.'"

Kennedy's plays reflect her view of the South as "a strange mesh of dark kinship between the races." Her fascination with European culture provides multiple influences and allusions in her plays. The great icons of Hollywood, for example, have long fascinated Kennedy. In her memoir, she remarks that she read *Modern Screen* magazine in secret and "in the evenings after I'd done my homework I'd sit at the kitchen table and write penny postcards to the movie stars to get their autographed photos." Many of these movie stars—Ingrid Bergman, Orson Welles, and Bette Davis—would later appear as characters in her works.

Despite her deep connection with Western culture, Kennedy suffered no illusions about the brutality of white racists. In high school, she aspired to be a journalist, but her teacher discouraged her because of her skin color. Attending Ohio State University was painful. "Often from southern Ohio towns, white students were determined to subjugate the Negro girls," she remembered. "They were determined to make you feel that it was a great inequity that they had to live in the same dorm with you . . . an injustice." Although Kennedy realized early on that whites "tried to hold you back," she believed that implied a "great challenge existed in life."

She began writing plays while her husband, Joseph C. Kennedy, whom she married in 1953, was stationed at a U.S. Army base in Korea. During his absence she "sometimes began to daydream of being a writer, perhaps a famous writer." Her chance of becoming a "famous writer" began with her trip in the early 1960s to West Africa, where she began *Funnyhouse of a Negro,* the play that would ultimately be produced by Edward Albee. Africa gave Kennedy direction. She became deeply affected by the continent's art and political landscape. Her plays reflect her deep interest in African ritual drama, especially the Kuntu form. Her experience "gave [her] the images that dominated [her] work for a long time."

Funnyhouse of a Negro (1964), for which she won the Obie, broke new ground in American drama. Kennedy uses a fragmented collage of dialogue and image in the play to reveal the tortured soul of its protagonist Sarah. For Kennedy, surrealism and expressionism present reality as "a thin line between fantasy and consciousness." Employing the dreamlike, non-linear form of *Funnyhouse of a Negro,* Kennedy also wrote *The Owl Answers* (1969), *A Beast's Story* (1969), *A Rat's Mass* (1969), and *A Lesson in Dead Language* (1968). As with *Funnyhouse,* poetic dialogue and phantasmagoric images evoke the conflicts of racial identity within the context of the black and American experience.

Many critics, such as Clive Barnes, have recognized that in her "dream" plays Kennedy "was weaving some kind of dramatic fabric of poetry." Yet her surreal plays have also confounded some critics who were disturbed by their severe departure from realism and complex symbolism. Furthermore, many in the black community, especially those active in the early black movement, criticized her theater because of her emphasis on the negative aspects of the black experience. Yet, increasingly, scholars have begun to recognize the importance of Kennedy's work and her influence on postmodernism. Herbert Blau argues that Kennedy is "the most original black dramatist of her generation and, along with [Sam] Shepard, the most original."

In the last few years, Kennedy has been in demand as a university lecturer, teaching at such prestigious schools as Yale, Princeton, Brown, the University of California at Berkeley, Stanford, and Harvard. She has been commissioned to write plays for Joseph Papp's Public Theatre, Jerome Robbins, The Royal Court, the Mark Taper Forum, and Juilliard. Several of her recent plays have won prestigious awards: *The Ohio State Murders* won the 1993 Lecomte de Nouy Award and an honorable mention in 1991 for Best New American Play from the American Theatre Critics Association, and *June and Jean in Concert* and *Sleep Deprivation Chamber* won Obies for Best New Plays in 1996. The Signature Theatre Company devoted its 1995/1996 season to Kennedy's plays at Joseph Papp's Public Theatre in New York. These plays reflect Kennedy's continuing exploration of conflicted protagonists and disturbing actions, but the violence is subtler than in her earlier plays. However subtle, Kennedy's later plays are, as Alisa Solomon maintains, "paradoxically more ominous . . . [If the haunted images] are less aggressive than the demons pursuing Sarah and Clara and sister Rat, it is only because they have been at it longer."

Profiles and Interviews

"Adrienne Kennedy." In *Black Literature Criticism: Excerpts from Criticism of the Most Significant Works of Black Authors over the Past 200 Years,* Vol. 2. Edited by James P. Draper, 1156–1158. Detroit: Gale Research,1992.

This article includes a survey of Kennedy's life and work, along with several excerpts from writings discussing Kennedy's plays.

Betsko, Kathleen and Rachel Koenig. *Interviews with Contemporary Women Playwrights.* New York: Beech Tree Books, 1987. [Excerpt reprinted in *Black Literature Criticism: Excerpts from Criticism of the Most Significant Works of Black Authors over the Past 200 Years,* Vol. 2. Edited by James P. Draper, 1156–1158. Detroit: Gale Research, 1992.]

Betsko and Koenig's landmark volume includes Kennedy in a collection of dynamic and diverse interviews with women playwrights. The playwrights explore their experience in writing for a theater considered the preserve of their male counterparts. The dramatists discuss the presence of a "female aesthetic," their associations with directors and members of the theater community, and the forces that have influenced their writing.

Binder, Wolfgang. "A *Melus* Interview: Adrienne Kennedy." *Melus* 12, no. 3 (Fall 1985): 99–108.

Binder's questions touch upon several facets of the playwright's life and work. Kennedy speaks of how her home environment influenced her early themes. She recalls, for example, "inside our house we had these seemingly endless conflicts, these arguments. How could we be a certain way on the outside and another inside our house?" The dramatist also describes the evolution of the production of *Funnyhouse of a Negro,* how it evolved from a workshop presentation to Edward Albee's production in 1964, and its controversial reception by critics and audiences. Kennedy also speaks of her activities after winning the Obie in 1964. Binder includes a selective bibliography of primary and secondary sources.

Blumenthal, Ralph. "A Writer Braces for the Attention." *New York Times* (July 25, 1995): C13.

Blumenthal profiles Kennedy shortly before the Signature Theatre Company presented a series of her plays for the 1995/1996 season at the Joseph Papp Public Theatre. Kennedy talks of the anxiety and ambivalence she experiences with her plays. "I don't like to watch my plays," she explains. "I've never come to terms with the stuff that pours out of me. I get upset when I see that material." Despite prior unpleasant experiences of being produced professionally, Kennedy says that "she relished renewing some professional friendships."

Diamond, Elin. "An Interview with Adrienne Kennedy." *Studies in American Drama, 1945–Present* 4 (1989): 143–157.

Diamond uses Kennedy's memoir, *People Who Led to My Plays,* as a basis from which to awaken reflections from the playwright. According to Kennedy, many individuals have proved to be powerful forces in her life and work, not all of them real. Humpty-Dumpty and the figures on the Old Maid cards, for example, created strong impressions: "[They] were as real to me as my brother." Interspersed throughout the interview, Kennedy talks about encounters with racism that have affected her life, contending that she has "come to grips with that." Kennedy's plays are discussed to a very limited extent throughout the interview. A biographical profile prefaces the interview.

"Dramatus Instructus: How Six Playwriting Teachers Fire Up Their Students' Imaginations." *American Theatre* 6 (Jan. 1990): 22–26.

Six playwrights, including Kennedy and Maria Irene Fornes, talk about the methods they use to inspire experimentalism and individuality.

Dunning, Jennifer. "Kennedy Decides That the Classroom's the Thing." *New York Times* (Dec. 29, 1977): sec. 3:13.

Dunning interviewed Kennedy shortly before Kennedy began teaching a playwriting course at the Women's Interart Center in New York. Kennedy comments that an essential part of her teaching approach is for her students to explore repetitive images that occur in their dreams: "I'm against people choosing a writing subject from a purely intellectual viewpoint." The source of most of Kennedy's plays emerge from images from her own dreams, which she regularly records in journals. She empathizes with women artists, but "she does not see herself as a feminist playwright whose role is to encourage other women to write."

Evett, Marianne. "Ex-Cleveland Playwright Hits Bonanza in Big Apple." *The Plain Dealer* (Oct. 1, 1995): sec. Arts: 1J.

Evett profiles Kennedy during the Signature Theatre 1995/1996 season, which was devoted to Kennedy's plays *(Funnyhouse of a Negro, A Movie Star Has to Star in Black and White, June and Jean in Concert, Sleep Deprivation Chamber, The Alexander Plays,* and *Motherhood 2000).* See also Evett's article, "Cleveland Native's Plays are Heading for Off-Broadway." *The Plain Dealer* (July 26, 1995): Arts: 5E.

Kennedy, Adrienne. "Becoming a Playwright." *American Theatre* 4 (Feb. 1988): 26–27.

Kennedy reminisces about the original production of *Funnyhouse of a Negro* at the Circle in the Square, which evolved from a class on playwriting taught by Edward Albee. She recollects telling Albee that she was going to drop the class because she was unable to stage her play—she was embarrassed because she felt the piece was "too revealing." Although terrified at the prospect of staging *Funnyhouse,* Kennedy, after talking to Albee, decided to witness the "anguish that most often I had carefully blotted out as it unfolded on the stage."

———. *Deadly Triplets: A Theatre Mystery and Journal.* Minneapolis: University of Minnesota, 1990.

Deadly Triplets is a journal that Kennedy kept of the theater people she encountered. Highlighted is Playwright Edward Albee, who greatly influenced Kennedy. She had submitted the script of *Funnyhouse of a Negro* to Albee's playwriting workshop. However, before its workshop production, Kennedy informed Albee that she was dropping the class because, as she explained, "my play seemed far too revealing and much to my own shock, I had used the word 'nigger' throughout the text." Albee responded by pointing to the stage and asking her to look at it. "Well, do you know what a playwright is?" he said. "A playwright is someone who lets his guts out on the stage, and that's what you've done in this play."

———. "A Growth of Images." *Modern Drama* 21, no. 4 (Dec. 1977): 41–48. [Excerpt reprinted in *Black Literature Criticism,* Vol. 2. Edited by James P. Draper, 1156–1158. Detroit: Gale Research,1992.]

Kennedy discusses her playwrighting techniques in this article. Although autobiographical topics concern her the most, Kennedy wishes that she could refrain from writing about her family. However, writing helps her work out her "psychological confusion" about family problems, which "overwhelm" her. Kennedy believes her dramas develop from images emanating from her unconscious, which she records in her journals. For example, *A Rat's Mass* originated from a dream she had in which she was "being pursued by red, bloodied rats." According to the playwright, her admiration for Tennessee Williams and Federico Garcia Lorca influenced *Funnyhouse of a Negro,* whose protagonist struggles with the ambivalent forces within herself.

———. *People Who Led to My Plays.* New York: Knopf, 1987.

In this experimental memoir of a playwright "slowly find[ing] her direction," Kennedy describes the motley collection of family, friends, writers, movies stars, storybook characters, souls, and witches who have given a profound "impetus and energy to [her] writing." As Ben Brantley (8.143) of the *New York Times* comments, Kennedy's "singular memoir . . . lays out the bricks . . . from which [she] builds her disturbing, haunted dream houses of plays." Kennedy's *June and Jean in Concert* is based on this memoir. In 1992 the Great Lakes Theater Festival premiered a dramatic adaptation of *People Who Led to My Plays.* For a discussion of how Kennedy's autobiographical self-representation influences her plays, see Werner Sollors' "*People Who Led to My Plays:* Adrienne Kennedy's Autobiography." In *Intersecting Boundaries: The Theatre of Adrienne Kennedy.* Edited by Paul K. Bryant-Jackson and Lois More Overbeck, 13–20. Minneapolis: University of Minnesota Press, 1992.

Robinson, Alice M., Vera Mowry Roberts, and Milly S. Barranger. *Notable Women in the American Theatre: A Biographical Dictionary.* New York: Greenwood, 1989.

The first of its kind, this handbook focuses on the contributions of women in the theater. Represented here are playwrights, producers, actresses, directors, designers, critics, and managers. For playwrights, including Adrienne Kennedy, each signed entry includes a biographical sketch as well as a cursory discussion of selected plays. Also included is a list of primary and secondary sources.

Solomon, Alisa. "Foreword." In Adrienne Kennedy's *The Alexander Plays.* Minneapolis: University of Minnesota Press, 1992.

Solomon observes that while *The Alexander Plays* "seem calm, centered," as compared to Kennedy's earlier plays, such as *Funnyhouse of a Negro* and *A Rat's Mass,* the ubiquitous "sense of threat that careened headlong from the previous works . . . lurks in [these new plays] as well. . . . They seethe quietly with the same sense of violence and disjuncture, like tranquil waters where reptiles rage hungrily beneath the surface."

Splawn, P. Jane. "Adrienne Kennedy." In *Critical Survey of Drama: Supplement.* Edited by Frank Magill, 212–217. Pasadena, Calif.: Salem Press, 1987.

Splawn provides a biographical sketch of Kennedy's life and achievements as well as a cursory analysis of her major plays.

Views of a Changing Cluture: An Exhibition Catalogue. Austin: Harry Ransom Humanities Research Center, University of Texas, 1994.

This exhibit highlights the contributions of several American writers, including Kennedy. Includes typescripts and photographs. Also included is a description of *Pale Blue Flowers,* one of Kennedy's earliest dramatic efforts.

Wilkerson, Margaret B. "Adrienne Kennedy." In *Dictionary of Literary Biography:* Vol. 38. *Afro-American Writers After 1955: Dramatists and Prose Writers.* Edited by Thadious M. Davis and Trudier Harris, 162–168. Detroit: Gale Research, 1985.

This introductory article includes an extensive biographical and critical survey of Kennedy's achievements. A primary and secondary bibliography of her works is included.

Additional Biographical Entries

Als, Hilton. "Stardust Memories: Adrienne Kennedy Shows and Tells." *Village Voice* (Nov. 3, 1967): 61, 65.

Black Writers: A Selection of Sketches from Contemporary Authors. Edited by Linda Metzger, 320–321. Detroit: Gale Research, 1989.

Contemporary Authors: A Bio-Bibliographical Guide: Vol. 26. New Revision Series. Edited by Hal May, 199–201. Detroit: Gale Research, 1989.

Contemporary Black American Playwrights and Their Plays: A Biographical Directory and Dramatic Index. Edited by Bernard L. Peterson, 287–290. New York: Greenwood Press, 1988.

Diamond, Elin. "Adrienne Kennedy." *Contemporary American Dramatists.* Edited by K.A. Berney, 304–307. London: St. James Press, 1994.

Contemporary Dramatists, 3rd Ed. Edited by James Vinson, 293–294. New York: St. Martin's Press, 1982.

Great Writers of the English Language: Dramatists. Edited by James Vinson, 271–273. New York: St. Martin's Press, 1979.

General Criticism

Barnett, Claudia. "Adrienne Kennedy and Shakespeare's Sister." *American Drama* 5, no. 2 (Spring 1996): 44–65.

Kennedy's plays lack the "freedom" exhorted by Virginia Woolf, who assumed that women would begin to write in response to the new laws governing women's political and economic emancipation. Kennedy's heroines are "thwarted by their identities and their births; they are trapped by mental and emotional prisons imposed on them from without and within." See also Barnett's "This Fundamental Challenge to Identity." *Theatre Journal* 48 (May 1996): 141–155.

Benston, Kimberly W. "Locating Adrienne Kennedy: Prefacing the Subject." In *Intersecting Boundaries; The Theatre of Adrienne Kennedy.* Edited by Paul K. Bryant-Jackson and Lois More Overbeck, 113–130. Minneapolis: University of Minnesota Press, 1992.

To study Kennedy's "'own' taking of herself as subject," Benston discusses three recent books that include prefaces written by Kennedy: *People Who Led to My Plays, Adrienne Kennedy in One Act,* and *Deadly Triplets.*

Burke, Sally. *American Feminist Playwrights: A Critical History.* New York: Twayne Publishers, 1996.

In this first sociohistorical examination of American feminist dramatists, Burke includes a discussion of Kennedy's major plays.

Byrant-Jackson, Paul K. "Kennedy's Travelers on the American and African Continuum." In *Intersecting Boundaries: The Theatre of Adrienne Kennedy.* Edited by Paul K. Bryant-Jackson and Lois More Overbeck, 54–57. Minneapolis: University of Minnesota Press, 1992.

Bryant-Jackson discusses Kennedy's plays *(Funnyhouse, Owl, She Talks to Beethoven, A Movie Star)* with respect to their affinity with the European-American transcendentalists, the Absurdists, and black writers of the diaspora.

Case, Sue-Ellen. *Feminism and Theatre.* New York: Methuen, 1988.

In this landmark introduction to feminist theater and theory, Case includes brief discussions of Kennedy's *Funnyhouse of a Negro, The Owl Answers,* and *A Movie Star Has to Star in Black and White*

Cohn, Ruby. *New American Dramatists, 1960–1980.* New York: Grove, 1982.

In terms of its treatment of women dramatists, Cohn's book is a disappointment; although Cohn includes sections on gay and black playwrights, she fails to include one assessing the contributions of women in the theater . Nevertheless, she does discuss the work of several female dramatists throughout the book. And in the sixth chapter Cohn includes Adrienne Kennedy, Ed Bullins, and Amiri Baraka as writers "for whom Blackness is an obsessive theme."

Curb, Rosemary. "(Hetero)Sexual Terrors in Adrienne Kennedy's Early Plays." In *Intersecting Boundaries: The Theatre of Adrienne Kennedy.* Edited by Paul K. Bryant-Jackson and Lois More Overbeck, 142–156. Minneapolis: University of Minnesota Press, 1992.

Curb examines Kennedy's early plays *(Funnyhouse of a Negro, The Owl Answers, A Rat's Mass, A Lesson in Dead Language)* according to three "interrelated consequences of (hetero)sexual terrors: (1) obsessive fear of rape, (2) guilt stemming from culturally learned dualisms, and (3) loss of history, ancestry, identity." According to Curb, Kennedy's "foregounding of women's terrors disrupts dominant ideologies of gender, race, and class rooted in heterosexualism."

Diamond, Elin. "Mimesis in Syncopated Time: Reading Adrienne Kennedy." In *Intersecting Boundaries: The Theatre of Adrienne Kennedy.* Edited by Paul K. Bryant-Jackson and Lois More Overbeck, 131–147. Minneapolis: University of Minnesota Press, 1992.

Diamond's title is derived from Gertrude Stein's "Plays," in which she describes her nervousness at the theater because "the thing seen and the thing felt about the thing seen [were] not going on at the same tempo." Diamond analyzes *Funnyhouse of a Negro, A Movie Star Has to Star in Black and White,* and *An Owl Answers* according to mimetic criticism, "which eliminates the syncopation between subject and object, because it needs to appropriate the object for the enterprise of critical truth-telling."

———. "Rethinking Identification: Kennedy, Freud, Brecht." *The Kenyon Review* 15 (Spring 1993): 86–99.

No dramatist, Diamond contends, comes close to Kennedy's acute treatment of identity and identification, what she calls the playwright's "*imbrication* of identity and identification." To explore Kennedy's use of identification, Diamond juxtaposes the theories of Sigmund Freud and Bertolt Brecht's theater practice. Her motive is not to interpret Kennedy according to psychoanalytic theory but "to press psychoanalysis . . . on this question: what social and cultural meanings are embeded in acts of identification?" As for Brecht, Diamond acknowledges that Kennedy's drama has little in common with his theater practice; however, "her plays . . . are no less promising as invitations to political self-consciousness. . . . Kennedy offers us a radical revision of Brechtian historicization: the historicizing power of identification." Kennedy's plays included in Diamond's discussion are *Funnyhouse of a Negro, The Owl Answers, A Movie Star Has to Star in Black and White,* and *The Alexander Plays.*

Forte, Jeanie. "Kennedy's Body Politic: The Mulatta, Menses, and the Medusa." In *Intersecting Boundaries: The Theatre of Adrienne Kennedy.* Edited by Paul K. Bryant-Jackson and Lois More Overbeck, 157–169. Minneapolis: University of Minnesota Press, 1992.

Forte is not interested in examining Kennedy's protagonists as tragic individuals but in how they resist racist acculturation, and "how they operate both to frame and deconstruct history and perceptions of race." In her attempt, Forte hopes to break through racist and/or narrow discussions of Kennedy's early plays, *Funnyhouse of a Negro, The Owl Answers, A Movie Star . . .*, and *A Rat's Mass.* She particularly addresses the question of what saves Kennedy's heroines from the marginalized, regressive, and negative figures prevalent in the writing of black American women. Forte asserts that Kennedy's heroines are "not merely tragic characters; rather, they frame/demarcate the problematics of a specific historical juncture, operative as tropes of resistance within that historical context."

Gillespie, Patti. "American Women Dramatists, 1960–1980." In *Essays on Contemporary American Drama.* Edited by Bock Hedwig and Albert Wertheim, 111. Munich: M. Hueber, 1981.

Introducing the reader to the contemporary American theatrical scene, Gillespie's straightforward essay surveys the work of women playwrights writing and producing plays from the late 1950s through the 1970s. Gillespie briefly examines the work of several women dramatists, including Adrienne Kennedy and Ntozake Shange. Following her essay, Gillespie provides a list of the women dramatists discussed, their major works, and a list of anthologies and collections of plays.

Herman, William. *Understanding Contemporary Drama.* Columbia: University of South Carolina Press, 1987.

Herman introduces the reader to the personalities, forces, and trends that have pushed the American theater to innovative heights since the early 1960s. Unfortunately, Herman fails to devote much space to a discussion of the contributions of women dramatists; however, he does provide general critical remarks on the work of Adrienne Kennedy and Marsha Norman.

Intersecting Boundaries: The Theatre of Adrienne Kennedy. Edited by Paul K. Bryant-Jackson and Lois More Overbeck. Minneapolis: University of Minnesota Press, 1992.

An important addition to the Kennedy critical canon, this volume is the first full-length work on the life and work Adrienne Kennedy. Part 1 includes an interview with Kennedy and a well-researched chapter on the production history of Kennedy's plays. Part 2, "Intersecting Dramatic Traditions," places her plays within the context of theater history. Part 3, "Changing Boundaries," includes critical interpretations of her plays and an essay by feminist critic and theorist, bell hooks. Part 4 provides interviews with directors, dramaturges, and performers, including Michael Kahn, Gaby Rodgers, Gerald Freedman, Billie Allen, and Robbie McCauley.

Jenkins, Linda Walsh. "Locating the Language of Gender Experience." *Women & Performance* 2, no. 1 (1984): 5–20.

Jenkins discusses what she refers to as "the language of gender experience." That is, she asserts that although men and women use the same language, they "tend to image and enact [words] in different ways." In short, females speak the "mother tongue" and males speak the "father tongue." Drawing upon her investigations in women's studies and gender research, Jenkins concludes that the reason both sexes name and perceive in distinct ways is not primarily biological but because of the social roles prescribed to each sex. Consequently, the individual "grows up with the engendered language" of that social role. The author illustrates her assertions with excerpts from the works of several playwrights, including Adrienne Kennedy.

Kintz, Linda. *The Subject's Tragedy: Political Poetics, Feminist Theory, and Drama.* Ann Arbor: University of Michigan Press, 1992.

Kintz disagrees with Herbert Blau in Kennedy's positioning of white history in her plays. Blau, says Kintz, contends that Kennedy "writes from a colonized psyche," which reflects the playwright's appreciation of white culture over black art. Kintz insists that Kennedy's plays "are obsessively, unwaveringly about the impossibility of any kind of definitive separation of African culture from the romance of the Western tradition." Plays included in Kintz's analysis are *Funnyhouse of a Negro, A Lesson in Dead Language, The Owl Answers,* and *A Movie Star Has to Star in Black and White.*

Meigs, Susan E. "No Place But the Funnyhouse: The Struggle for Identity in Three Adrienne Kennedy Plays." In *Modern American Drama: The Female Canon.* Edited by June Schlueter, 172–183. Rutherford, N.J.: Fairleigh Dickinson University Press,1990.

Meigs argues that Kennedy's fragmented protagonists represent the sociopolitical forces of white society that disrupt the construction of a viable black community. At a deeper level this fragmented identity points to the deeper problem of black women's fragmented psyche. These tortured women's equally damaged community has "failed to provide them with the ritual means for locating themselves and have made them feel guilty for recognizing the extra measure of alienation assigned to black women." Meigs shows how Kennedy perverts the use of African ritual masks, traditionally used as symbols of power and mystery. Kennedy undermines the empowerment of masks and "transforms [them] into . . . image[s] of imprisonment and terror." Meigs bases her analysis on Kennedy's early plays, *Funnyhouse of a Negro, The Owl Answers,* and *A Movie Star Has to Star in Black and White.*

Miller, Jeanne-Marie. "Black Women Playwrights from Grimké to Shange: Selected Synopses of Their Works." In *But Some of Us Are Brave: Black Women's Studies.* Edited by Gloria T. Hull, P.B. Scott, and Barbara Smith, 280–290. Old Westbury, N.Y.: Feminist Press, 1982.

Miller surveys the work of several African-American women whose plays "offer a unique insight into the Black experience," including Angelina Weld Grimké, Marita Bonner, Georgia Douglas Johnson, Mary Burrill, Lorraine Hansberry, Alice Childress, Ntozake Shange, Adrienne Kennedy, Sonia Sanchez, J.E. Franklin, and Martie Charles.

Olauson, Judith. *The American Woman Playwright: A View of Criticism and Characterization.* Troy, N.Y.: Whitson, 1981.

Olauson's general examination focuses on women playwrights, active over a forty-year period (1930–1970), who have created roles that deviate from the conventional one-dimensional, submissive women characters traditionally portrayed in the past. Olauson surveys the major work of five contemporary female playwrights: Adrienne Kennedy, Rosalyn Drexler, Megan Terry, Rochelle Owens, and Myrna Lamb.

Overbeck, Lois More. *Contemporary Authors Bibliographical Series: American Dramatists,* Vol. 3. Edited by Matthew C. Roudane, 109–124. Detroit: Gale Research, 1989.

This essay assesses the critical reputation of Kennedy's work and includes a primary and secondary bibliography of sources. See also Overbeck's "bio-theatrical" article (8.37) covering the production history of Kennedy's works.

Where Are the Women Playwrights?" *New York Times* (May 20, 1973): sec. 2: 1, 3.

In 1973, *Times*'s curiosity was piqued by the fact that so few women were writing for the theater, so the newspaper asked several prominent female playwrights to discuss the issue of the scarcity of women dramatists. For Gretchen Cryer, the problem is guilt: "[Who] knows how many potential playwrights there may be out there fixing bag lunches for their children who would be attempting to write their plays, and get them on, were it not for the fact that they would guiltily consider their efforts self-indulgent folly." Adrienne Kennedy adds that women are not encouraged by society to pursue the solitary course of creative endeavor: "[A] woman listens to several voices . . . women are taught to answer the voices and needs of others, to surrender to the desires of those we love." And Rochelle Owens declares that there are many "latent playwrights, [women who] deplete their creative force and inspiration in the eons-old traditional habit of overnurturing and pampering their 'genius' husbands who are driven to kvetching out 'The Novel.'" Other playwrights included in the article are Rosalyn Drexler, Lillian Hellman, Renee Taylor, Clare Boothe Luce, and Jean Kerr.

The Alexander Plays

(Includes a quartet of plays: *She Talks to Beethoven, The Ohio State Murders*; *The Film Club* (A *Monologue* by Suzanne Alexander) and *The Dramatic Circle;* see individual titles)

A Beast's Story

(Part of *Cities in Bezique: Two One-Acts,* Public Theater, 1969)

Playscripts

see *Cities in Bezique*

Summary of Play

This is surreal drama about a young Beast woman who is raped by her young husband, Human, to consummate the marriage. A baby is conceived of the union (Beast woman is also the product of such a union). The Beast woman's parents, who despise her husband, urge their daughter to kill her baby as well as Human.

Criticism and Performance Reviews

see *Cities in Bezique*

Cities in Bezique: Two One-Acts

(Includes the one-acts *A Beast's Story* and *The Owl Answers;* Public Theater New York, 1969.)

Playscripts

Cities in Bezique: Two One-Act Plays. New York: Samuel French, 1969

Kuntu Drama: Plays of the African Continuum. Edited by Paul Carter Harrison, 169–202. New York: Grove Press, 1974.

Criticism and Performance Reviews

Barnes, Clive. "Theater: *Cities in Bezique* Arrives at the Public." *New York Times* (Jan. 13, 1969): 26.

Barnes praises these "weirdies" (i.e., *The Owl Answers* and *A Beast's Story)* as "moving" and as works that clearly indicate that Kennedy's vision is headed in the right direction.

Benston, Kimberly W. "*Cities in Bezique*: Adrienne Kennedy's Expressionistic Vision." *CLA Journal* 20, no. 2 (Dec. 1976): 235–244. [Excerpt reprinted in *Black Literature Criticism,* Vol. 2. Edited by James P. Draper, 1153–1156. Detroit: Gale Research, 1992.]

Benston asserts that Kennedy's expressionistic work anticipated Amiri Baraka's in its break from naturalism. Kennedy's surreal vision of the black psyche and the "strange power" and "otherworldliness" of her dramas, such as *Cities of Bezique,* and two one-acts, *The Owl Answers* and *A Beast's Story,* emanate from her unique dramatic method, which includes "the breakdown of autonomous characters; the elaboration of a pattern of verbal themes; and rejection of the representational stage." The plays complement each other thematically (sexuality, family structure, death) and symbolically (animals, light and dark, music). The surreal use of theme and symbol converts action into "another signature of emotion . . . invok[ing] . . . the intimacies, ecstasies, and anguish of the Afro-American's soul-life."

Cooke, Richard P. "The Theater: World of Fantasy." *Wall Street Journal* (Jan. 14, 1969):18.

Kennedy's poetic drama "is well worth observing," but Cooke suggests that in the future she should "direct her fantasies into more comprehensible form."

Curb, Rosemary K. "Fragmented Selves in Adrienne Kennedy's *Funnyhouse of a Negro* and *The Owl Answers.*" *Theatre Journal* 32, no. 2 (May 1980): 180–195.

Curb asserts that Kennedy's uniqueness lies in her startling symbolic representations of "archetypal female obsessions" as well as her innovative use of space and time on stage. Kennedy breaks away from the traditional linear plot, dramatizing her theme of the double horror of being black and female by depicting the fragmented selves of Sarah and She symbolically as other personalities, such as Queen Victoria and Anne Boleyn. Noting that the dramatic structure of *Funnyhouse* and *Owl* is concentric rather than linear, Curb says the "concentric accumulation of images and symbols creates poetic unity."

Duberman, Martin. "Black Theater." *Partisan Review* 36, no. 3 (1969): 483–500.

Duberman finds that Kennedy is "absorbed by her fantasies." Although she prefers poetic to realistic drama, he complains that Kennedy is "not a good poet." Her imagery is vague and her language so private that it excludes the spectator.

Forte, Jeanie. "Realism, Narrative, and the Feminist Playwright—A Problem of Reception." *Modern Drama* 32 no. 1 (March 1989): 115–127. [Reprinted in *Feminist Theatre and Theory.* Edited by Helene Keyssar, 19–34.]

Forte's article reflects the ongoing debate concerning the relationship of classic realist dramatic texts and feminism. Forte asserts that if a playwright subverts the dominant ideology, which realism embraces, then "strategies must be found within the realm of discourse, particularly *vis-à-vis* narrative, which can operate to deconstruct the imbedded ideology." To illustrate her points, Forte analyzes several plays, including Adrienne Kennedy's *The Owl Answers.*

Kerr, Walter. "*Cities of Bezique.*" *New York Times* (Jan. 19, 1969): sec. 2: 3.

Kerr concedes that there is a "spare, unsentimental intensity about Kennedy that promises to drive a dagger home," but he feels that these plays do not work because the fragments fail to integrate themselves: "The rain drops are there, but they are too far apart to make a rain." Furthermore, says Kerr, the spectator feels too far removed from the stories.

Keyssar, Helene. "Rites and Responsibilities: The Drama of Black American Women." *Feminine Focus: The New Women Playwrights.* Edited by Enoch Brater, 226–240. Cambridge: Oxford University Press, 1989.

Keyssar maintains that there is "potential power" in the plays of black women playwrights because of their duality of perception: they "see the world as an American *woman* and as a black *woman.*" Thus the duality of perceptions results in viewing experiences prismatically. To express their mulitplicity of views, "in which diverse voices and world views collide," many black playwrights have used a variety of dramatic strategies, often incorporating song, dance, music, and visual imagery. Keyssar assesses the works of earlier twentieth-century playwrights as well as contemporary dramatists, including Kennedy *(The Owl Answers),* Ntozake Shange (*Boogie Woogie Landscapes),* and Sonia Sanchez' *(Sister Son/ji).*

Miller, Jeanne-Marie. "Images of Women in Plays by Black Playwrights." *CLA Journal* 20, no. 4 (June 1977): 494–507. [Reprinted in *Women in American Theatre.* Edited by Helen Krich Chinoy and Linda Walsh Jenkins, 256–262. New York: Theatre Communications Group, 1987.]

Miller discusses the position of the black woman in selected plays of several African-American playwrights, including Kennedy (*The Owl Answers* and *Funnyhouse of a Negro),* Alice Childress *(Trouble in Mind, Wedding Band, Wine in the Wilderness,* and *Florence),* and J.E. Franklin *(Black Girl).*

Oliver, Edith. "Off Broadway." *The New Yorker* 44 (Jan. 25, 1969): 77.

Oliver observes that productions of *The Owl Answers* and *The Beast's Story* are well done but complains that "since Expressionism . . . tends to cancel the humanity of the characters . . . it is almost impossible to assess the work of the individual actors."

Pasolli, Robert. "*Cities in Bezique*: An Open Letter to Joseph Papp." *Village Voice* (Jan. 23, 1969): 43.

Pasolli views Joseph Papp's production of *Cities in Bezique* as a "dud." The critic complains that the production team failed to address the problems inherent in staging poetic dramas.

Rudin, Seymour. "Theatre Chronicle: Winter-Spring, 1969." *Massachusetts Review* 10 (Summer 1969): 583–593.

Rudin notes that Kennedy's surreal one-acts *(The Owl Answers* and *A Beast's Story)* "revealed a measure of poetic sensibility;" however, Kennedy fails to "mak[e] dramatic use of this sensibility." Unlike her black counterparts LeRoi Jones and Douglas Turner Ward, Kennedy is unable to dramatize black issues in a nonrealistic style.

Simon, John. *Uneasy Stages: A Chronicle of the New York Theater, 1963–1973,* 181. New York: Random House, 1975.

Simon complains that the language in *The Owl Answers* "is all desperate pseudopoetry, and the tone is harrowing, harried self-accusation." *A Beast's Story,* as arcane as its companion piece, "tries to prop up its poetastery with theater devices for buttresses. . . . which can knock you unconscious." Simon thinks little of Kennedy's capability of combining poetry with drama. See also Simon's review of both plays in "Whirled Without End." *New York* (Feb. 3, 1969): 54.

Tener, Robert L. "Theatre of Identity: Adrienne Kennedy's Portrait of the Black Woman." *Studies in Black Literature* 6, no. 2 (1975): 1–5. [Excerpted in *Black Literature Criticism,* Vol. 2. Edited by James P. Draper, 1150–1153. Detroit: Gale Research, 1992.]

The Owl Answers is a complex mosaic of image, myth, and metaphor used to portray the character She's fragmented self and her quest for psychic integration. Tener explores Kennedy's use of the complex symbolic associations of the owl as a controlling metaphor, which "anchors the heroine's problem of identity with the worlds of her white and black parents and her many self-images."

An Evening with Dead Essex

(American Place Theater, 1973)

Playscript

"An Evening with Dead Essex." Theater 9, no. 2 (Spring 1978): 66–78.

Summary of Play

A group of actors gather on stage to rehearse an emotionally intense piece on the life and death of Mark Essex. Essex, a former U.S. Navy sailor and a black revolutionary, killed several people from atop a Howard Johnson's in New Orleans. He was later killed by police, who riddled his body with over a hundred bullets. The characters are black except for the projectionist, who is white.

Adrienne Kennedy came to write this play after reading about Mark Essex in the January 22, 1973, issue of *Time* magazine. She was intrigued with this "quiet little guy who went berserk and shot those people." *An Evening with Dead Essex* departs in structure and theme from most of Kennedy's earlier work. Instead of focusing on the personal, surreal, and female, *Evening* is realistic, political, and focuses on the male.

Criticism and Performance Reviews

Asahina, Robert. "The Basic Training of American Playwrights: Theater and the Vietnam War." *Theater* 9, no. 2 (1978): 30–37.

In this discourse on the interrelationship of theater, television journalism, and the Vietnam War, Asahina analyzes several experimental and traditional plays, including Kennedy's *An Evening with Dead Essex* and Megan Terry's *Viet Rock.*

Brustein, Robert. *Making Scenes: A Personal History of the Turbulent Years at Yale, 1966–1979,* 176–177. New York: Random House, 1981.

Brustein, the founding director of the Yale Repertory Theatre, recounts the production of *An Evening with Dead Essex* by the Rep. Brustein comments that mounting this play was "a bad mistake" on his part. Apparently, he took umbrage at the stage interpretation of the protagonist, the black revolutionary Mark Essex, whom he thought was being converted from a "symbol of violence" to a "symbol of martyrdom." The director's interpretation, Brustein thought, was highly inflammatory, especially given the political atmosphere of 1974.

Gussow, Mel. "Theater." *New York Times* (March 18, 1974): 42.

The critic finds the play's "material undigested" and the "impact diluted" but concedes that at "the end there is a moment that makes us realize how striking the work could be."

Murray, Timothy. "Facing the Camera's Eye: Black and White Terrain in Women's Drama." *Modern Drama* 28, no. 1 (March 1985): 110–124. [Reprinted in *Reading Black, Reading Feminist: A Critical Anthology.* Edited by Henry Louis Gates, Jr., 155–175. New York: Meridian, 1990.]

Murray examines Adrienne Kennedy's *An Evening with Dead Essex* and Ntozake Shange's *photograph: lovers in motion* from the perspective of the "fixating camera and desirous male [that] come together in a performance of masculine entrapment as deeply oppressive as is the racism from which the characters all hope to escape."

Sollors, Werner. "*People Who Led to My Plays:* Adrienne Kennedy's Autobiography." In *Intersecting Boundaries: The Theatre of Adrienne Kennedy*. Edited by Paul K. Bryant-Jackson and Lois More Overbeck, 13–20. Minneapolis: University of Minnesota Press, 1992 and "Owls and Rats in the American Funnyhouse: Adrienne Kennedy's Drama." *American Literature* 63 (Jun. 3 1991): 507–32.

Within the context of Kennedy's memoir, *People Who Led to My Plays,* Sollors shows, in this pair of essays, how Kennedy weaves autobiographical elements of family history, racial ambivalence, and cultural icons to shape her aesthetic vision.

Zinman, Toby Silverman. "'in the presence of mine enemies': Adrienne Kennedy's *An Evening with Dead Essex.*" *Studies in American Drama, 1945–Present 6,* no. 1 (1991): 3–13.

Zinman finds *An Evening with Dead Essex* "odd and intriguing." Although the script was not included in Kennedy's collection of plays, *One Act,* this play raises questions regarding the Vietnam War, racial oppression, violence, and using the theater as a political tool. Zinman concludes that the play is interesting on several levels, but maintains that "the play seems empty not because of Essex's absence but because Kennedy has not found a satisfying way to present absence on stage. Her "play fails aesthetically to create either presence or absence, just as it fails politically to create either an incendiary call to arms or a healing call to peace. . . . Polarities dwindle into irresolution."

Funnyhouse of a Negro

(East End Theatre, 1964)

Playscripts

Anthology of the American Negro in the Theatre: A Critical Approach. Edited by Lindsay Patterson, 280–290. New York: Publishers, 1969.

The Best Short Plays of 1970. Edited by Stanley Richards, 123–147. Philadelphia: Chilton, 1970.

Black Drama: An Anthology. Edited by William Brasmer, 247–272. Columbus, Ohio: Charles S. Merrill, 1970.

Black Theatre U.S.A.: Plays by African Americans. Rev. Ed. Edited by James Hatch and Ted Shine, 741–751. New York: Free Press, 1996.

Contemporary Black Drama. Edited by Clinton F. Oliver New York: Charles Scribner's, 1971.

Kennedy, Adrienne. *Adrienne Kennedy in One Act.* Minneapolis: University of Minnesota Press, 1988. (Includes *Funnyhouse of a Negro, The Owl Answers, A Lesson in Dead Language, A Rat's Mass, Sun, A Movie Star Has to Star in Black and White, Electra* and *Orestes.)*

Summary of Play

Sarah, the "Negro" of *Funnyhouse,* fragments as she agitates over her disturbing ancestry. Sarah was conceived when her dark-skinned father raped her lighter-skinned mother. Before her birth, Sarah's parents marry and at the behest of her father's mother, a devout woman who believes her son to be the savior of the black race, move to Africa to build a Christian mission. While in Africa, Sarah's mother becomes emotionally estranged from her father, and he subsequently rapes her while drunk. Sarah's mother goes mad and is committed to a mental institution. Her father moves back to New York and begs Sarah's forgiveness. Sarah rejects his entreaties and he kills himself. Tormented by guilt, anger, and resentment that her blackness excludes her from the fruits of white society, Sarah, too, destroys herself.

Criticism and Performance Reviews

Berson, Misha. "*Funnyhouse of a Negro:* Unusual Play That Keeps Kicking." *San Francisco Chronicle* (June 19, 1983): Datebook: 45.

Berson discusses *Funnyhouse* prior to its opening at the Lorraine Hansberry Theater in San Francisco. Kennedy remarks that *Funnyhouse* "represents to me 10 years of writing and struggling with concepts." Although the play has continued to be produced over the last twenty years, Kennedy was so "devastated" by the hostile reaction of the critics to the first commercial Off-Broadway production that she avoided the theater and went to England to recover.

Blau, Herbert. "The American in American Gothic: The Plays of Sam Shepard and Adrienne Kennedy." *Modern Drama* 27, no. 4 (Dec. 1984): 520–539. [Reprinted in Blau's *The Eye of Prey: Subversions of the Postmodern,* 42–64. Bloomington: Indiana University Press, 1987.]

Blau examines the work of Shepard and Kennedy, whom he considers to be the "most original" writers of their generation, to discuss "the persistence of desire in language to overcome the failed promise" of the American Dream. Kennedy, Blau asserts, was "out of place" with the black activists of the sixties, using indirect modes of expressing issues of racial prejudice, miscegenation, and black nationalism on stage. Kennedy's highly expressionistic style, Blau contends, depends on a complex symbolic system using arcane and enigmatic images. Blau further argues Kennedy "is . . . [not] entirely sure . . . that she wouldn't rather be white. Whiteness is very much engrained, maybe against her wishes, in her lyrical quest for roots." Linda Kintz (*The Subject's Tragedy,* 1992. See General Criticism or "The Sanitized Spectacle," 1992. See *A Movie Star Has to Star in Black and White,* Criticism and Performance Reviews) disagrees with Blau on Kennedy's positioning of white culture in her plays.

Brown, Lorraine A. "For the Characters of Myself": Adrienne Kennedy's *Funnyhouse of a Negro.*" *Negro American Literature Forum* 3 (Sept. 1975): 86–88.

Brown maintains that Kennedy's plays "have gone unheralded and unappreciated" and considers her to be one of the most significant contemporary American playwrights. The author describes how Kennedy employs surrealistic and expressionistic modes, dramatizing the struggle of Sarah, the educated daughter of a black father and white mother in overcoming the obstacles to achieving psychic integration caused by her color, gender, and intellectual enlightenment. The play demonstrates through Sarah's fragility "the age-old necessity of possessing one's own soul. Her view that the modern world is oblivious, if not downright hostile, to spiritual struggles links her work to that of many others writing for the contemporary theater."

Clurman, Harold. "Theatre." *Nation* 198 (Feb. 10, 1964):154.

Clurman recognizes Kennedy as a "playwright of talent."

Curb, Rosemary K. "Re/cognition, Re/presentation, Re/creation in Woman-Conscious Drama: The Seer, the Seen, the Scene, the Obscene." *Theater Journal* 37, no. 3 (Oct. 1985): 302–316.

Curb defines "woman-conscious" drama as being "by and about women . . . [and] that characterized by multiple interior reflections of women' s lives and perceptions." She draws upon the ideas of authors N.O. Keohane and Barbara C. Gelpi, who "distinguish three lives of women's self-consciousness: feminine, female, and feminist." The feminine consciousness is defined by male desire, that is, woman as sex object.

The female consciousness, although "less inert and passive" but still deeply rooted in the male tradition, is the "age-old experience of women in giving and preserving life, that is, woman as earth mother." And the feminist consciousness focuses on women's experience within the patriarchal system, yet "envisions alternative levels of consciousness that operate in drama." Curb examines several plays, including Adrienne Kennedy's *Funnyhouse of a Negro* and Ntozake Shange's *for colored girls who have considered suicide/ when the rainbow is enuf.*

Dodson, Owen. "Who Has Seen the Wind? Playwrights and the Black Experience." *Black American Literature Forum* 11, no. 3 (Fall 1977): 108–116.

Dodson includes *Funnyhouse* in his survey of major works of several contemporary African-American dramatists. He observes that "[b]ecause we see the play in print or live on stage, some force within us will not admit that we are in the midst of the most agonizing search for identity since Sophocles' *Oedipus.*" Dodson also discusses Ntozake Shange's *for colored girls who have considered suicide/when the rainbow is enuf.*

Elwood, William R. "Adrienne Kennedy Through the Lens of German." *Intersecting Boundaries; The Theatre of Adrienne Kennedy.* Edited by Paul K. Bryant-Jackson and Lois More Overbeck, 76–84. Minneapolis; University of Minnesota Press, 1992.

Elwood contends that German expressionism informs Kennedy's plays *(Funnyhouse of a Negro, A Rat's Mass, A Movie Star Has to Star in Black and White,* and *A Lesson in Dead Language)* despite the fact that Kennedy's perception of reality differs from that of expressionism. Kennedy seems to be attracted to expressionism because of its vision of transgressing cultural and physical boundaries. As with expressionism, much of Kennedy's work is based on the belief that social reality is grounded too much in materialism. According to Elwood, whereas the German expressionists desired "to disassemble the materialist reality, Kennedy transmutes it through rhythm." Both Kennedy and the expressionists wanted a creative form that would enable the human spirit to transcend to a "'safer' level of meaning." See also Elwood's "*Mankind* and *Sun:* German-American Expressionism." *Text and Presentation* 11 (1991): 9–13, in which he compares the German expressionist piece *Die Menschen (Mankind)* by Walter Hasenclever with Kennedy's *Sun* to explore the German and American attitudes toward the expressionist view of reality.

Fletcher, Winona. "Who Put the 'Tragic' in the Tragic Mulatto?" In *Women in*

American Theatre. Edited by Helen Krich Chinoy and Linda Walsh Jenkins, 262–268. New York: Theatre Communications Group, 1987.

Fletcher traces the history of the portrayal of the "tragic mulatto" by black and white writers of the American theater: "The myriad associations of 'white' with right, might, and superiority and 'black' with backwardness and inferiority set the stage for the entrance of the tragic mulatto." The author highlights some of the mulatto characters in American drama that represent the older stereotype of the mulatto as "docile, saintly, noble, forgiving," as seen in Dion Boucicault's plays to the "new tragic mulatto" and in Adrienne Kennedy's works, in which she "displays[s] the tortures and nightmares . . . of a tragic mulatto searching for an identity that is . . . torn by the paradoxes of living in a no man's (nor woman's) land." Ultimately, Fletcher does not accuse any one party of "put[ting] the tragic in the mulatto," and its portrayal, Fletcher predicts, will continue to appear on stage, as long as "the mulatto is viewed as a social problem rather than as [a] human being."

Kolin, Philip C. "From the Zoo to the Funnyhouse: A Comparison of Edward Albee's *The Zoo Story* with Adrienne Kennedy's *Funnyhouse of a Negro*." *Theatre Southwest* (April 1989): 8–16.

Kolin sees a gap in criticism concerning the parallels between Edward Albee's *The Zoo Story* and Kennedy's work. This is strange given the close creative and financial relationship they had in the early 1960s. Although the playwrights' approaches differ, their plays share similar settings, symbols, and confrontations. For example, both are set in dingy rooming houses, which Kolin sees as symbolically "a living hell . . . [and an] infernal torture chamber."

Oliver, Edith. "The Theatre." *The New Yorker* 39 (Jan. 25, 1964): 76–77.

Generally, Oliver dislikes expressionism because "its built-in weirdness and distortion tend to make the material it deals with seem more important than it really is." However, because Kennedy's subject matter is significant, Oliver concedes that the expressionistic approach is suitable. *Funnyhouse*, observes Oliver, "is quite strong and original . . . [and Kennedy] . . . has wit."

Oppenheimer, George. "*Funnyhouse of a Negro* at the East End." *Newsday* (Jan. 15, 1964): 2c.

Funnyhouse of a Negro is an "inept enigma," according to Oppenheimer, and he predicts it will cause the demise of the Theatre of the Absurd. He faults the plays for its incomprehensiveness, unfunny jokes, and lack of plot.

Patsalidis, Savas. "Adrienne Kennedy's Heterotopias and the (Im)possibilities of the (Black) Female Self." In *Staging Difference: Cultural Pluralism in American Theatre and Drama.* Edited by Marc Maufort, 301–321. New York: Peter Lang, 1995.

Patsalidis contends that Kennedy's *Funnyhouse* and *The Owl Answers* reflect Kennedy's "attempt to stage the impossibilities of racial difference" . . . and dramatize through this "difference the crisis of the new age that is marked by a crisis of self-authenticating knowledge, authority, identity and ethics." Postmodern subjectivity, as it is grounded in these two plays, Patsalidis maintains, is not relegated to apolitical essentialism, but rather is "multiple, layered and non-unitary."

Scanlon, Robert. "Surrealism as Mimesis: A Director's Guide to Adrienne Kennedy's *Funnyhouse of a Negro.*" In *Intersecting Boundaries: The Theatre of Adrienne Kennedy.* Edited by Paul K. Bryant-Jackson and Lois More Overbeck, 76–84. Minneapolis: University of Minnesota Press, 1992.

In analyzing *Funnyhouse,* Scanlon divides the play into ten segments. From these, he identifies three types of segments: (1) pure stage effects (tableaux, stage gimmicks, pantomimes, pop-up horror visuals; (2) groupings of characters engaged in dialogue in location settings; and (3) pure writing or text in monologue forms. These segments, Scanlon asserts, "add up very clearly to the imitation of a single-minded action: to escape the ever-recurring return of the black father."

Sontag, Susan. "Going to the Theatre." *Partisan Review* 31 (Spring 1964): 284–293.

Sontag complains that *Funnyhouse* is "derivative, excessive, and full of mistakes" and fails as a play "about the Negro problem." However, she is impressed by Kennedy's treatment of insanity, which is "sensitive and promising."

Sullivan, Dan. "Staircase Co. in Two Plays." *Los Angeles Times* (Dec. 22, 1972): sec. 4: 21.

Funnyhouse (Staircase Company, MET Playhouse), according to Sullivan, is dated, clichéd, and not terribly arresting. Kennedy's approach is "as old as 'Oedipus' and can be gripping, if we feel that with each turn of the screw we are getting closer to the truth. *Funnyhouse* doesn't convince us." The images and soliloquies do not increase with intensity, "but remain on the same level—a rather weakly-imagined one." Sullivan also reviews *A Beast's Story.*

Talbot, William. "Every Negro His Place." *Drama Critique* 7 (Spring 1964): 92–96.

Talbot, an editor for Samuel French, included *Funnyhouse* in his survey of modern black theater because "a lot of critics like it a lot." He claims he finds the play "unsatisfying" but fails to give any substantiated reasons beyond its "subconscious rationale."

Tapley, Mel. "*Funnyhouse of the Negro,* with Music, Is at NYU." *N.Y Amsterdam News* (Dec. 1, 1984): 26.

Tapley interviews Kennedy and composer Carman Moore, who wrote the score for a new production of *Funnyhouse,* as performed by students in the drama department of New York University. Moore comments that "I heard the music immediately. The logic of how it's written—its kind of stream of consciousness is the way I write." Moore includes ragtime, jazz, synthesizers, and African drums. See also Tapley's "*Funnyhouse* Reveals America's Obsession." *N.Y Amsterdam News* (Sept. 30, 1995): 21.

Taubman, Howard. "The Theater: *Funnyhouse of a Negro.*" *New York Times* (Jan. 15, 1964): 25.

Taubman acknowledges that in *Funnyhouse,* Kennedy is exploring "unknown territory."

Turner, Beth. "Beyond *Funnyhouse:* Adrienne Kennedy." *Black Masks* 1 (Dec. 1984): 1, 8–9.

Turner profiles Kennedy's playwriting activities, focusing on *Funnyhouse.* This play, according to Turner, established Kennedy as a gifted dramatist and "catapulted [her] into the upper echelon of avant-garde playwrights," despite the fact that Kennedy was heavily criticized for the surreal and expressionistic forms she used to depict the tortured protagonist, Sarah.

Turner, Darwin T. "Negro Playwrights and the Urban Negro." *CLA Journal* 12, no. 1 (Sept. 1968): 19–25.

Turner examines the ways in which African-American playwrights dramatize the conflicts blacks face in the city. Kennedy's *Funnyhouse of a Negro* and Alice Childress's *Trouble in Mind* are among the plays discussed.

Wilkerson, Margaret B. "Diverse Angles of Vision: Two Black Women Playwrights." *Theatre Annual* 40 (1985): 91–114. [Reprinted in *Intersecting Boundaries: The Theatre of Adrienne Kennedy.* Edited by Paul K. Bryant-Jackson and Lois More Overbeck, 58–75. Minneapolis: University of Minnesota Press, 1992.]

Wilkerson contends that Kennedy and Lorraine Hansberry are mutually concerned with dramatizing the sociopolitical forces that affect an individual, making a statement about the human condition. However, the playwrights' approach to style, language, and the depiction of the perceptions of their characters are entirely different. Hansberry's method was grounded in realism: "[S]he insisted on meaning, on affirmation, willing it into being, even though she was deeply aware of the absurdity and irrationality of human beings." Kennedy, however, set her dramas "in the thin line between fantasy and consciousness, between dream and reality."

Winn, Steven. "Surrealistic Black Nightmare." *San Francisco Chronicle* (June 30, 1983): 64.

Winn praises SEW Productions, a black theater in the Bay Area, for "pull[ing] off the tricky business of reviving a difficult, somewhat time-bound play without undue reverence or condescension."

The Lennon Play: *In His Own Write*

(National Theatre, London, 1968; Arena Summer Theatre, 1969)

Playscript

Best Short Plays of the World Theatre, 1968–1973. Edited by Stanley Richards. New York: Crown, 1973.

Summary of Play

The hero, "Me," a postwar British kid submerged in the life and lingo of mass media, vacillates between his environment and his fantasy life.

The Lennon Play emerged from Kennedy's fascination with the nonsense books of John Lennon, *A Spaniard in the Works* and *In His Own Write.* Kennedy began writing *The Lennon Play,* ironically, in the building where Lennon was later murdered. She continued working on the play in London, where she met Victor Spinetti, an actor in the Beatles movies. He assisted Kennedy in adapting the Lennon books and was interested in directing the play. However, Kennedy found herself dropped from the project. As she explains in "A Theatre Journal," she sat with the actor

Laurence Olivier during a tryout performance of the play. Olivier was to decide if he wanted to continue with the piece. Olivier liked the piece and "definitely wanted to go on with the project," but without Kennedy.

Criticism and Performance Reviews

Barnes, Clive. "Theater: Irreverence on London Stage." *New York Times* (July 9, 1968): 30.

Barnes finds the outrageousness of *In His Own Write* "appealing" and the hero a "pure delight."

Esslin, Martin. "Two Trifles and a Failure." *New York Times* (July 14, 1968): sec. 2:4.

Esslin maintains that *In His Own Write* "is [almost] ingenious . . . but ultimately less than satisfying."

Wardle, Irving. "John Lennon Play, *In His Own Write,* Is Staged in London." *New York Times* (June 20, 1968): 50.

Wardle is lukewarm in his opinion of John Lennon's text, however, he concedes that cowriter Kennedy and director Victor Spinetti have been able to create a "loose but workable stage form."

A Lesson in Dead Language

(English Stage Society, Royal Court, London, 1968, Theater Genesis, New York, 1970)

Playscripts

Adrienne Kennedy in One Act. Minneapolis: University of Minnesota Press, 1988.

Collision Course. Edited by Edward Parone, 33–40. New York: Random House, 1968.

Summary of Play

A Lesson in Dead Language dramatizes the trauma of a girl's sexual maturation. The setting is a classroom in which the teacher, portrayed as a "great white dog," is seated at a huge dark desk. Her pupils, also seated at desks, are dressed in white organdy dresses, stained in the back with a "great circle of blood." The classroom is ringed by statues of Jesus, Joseph, Mary, two Wise Men, and a shepherd. White Dog teaches the girls the meaning of menstruation and the severe limitations it will impose on the girls.

Criticism

Curb, Rosemary. "'Lesson I Bleed': Adrienne Kennedy's Blood Rites." In *Women in American Theatre.* Edited by Helen Krich Chinoy and Linda Walsh Jenkins, 50–56. New York: Theatre Communications Group, 1987.

Curb asserts that Kennedy employs the image of blood, charged with symbolic meaning, to "dramatize the horrors attendant on female adolescent rites of passage under patriarchy" in five of her plays: *A Lesson in Dead Language, A Rat's Mass, A Beast's Story, The Owl Answers,* and *Funnyhouse of a Negro.* In these plays, blood represents the ambiguousness of the teenage girl's transition to womanhood. On the one hand, the bleeding resulting from the menstrual cycle is natural. On the other hand, because the menstrual process is regarded as a "curse," and therefore should be hidden from the male-dominated society, the young girl "learns to hate her imperfect and uncontrollable body . . . menstrual blood is the sin . . . of the inherited guilt of womanhood."

A Movie Star Has to Star in Black and White

(New York Shakespeare Theatre, Public Theatre, 1976)

Playscripts

Adrienne Kennedy in One Act. Minneapolis: University of Minnesota Press, 1988.

Norton Anthology of African American Literature. Edited by Henry Louis Gates, Jr., and Nellie McKay, 2079–2094. New York: W.W. Norton, 1997.

Wordplays 3: An Anthology of New American Drama, 51–68. New York: PAJ Publications, 1984.

Summary of Play

In this collage-like drama, Clara (seen earlier in Kennedy's *The Owl Answers*), a writer raising a child, visits her hometown where her brother lies in a coma as a result of injuries suffered in a car accident. To cope with her family and pregnancies and the constraints they impose on her art, she tries to insert herself into an ideal world as constructed by Hollywood. The characters include the protagonist, Clara, and what Kennedy calls the "leading roles," actors who look like Bette Davis, Paul Henreid, Jean Peters, Marlon Brando, Montgomery Clift, and Shelley Winters. The "supporting roles" are the mother, the father, and the husband. Kennedy juxtaposes scenes with those from the movies *Now, Voyager* (1942), *Viva Zapata!* (1952), and *A Place in the Sun* (1951).

Criticism and Performance Reviews

Brantley, Ben "Glimpsing Solitude In Worlds Black and White." *New York Times* (Sept. 25, 1995): C11.

Brantley praises *A Movie Star* and *Funnyhouse of a Negro* (both plays staged by Signature Theatre at the Joseph Papp Public Theatre, New York). He comments that "Kennedy has carefully forged an emotional bridge that one cannot avoid crossing, regardless of race, age or sex. She is unmistakably the real thing: a strong, utterly individual voice in the American theater."

Geis, Deborah R. "'A Spectator Watching My Life': Adrienne Kennedy's *A Movie Star Has to Star in Black and White.*" In *Intersecting Boundaries: The Theatre of Adrienne Kennedy.* Edited by Paul K. Bryant-Jackson and Lois More Overbeck, 170–178. Minneapolis: University of Minnesota Press, 1992.

Geis focuses on the torment Clara experiences while identifying with cinematic icons yet, at the same time, repudiating them. Clara's tension signifies the ambivalence of identifying with the products of an industry that has traditionally excluded blacks: "However compelling the movie-star fantasies may appear to be, their attractiveness originates from a Hollywood world sustained by a mythology that is ultimately oppressive in its unassailability." For Clara to understand and control a chaotic world, she must filter her real world through "the lying eye" of the camera's idealized images. Geis suggests that "Clara desire[s] to insert herself and her family into the context of the Hollywood narratives [so that she might attain a] seemliness and coherence promised by the machinations of the visible, the eye/I of the camera."

Graham-White, Anthony. *"A Movie Star Has to Star in Black and White."* In *Contemporary American Dramatists.* Edited by K.A. Berney, 704–705. London: St. James Press, 1994.

Graham-White presents a brief explication of *A Movie Star.*

Jacobson, Aileen. "Adrienne Kennedy's Signature Season." *Newsday* (Sept. 25, 1995): sec. 2: B6.

Jacobson observes that *A Movie Star* "is not a good match for *Funnyhouse of a Negro*" (both presented by the Signature Theatre Company). The critic acknowledges that while the play is entertaining, it is simply an echo of *Funnyhouse.*

Kintz, Linda. "The Sanitized Spectacle: What's Birth Got to Do With It? Adrienne Kennedy's *A Movie Star Has to Star in Black and White.*" *Theatre Journal* 44 (1992): 67–86.

Kintz credits Kennedy as anticipating postmodernist discussions of the legitimate position of the female in society. Kennedy "was a feminist in a period of masculinist Black nationalism, she was also a postmodern experimentalist in a period of realist political drama and women writing very specifically about the consequences of the physicality of blackness and the bleeding, pregnant female body when theoretical discourse could not account for those differences." In *A Movie Star,* Kennedy "displaces the sanitized version of the reproductive female in the black- and-white movies of Hollywood." She fragments the personal identities of Clara and her family members by inserting them into scenes of movies, what Kintz calls "the most public space of all in American culture." The insertion, Kintz argues, "sets up a shimmering, wavering movement between sites of subjectivity which simply don't match up, which won't fit."

Kissel, Howard. "Plays' Mind-Set Is Way Too Brainy: *Funnyhouse* and *Movie Star* Aim for the Head But Don't Touch the Heart." *Daily News* (New York) (Sept. 29, 1995): 39.

Although *A Movie Star* and *Funnyhouse of a Negro* (both staged by Signature Theatre Company at the Joseph Papp Public Theatre, New York) have been "splendidly mounted," Kissel complains that despite "a certain wit, a certain brittle poetry, [these plays] are nothing more than mind games without much emotional depth."

Sainer, Arthur. "Gavella Orchestrates a Sigh." *Village Voice* (Nov. 29, 1976): 97, 99.

Sainer comments that Kennedy verges on saying something of import about human endeavors. However, her characters become mired in the convoluted script. He complains that "her forcefulness" is aimless, her verbal images are "overheated," and "she painstakingly invokes images and rituals that . . . *almost* mean something." Despite her sympathetic manner, her confessional style is so private that he is a spectator excluded from understanding in a truly meaningful way. Sainer suggests that Kennedy allow more joy into her dense, heated dialogue, so that "more life flow[s] in, and thus a possible way to joy."

Stein, Ruthe. "She's Got Her Own Place in the Sun." *San Francisco Chronicle* (Jan. 31, 1980): 22.

Kennedy, whose play *A Movie Star Has to Star in Black and White* opened in February at the Durham Studio Theater in Berkeley, remarks that it took many years to work through the fact that she would never "be a really famous playwright." But, Kennedy claims, she has "made peace" with herself.

The Ohio State Murders

(Commissioned by the Great Lakes Theater Festival, 1992)

Playscripts

Kennedy, Adrienne. *The Alexander Plays*. Minneapolis: University of Minnesota Press, 1992.

Related material: Kennedy, Adrienne. "Letter to My Students on my Sixty-First Birthday by Suzanne Alexander." *Kenyon Review* 15, no. 2 (Spring 1993): 100–130.

Summary of Play

A well-known black writer, Suzanne Alexander, visits Ohio State University to discuss the violent imagery in her work. In a series of flashbacks, she recalls the years she attended Ohio State as a student. She was not prepared for the racist attitudes she encountered on campus, those of the white girls in her dorm to those of members of the English department, where "[i]t was thought that [blacks] were not able to master the program." Suzanne has an affair with Robert Hampshire, a white English teacher who reads Hardy. She becomes pregnant. Hampshire and her parents distance themselves from her, and the university expels her. She moves in with her aunt Louise in Harlem and has twins, Cathi and Carol. Over the objections of her aunt, Suzanne moves back to Columbus and stays at Mrs. Tyler's boarding house. Someone kidnaps and kills Cathi. The police are unable to find the killer. In the meantime, Suzanne meets a young law student, David. She tells him about everything except the identity of the father of her twins. They agree to marry. One day, when Suzanne is out, Robert Hampshire, posing as a researcher, gains access to Carol, the other twin. He murders her and himself. It is revealed that he feared that ultimately Suzanne would reveal that he fathered her twins. The truth, he felt, would ruin his life and career. The play closes when Suzanne tells her audience that her experiences as a young woman attending Ohio State gave birth to the violent imagery in her work.

Performance Reviews

Grossberg, Michael. "Memories in Black and White: College Days Haunt Playwright into Creating *Ohio State Murders*." *The Columbus Dispatch* (March 1, 1992): Accent: 1I.

Ohio State Murders signals Kennedy's willingness to confront the pain she endured thirty years ago while attending Ohio State University. While a student, she felt isolated because of race. However, Kennedy warns that the play is "totally fictional," declaring that "most of my plays express fears and emotions, dreams and images that I am haunted by. *Murder* is used as a metaphor in the play," [says Kennedy]. "I tried to capture the feeling of violence through the use of imagery in a fictionalized story about an English professor who eventually murders his twins." The play also dramatizes blacks' grappling with racial oppression during the 1940s and 1950s.

Kolin, Philip C. "The Adrienne Kennedy Festival at the Great Lakes Theater Festival: A Photo Essay." *Studies in American Drama, 1945–Present* 8 (1993): 85–94.

The Great Lakes Theater Festival held the first Adrienne Kennedy Festival, which included the premiere of *The Ohio State Murders* and a dramatic adaptation of *People Who Led to My Plays.*

The Owl Answers

(Part of *Cities in Bezique: Two One-Acts,* Public Theater, 1969)

Playscripts

Black Theater U.S.A.: Forty-Five Plays by Black Americans, 1847–1974. Edited by James V. Hatch and Ted Shine, 756–764. New York: The Free Press, 1974.

Cities in Bezique: Two One-Act Plays. New York: Samuel French, 1969.

Adrienne Kennedy in One Act. Minneapolis: University of Minneosta Press, 1988.

New American Plays II. Edited by William Hoffman, 249–268. New York: Hill & Wang, 1968.

Summary of Play

The story revolves around "She who is CLARA PASSMORE who is the VIRGIN MARY who is the BASTARD who is the OWL." Clara, a black teacher, is the child of a black cook and a wealthy white employer. She is adopted by a black minister and his cold wife, who constantly reminds Clara that her illegitimacy will restrict her ambitions. Her blood father dies while she attends college; she is excluded from his funeral. To connect with him, she visits her father's ancestral home in England, but she is shunned there as well. On a "New York subway is the Tower of London is a Harlem hotel room is St. Peter's" she encounters white figures associated with Western culture: Shakespeare, William the Conqueror, Chaucer, and Anne Boleyn. She induces a black man to have sex with her, but she rejects his sexual advances. Unable to reconcile being tormented by those who reject her and shunning the one that desires her, she goes mad.

Criticism and Performance Reviews

(see *Cities in Bezique*)

A Rat's Mass

(La Mama ETC, New York, 1969)

Playscripts

Adrienne Kennedy in One Act. Minneapolis: University of Minnesota Press, 1988.

More Plays from Off-Off Broadway. Edited by Michael Smith, 345–357. New York: Bobbs-Merrill, 1972.

New Black Playwrights. Edited by William Couch, Jr., 61–69. Baton Rouge: Louisiana State University Press, 1968.

The Off-Off Broadway Book: The Plays, People, Theatre. Edited by Albert Poland, 352–356. New York: Bobbs-Merrill, 1972.

Summary of Play

In this expressionistic drama, Sister Rat and Brother Rat, both black, reminisce about Rosemary, their playmate and later girlfriend, who is white,

Catholic, and Italian. Sister Rat, with her rat's belly, and Brother Rat, with his rat's head, obsess about Rosemary and her "insidious control over their lives." According to Kennedy, the images for this play emanated from a dream that haunted her for years, in which she was being chased by "big, bloodied rats."

Criticism and Performance Reviews

Ansorge, Peter. "La Mama." *Plays and Players* 17 (July 1970): 51.

Ansorge reviews La Mama Cafe's production of *A Rat's Mass* at the Royal Court, London.

Barnes, Clive. "*A Rat's Mass* Weaves Drama of Poetic Fabric." *New York Times* (Nov. 1, 1969): 39.

Upon a first reading of *A Rat's Mass,* Barnes admits that he found it incomprehensible. However, when performed, the nonsensical dialogue "float[s] accusingly in the mind like the perfume of a girl whose name you have forgotten." Barnes distinguishes Kennedy's work from that of her black counterparts in two ways. First, Kennedy's dramatic approach is not grounded in realism but in poetic images. Second, she is "most concerned with white, with white relationship, with white blood. She thinks black, but she remembers white."

Fuchs, Elinor. "Adrienne Kennedy and the First Avant-Garde." In *Intersecting Boundaries: The Theatre of Adrienne Kennedy.* Edited by Paul K. Bryant-Jackson and Lois More Overbeck, 76–84. Minneapolis: University of Minnesota Press, 1992.

Fuchs discusses the parallels of Kennedy's early plays *(A Rat's Mass, The Owl Answers,* and *Funnyhouse of a Negro)* to the ritual theater of Artaud and Genet, as well as the symbolists of the early twentieth century. Like the symbolists, Kennedy is not interested in the realities of social interaction but "the mystery of the isolated soul."

Gussow, Mel. "*A Rat's Mass.*" *New York Times* (March 11, 1976): 42.

Gussow reviews a musicalized version of *A Rat's Mass* performed in New York at La Mama. The critic feels that this "muscial procession" is not easily accessible but he praises the attempt at "cross-breeding experimental theater and experimental music."

Hughes, Catharine R. "New York: Theatre." *Plays and Players* 17 (Nov. 1969): 14–15.

Hughes contends that Kennedy's power lies in her imagery—"[S]he is a poet far more than a playwright." Generally, however, *A Rat's Mass* (as staged by La Mama ETC) is too self-conscious and fraught with gimmicks to involve the audience. Yet Kennedy's imagery is powerful, and "that power is quite considerable." Hughes suggests that black theater in general could become forceful if blacks and whites "become a trifle less self-conscious about it all."

Sainer, Arthur. "Theatre: *A Rat's Mass*." *Village Voice* (Sept. 25, 1969): 42.

Sainer comments that although *A Rat's Mass* was "heavily charged with possibilities of meaning," his understanding could not get beyond the intellect to the gut. However, the critic encourages theatergoers to see the play because "it has its own sense of what it wants to do."

Scott, John S. "Teaching Black Drama." *Players* 47 (Feb.-March. 1972): 130–131.

Contrary to the view of many critics, Scott argues that the black characters in *A Rat's Mass* who seem weak or desire death do not indicate that blacks are grounded in despair. Rather, black theatergoers experience a "catharsis through death." For blacks, "witnessing a Black death for a Black cause" is an affirmation of life because "to risk or give life in benefit of other Black people is to live fully."

She Talks to Beethoven

(River Arts Repertory International Writers Festival, Woodstock, N.Y., 1989; reading at Harvard University, 1989)

Playscripts

Kennedy, Adrienne. *The Alexander Plays.* Minneapolis: University of Minnesota Press, 1992.

Plays in One Act. Edited by Daniel Halpern. Hopewell, N.J.: Ecco, 1991.

"She Talks to Beethoven." Antaeus No. 66 (Spring 1991): 248–258.

Related material: Kennedy, Adrienne. "Letter to My Students on My Sixty-First Birthday by Suzanne Alexander." *Kenyon Review* 15, no.2 (Spring 1993): 100–130.

Summary of Play

The play opens with Suzanne Alexander, (the protagonist in Kennedy's *Ohio State Murders),* an African-American writer, waiting at her house on the campus at Legon, Accra, Ghana, for her husband, a poet and activist, who has disappeared. As she waits, she reads from diary entries about Ludwig van Beethoven, about whom she is writing, Beethoven appears before her, and their conversation consoles her until her husband returns.

Criticism

Kolin, Philip C. "Orpheus Ascending: Music, Race and Gender in Adrienne Kennedy's *She Talks to Beethoven.*" *African American Review* 28, no. 2 (Summer 1994): 292–304.

Kolin argues that *She Talks to Beethoven* signifies a new direction in Kennedy's dramatic canon. While the play retains some of the conventions of her earlier work, it "offers healing consolation instead of the nightmarish world of fragmentation." Kennedy uses Suzanne's dialogue with Beethoven to show "that art and artists, questing for the creative acts that save, transcend the dichotomies of white and black, male or female. . . . [The play] expands the significance of the Orpheus myth to erase the taint of female marginality as well as racial and ethnic exclusivity." See also Kolin's "Color Connections in Adrienne Kennedy's *She Talks to Beethoven.*" *Notes on Contemporary Literature* 24, no. 2 (March 1994): 4–6.

Sleep Deprivation Chamber

(Cowritten with Adam Kennedy; won Obie for Best New Play, 1996; Signature Theater Company, Joseph Papp Public Theatre, 1996)

Playscripts

Kennedy, Adam P. and Adrienne Kennedy. *Sleep Deprivation Chamber.* New York: Theatre Communications Group, 1996.

Summary of Play

Teddy, a young, upper-middle-class black man, is stopped by police officers ostensibly for a broken taillight. Teddy ends up in jail on a trumped-up charge of beating the arresting officer. The surrealist nightmare of Teddy's arrest and trial is juxtaposed with Teddy's mother's nostagalic memories of growing up in a black middle-class family. And although Teddy is found innocent of the charges, the play ends with the realization that Teddy and his mother have paid dearly for the ordeal.

Kennedy and her son Adam wrote *Sleep Deprivation Chamber* in response to a "wrenching Kennedy family experience." Several years ago, Adam was beaten by a cop outside his father's home in Virginia, and subsequently arrested. Adam Kennedy later won a civil suit that he had filed against Arlington County.

Performance Reviews

Brantley, Ben. "Righting a Wrong in a World Out of Joint." *New York Times* (Feb. 27, 1996): C11.

Brantley observes that *Sleep Deprivation Chamber* is "imperfect, but it has unsettling power." The strength of the play lies in its dramatization of the feelings of despair of the falsely accused, "recalling the fearful, free-falling sensations of Hitchcock movies like *The Wrong Man*." Another strength is Kennedy's "careful, hypnotic orchestration." The last part of the play is weak; it turns into a conventional courtroom drama with its stereopyped characters of good and evil. According to Brantley, "It has a thudding quality that is out of sync with what has preceded it."

Jacobson, Aileen. "Raw Anger over Injustice: Drama Decries Beating, Betrayal of Black Man." *Newsday* (Feb. 26, 1996): sec. 2: B2.

Jacobson finds *Sleep Deprivation Chamber* too virulent: "There's so much raw, undigested anger in this play that it mars the artistic endeavor." Kennedy's use of fragmentation fails to work in this play; "[it] only serves to break apart instead of integrate various strands."

Kissel, Howard. "*Sleep* Deprived of Drama." *Daily News* (New York) (Feb. 27, 1996): 44.

Kissel points out that "although [*Sleep*] is carefully written and, for the most part, beautifully acted, [it] comes across more as an op-ed piece."

Sheward, David. "Record 35 Obies Handed Out in 41st Annual *Village Voice* Ceremony." *Back Stage* 37 (May 24, 1996): 3.

Kennedy received an Obie for Best New Play for *Sleep Deprivation Chamber* and *June and Jean in Concert.*

"Theater." *Back Stage.* (March 15, 1996): 60.

The reviewer complains that the realistic scenes are staged with the "brutal directness of a "Cops" videotape, but they go on endlessly and are repeated ad nauseum," while the nostalgic scenes with the mother "seem tangential and extraneous."

Other Plays by Adrienne Kennedy

Black Children's Day
(Commissioned by Brown University, Providence, R.I., 1980)

Boats
(Mark Taper Forum, Los Angeles, 1969)

Diary of Lights: A Musical Without Songs
(1987)

The Dramatic Circle
(A radio play dramatizing the events in the monologue *The Film Club,* commissioned by WNYC, New York)

Related material: Kennedy, Adrienne. "Letter to My Students on My Sixty-First Birthday by Suzanne Alexander." *Kenyon Review* 15, no. 2 (Spring 1993): 100–130.

Electra
(Adapted from Euripides, Juilliard School of Music, 1980)

Playscript
Adrienne Kennedy in One Act. Minneapolis: University of Minnesota Press, 1988.

Review
"Theater." *Village Voice* (April 22, 1981).

The Film Club (A Monologue by Suzanne Alexander)
(see *The Dramatic Circle*)

June and Jean in Concert
(Won Obie for Best New Play, 1996; adapted from Kennedy's *People Who Led to My Plays,* Signature Theater Company, Joseph Papp Public Theater, 1995)

Reviews
Backalenick, Irene. "*June and Jean in Concert.*" *Back Stage* 36 (Nov. 24, 1995): 52.

Brantley, Ben. "Restless voices of a Writer's Past." *New York Times* (Nov. 13, 1995): A21.

Jacobson, Aileen. "Twins Tracing Their Past; Amid '40s Music and Mainstream: Black Girls' Musings." *Newsday* (Nov. 15, 1995): sec. 2: B9.

June and Jean in Concert by Adrienne Kennedy. "*Armenian Reporter* (Dec. 9, 1995): 5.

A Lancashire Lad

(Empire State Youth Theatre, State University of New York, Albany, 1980)

Review

Rich, Frank. "Stage: *Lancashire Lad* for Children." *New York Times* (May 21, 1980): C3.

Motherhood 2000: Black Children's Day

(A ten-minute play commissioned in 1994 by the McCarter Theatre, Princeton, N.J.; Signature Theater Company, Joseph Papp Public Theater, 1996)

Orestes

(Adapted from Euripides; Juilliard School of Music, 1980)

Pale Blue Flowers

(unpublished, 1955). For background information on this early play, see *Twentieth-Century American Playwrights: Views of a Changing Cluture; An Exhibition Catalogue*, 110. Austin: Harry Ransom Humanities Research Center, University of Texas, 1994.

Solo Voyages

(Selected excerpts from *The Owl Answers, A Rat's Mass, and A Movie Star Has to Star in Black and White;* Interart Theater, 1985)

Reviews

Gussow, Mel. "Subway Sampler." *New York Times* (Sept. 20, 1985): C3.

Solomon, Alisa. "Sojourner's Truths." *Village Voice* (Oct. 1, 1985): 98.

Sun

(Some texts include the subtitle *A Poem for Malcolm X Inspired by His Murder*; commissioned by the Royal Court Theatre, London, 1968; La Mama ETC, 1970).

Playscripts

Kennedy, Adrienne. *Adrienne Kennedy in One Act.* Minneapolis: University of Minnesota Press, 1988.

Spontaneous Combustion: Eight New American Plays. Edited by Rochelle Owens, 3–13. New York: Winter House, 1972.

"Sun." *Scripts* 1 (Nov. 1971): 51–54.

Review

Elwood, William R. "*Mankind* and *Sun:* German-American Expressionism." *Text and Presentation* 11 (1991): 9–13.

Chapter Nine
May Miller

Brief Biography

The poet, playwright, and teacher, May Miller (1899–1995) grew up in genteel surroundings. Her father was an esteemed sociologist at Howard University, and her mother was also a teacher. Through her parents' connections she became acquainted with many of the writers and thinkers of the New Negro Renaissance, including W.E.B. Du Bois, Alain Locke, and Booker T. Washington. She was also a close friend of Georgia Douglas Johnson and studied with and was encouraged by Mary Burrill and Angelina Weld Grimké. Miller received training in the theater at Howard University, from which she graduated in 1920.

Miller won third prize in a *Opportunity* magazine contest in 1925, and Willis Richardson chose two of her plays for his anthology, *Plays and Pageants from the Life of the Negro* (1930). He considered her "one of the most promising of the Negro playwrights." She also coedited a play anthology on black heroes with Richardson entitled *Negro History in Thirteen Plays*.

As a teacher and playwright, Miller believed that black students needed greater exposure to the work and life of blacks. She wrote plays about key figures in black history, several of which she produced at Frederick Douglass High School, where she taught. Kathy A. Perkins observes that Miller is unique among contemporary female dramatists in that she wrote in a diversity of forms (folk, history, and propaganda); she portrayed blacks at different socioeconomic levels; and she often incorporated white characters "to stress a point" as in *Stragglers in the Dust* (1930) and *Nails and Thorns* (1933). In later life Miller devoted herself to composing poetry. She died in 1995.

Profiles and General Criticism

Brown-Guillory, Elizabeth. *Their Place on the Stage: Black Women Playwrights in America*. New York: Praeger, 1990.

Brown-Guillory includes discussions on several female playwrights active during the Harlem Renaissance: Marita Bonner, Mary Burrill, Angelina Weld Grimké, Georgia Douglas Johnson, and May Miller.

Burke, Sally. *American Feminist Playwrights: A Critical History.* New York: Twayne, 1996.

Burke provides a straightforward introduction to Miller's life and a discussion of her plays.

Miller, Jeanne-Marie A. "Georgia Douglas Johnson and May Miller: Forgotten Playwrights of the New Negro Renaissance." *CLA Journal* 33, (June 1990): 349–366.

Miller recognizes Johnson and Miller as two forgotten playwrights who contributed significantly to the drama of the New Negro Renaissance. She considers the plays of these women to be "among the best written by black playwrights during the 1920s and the early 1930s, and their works serve as important transition between the older extant black-authored plays—such as William Wells Brown's *The Escape* (1858) and Angelina Weld Grimké's *Rachel* (1916)—and the later works of black playwrights." The lynching plays, Miller observes, anticipate the later plays of social protest such as Theodore Ward's *Big White Fog* (1937) and Loften Mitchell's *A Land Beyond the River* (1957). Miller includes brief discussions of the following plays: Georgia Douglas Johnson's *Plumes, The Starting Point, Blue Blood, Blue Eyed Black Boy, A Sunday Morning in the South, William and Ellen Craft,* and *Frederick Douglass* and May Miller's *The Bog Guide, Graven Images, Moving Caravans, Christophe's Daughters, The Cuss'd Thing, Scratches,* and *Nails and Thorns.*

Peterson, Bernard L. *Early Black American Playwrights and Dramatic Writers; A Biographical Directory and Catalog of Plays, Films, and Broadcasting Scripts.* New York: Greenwood, 1990.

The entry on Miller includes a brief biography, plot summaries, staging history, and list of secondary sources.

Roses, Lorraine Elena, and Ruth Elizabeth Randolph. *Harlem Renaissance and Beyond: Literary Biographies of 100 Black Women Writers, 1900–1945.* Boston: G.K. Hall, 1990.

The entry on Johnson provides biographical information and a selected list of primary and secondary sources.

Shafer, Yvonne. "Georgia Douglas Johnson." In *American Women Playwrights, 1900–1950*. New York: Peter Lang, 1995.

Shafer provides a basic introduction to Miller and her work. The entries include quotes from key critics, synopses, and analyses of Miller's plays.

Stoelting, Winifred L. "May Miller." In *Dictionary of Literary Biography: Vol. 41. Afro-American Poets Since 1955.* Edited by Trudier Harris and Thadious M. Davis, 241–247. Detroit: Gale Research, 1985.

Stoelting provides an introductory article on Miller's life and work, emphasizing her poetry. Accompanying the article is a primary and secondary bibliography.

The Bog Guide

(Third prize, *Opportunity* magazine contest, 1925; Intercollegiate [Drama] Association at the Imperial Elks Auditorim, New York, 1926)

Playscript

Zora Neale Hurston, Eulalie Spence, Marita Bonner, and Others; The Prize Plays and Other One-Acts Published in Periodicals. Edited by Henry Louis Gates, Jr., 59–67. New York: G.K. Hall, 1996.

Summary of Play

The action begins with two English tourists, Rupert Master and Elwood Bealer, awaiting their guide, who will take them across a bog on the "great dark continent." Bealer wants to turn back, but Rupert entreats him to remain. Rupert confesses that he is trying to find Chauncey Bayne. According to Rupert's "ugly story," years ago Chauncey was to marry Audrian Waylon, the woman loved by Rupert but who loved Chauncey. Out of jealousy, Rupert reveals to Audrian that Chauncey's birth mother was a black. Audrian promptly breaks her engagement with Chauncey and marries Rupert. But Rupert's guilt over his deed inspires him to make things right by following Chauncey to Africa to bring him back The bog guide, Sabali, arrives. She turns out to be the daughter of Chauncey, who has just died. Rupert wants to assume paternal responsibility for Sabali and take her back to England so that he might "fight her battles," but Sabali has other ideas. She tells Rupert that she is not going, nor is he. "You see, " says Sabali, "I know you; you're Prejudice. Already Faraway Land has too many masqueraders and Prejudice must not go back." Both Sabali and Rupert slowly sink into the depths of the bog.

Criticism

(see *Profiles and General Criticism*)

Additional Plays

Christophe's Daughters
(1935)

Playscripts
Black Female Playwrights: An Anthology of Plays Before 1950. Edited by Kathy A. Perkins, 166–175. Bloomington: Indiana University Press, 1990.

Negro History in Thirteen Plays. Edited by Willis Richardson and May Miller, 241–265. Washington, D.C.: The Associated, 1935.

The Cuss'd Thing
(Honorable mention, *Opportunity* magazine contest, 1926; unpublished)

Graven Images
(1930)

Playscripts
Black Theater U.S.A.: Forty-Five Plays by Black Americans, 1847–1974. Edited by James V. Hatch and Ted Shine, 353–359. New York: The Free Press, 1974.

Black Theatre USA: Plays by African Americans, 1847 to Today. Rev. Ed. Edited by James V. Hatch and Ted Shine, 334–341. New York: The Free Press, 1996.

Plays and Pageants from the Life of the Negro. Edited by Willis Richardson, 109–139. Washington, D.C.: Associated Publishers,1930.

Harriet Tubman
(Dillard University, New Orleans, 1935–1936)

Playscripts

Black Female Playwrights: An Anthology of Plays Before 1950. Edited by Kathy A. Perkins, 176–186. Bloomington: Indiana University Press, 1990.

Black Heroes: 7 Plays. Edited by Errol Hill, 101–121. New York: Applause, 1989.

Negro History in Thirteen Plays. Edited by Willis Richardson and May Miller, 265–288. Washington, D.C.: Associated Publishers, 1935.

Nails and Thorns

(Won third prize, drama contest, Southern University, Baton Rouge, 1933)

Playscript

The Roots of African American Drama. Edited by Leo Hamalian and James V. Hatch, 307–327. Detroit: Wayne State University, 1991.

Riding the Goat

(Krigwa Players, Baltimore, 1932)

Playscripts

Black Female Playwrights: An Anthology of Plays Before 1950. Edited by Kathy A. Perkins, 153–165. Bloomington: Indiana University Press, 1990.

Plays and Pageants from the Life of a Negro. Edited by Willis Richardson, 141–177. Washington, D.C.: Associated Publishers, 1930.

Wines in the Wilderness: Plays by African American Women from the Harlem Renaissance to the Present. Edited by Elizabeth Brown-Guillory, 65–78. New York: Greenwood, 1990.

Samory

(1935)

Playscript

Negro History in Thirteen Plays. Edited by Willis Richardson and May Miller, 289–312. Washington, D.C.: Associated Publishers, 1935.

Scratches

(1929)

Playcripts
Miller, May. "Scratches." *Carolina Magazine* (April 1929): 36–44.

Zora Neale Hurston, Eulalie Spence, Marita Bonner, and Others: The Prize Plays and Other One-Acts Published in Periodicals. Edited by Henry Louis Gates, Jr., 68–78. New York: G.K. Hall, 1996.

Sojourner Truth
(1935)

Playscript
Negro History in Thirteen Plays. Edited by Willis Richardson and May Miller, 313–333. Washington, D.C.: Associated Publishers, 1935.

Stragglers in the Dust
(1930)

Playscript
Black Female Playwrights: An Anthology of Plays Before 1950. Edited by Kathy A. Perkins, 145–152. Bloomington: Indiana University Press, 1990.

Within the Shadow
(Won first prize in Harvard University's playwrighting contest, 1920)

Chapter Ten
Ntozake Shange

Brief Biography

It took Ntozake Shange's (1948–) smash hit *for colored girls who have considered suicide/when the rainbow is enuf* to jolt mainstream theater critics and academicians into an awareness of the work of black female dramatists. Considered by many in the theatrical and academic communities to be the "breakthrough" play for black female theater artists, the play won several awards, including an Obie in 1977, and inspired dozens of articles in the popular and scholarly press. Ntozake Shange is the first commercially successful playwright who has challenged the traditional view of black women without compromising their integrity.

Shange was born into a middle-class family on October 18, 1948, as Paulette Williams. Shange says of her upbringing that it "was one of the best lives America had to offer. . . . We were the American dream." But the wealth and culture that her parents gave her were not enough to erase the rage that roiled within her. At the age of eight she first experienced racism. In St. Louis she was bused to a previously all-white school. "I was not prepared for it," she later recalled. "I was rich and somewhat protected. Now I was being harassed and chased around by these white kids. My parents were busy being proud." Being raised as an "intellectual child," Shange felt alienated and frustrated at being limited because of her gender: "I had finished school, Black arts had taken on an incredibly antifemale aura. All the men I knew were running around getting ready to die. . . . I couldn't possibly sit up in nobody's kitchen forever baking nothing." At the age of nineteen, recently separated from her law-student husband, she attempted suicide.

In 1971 she rejected her middle-class upbringing. She changed her name to Ntozake Shange (pronounced En-toe-ZAH-kee Shon-GAY)—Zulu names meaning "she who comes with her own things" and "who walks like a lion," respectively. Shange maintains that "I had a violent,

violent resentment of carrying a slave name; poems and music come from the pit of myself and the pit of myself wasn't a slave."

She graduated from Barnard College in 1970 and in 1973 earned a master's degree in American studies from the University of Southern California. In an interview with Michele Wallace, Shange says her goal was to pursue a Ph.D but decided against it when she discovered that so few blacks had doctorates: "I became terribly afraid that I would be isolating myself from all the other blacks in the country, either educationally or economically, and would be left, essentially, with *nobody* to play with." Instead, Shange taught college courses. But she also wrote and performed her poetry, in collaboration with several other female poets, dancers, and musicians, in bars (she thought theaters were stuffy) in San Francisico and New York. Emerging from those performances was *for colored girls who have considered suicide/when the rainbow is enuf,* a "choreopoem" that explored the realities of black women living in a racist and sexist environment.

for colored girls ran on Broadway for 747 performances. Not all critics raved over the theater piece. Some viewed the choreopoem as "a slap in the face of [Shange's] collective black brethren."

Several black writers criticized Shange for presenting the male characters as one-dimensional while her female characters were full-bodied individuals. Shange remarks that the vehement reaction from many in the black male community blindsided her: "I was totally startled by the vociferousness of their response . . . I was coming out of this incredibly feminist environment in Oakland and then New York, and all of a sudden all these men were all upset. And I thought, this play had nothing to do with them! This is all about women!"

Shange's aesthetic is grounded in the affirmation that art is a tool. Art must do something other than act pretty. Shange's primary concern is with Third World women, that is, black women and other oppresed women of color whose "existence . . . is a political situation." She hopes that her art will encourage other Third World women to immerse themselves in themselves. "What I'm getting at, "says Shange," is the ability to be in your *woman's* body. . . . A lot of black and Latin women have not been allowed to be inside themselves, to really feel what that's about. Cause we've been so busy being revolutionaries or being reactionaries, or being 'ladies' that we forgot about it." Yet, because Shange's work touches upon universal problems such as rape, abortion, physical and emotional abuse, and infidelity, women across all cultures, ethnicities, and economic strata can relate to Shange's art and message.

Shange developed the choreopoem, an eclectic form of theater, to protest the traditional linear dramatic form, symbolic of the Western patriarchal system. Shange believes that Eurocentric theater is "overwhelmingly shallow/stilted & imitative":

for too long now afro-american[s] in theatre have been duped by the same artificial aesthetics that plague our white counterparts/"the perfect play" as we know it to be/a truly european framework for european psychology/cannot function efficiently for those of us from this hemisphere.(10.12)

This is why Shange refuses the label "playwright"; she prefers "poet" or "writer": "i am interested solely in the poetry of a moment/the emotional & aesthetic impact of a character or a line." For the most part, Shange's theater pieces follow the nonlinear, eclectic format she developed for *for colored girls.*

Shange conveys meaning, not through plot and character motivation, but through expressionism that is relayed through poetic language, movement, and music. As Mikell Pinkney points out, Shange has devised a "coded language":

i cant count the number of times i have viscerally wanted to attack deform n maim the language that i was taught to hate myself in/the language that perpetuates the notions that cause pain to every black child as he/she learns to speak of the world & the "self". . . . i haveta fix my tool to my needs. . . . leaving us space to literally create our own image.

As with language, movement and music are as vital to Shange's aesthetic as they are to her spirit: "With dance I discovered my body more intimately than I had imagined possible. With the acceptance of the ethnicity of my thighs & backside, came a clearer understanding of my voice as a woman & as a poet." Music and movement are vital to Shange's expressionistic structure—they reflect her need to "create an emotional environment/[a] felt architecture."

In addition to writing dramatic pieces, Shange has directed some of her own plays as well as the plays of others, including Richard Wesley's *Mighty Gents* (1979) and Bertolt Brecht's *Mother Courage* (1980). She is also a noted poet and novelist; her published works include *Sassafrass, Cypress and Indigo, nappy edges, Betsey Brown: A Novel, A Daughter's Geography, From Okra to Greens, Ridin' the Moon West: Word Paintings,* and *Liliane: Resurrection of a Daughter.*

Profiles and Interviews

Blackwell, Henry. "An Interview with Ntozake Shange." *Black American Literature Forum* 13, no. 4 (Winter 1979): 134–138.

Blackwell's interview is the rare one that focuses on Shange's aesthetics. The writer candidly responds to Blackwell's queries: What makes a good poet? Does living in the South influence black writers in "distinctive ways"? Who are your role models? Has diminishment and neglect in and out of literature forced black women to look at life in a special way, forced them to devise a special aesthetic? And for whom did you write *for colored girls ?*

Brown, Elizabeth. "Ntozake Shange." In *Dictionary of Literary Biography:* Vol. 38. *Afro-American Writers After 1955: Drama and Prose Writers.* Edited by Thadious M. Davis and Trudier Harris, 240–250. Detroit: Gale Research, 1985.

This article introduces the reader to Shange's life and work and provides a general assessment of her poetry and choreopoems.

Buckley, Tom."The Three Stages of Ntozake Shange." *New York Times* (Dec. 16, 1977): C6.

Buckley writes about Shange's recent activities: writing a new play *(In the Middle of a Flower);* lecturing at Rutgers; changing her "slave name" Paulette Williams to Ntozake Shange; and "formalizing her relationship" with David Murray, a musician who performs in *Where the Mississippi Meets the Amazon,* a play Shange cowrote with two other writers. Shange also talks about her "determined" feminism and the influence of the Vietnam War on her political ideology.

Contemporary Authors: A Bio-Bibliographical Guide, Vol. 27. New Revision Series. Edited by Hal May, 426–430. Detroit: Gale Research, 1989.

The entry includes a biographical sketch, general critical remarks on Shange's work, and a list of her works.

Dong, Stella. "Ntozake Shange." *Publisher's Weekly* 227 (May 3, 1985): 74–75.

Dong's portrait of Shange was written after the publication of Shange's novel *Betsey Brown,* which, Dong claims, will reappear as a musical at Joseph Papp's Public Theatre. In addition to discussing biographical details, Dong describes Shange's work. Dong observes, for example, that "from *for colored girls,* Shange began to dissect her earlier theme of sisterhood and feminism to analyze smaller themes." She quotes Shange as saying that "in my successive pieces [e.g., *a photograph, spell #7,* and *boogie woogie landscapes*] I've tried to look at the choices available to their characters."

Fraser, C. Gerald. "Theater Finds an Incisive New Playwright." *New York Times* (June 16, 1976): 27.

Shange talks of her life before *for colored girls.* While Shange says that her life "was one of the best lives America had to offer," she felt uprooted and at odds with her parents over the "the class thing"; they discouraged her from interacting with the "regular colored kids." She relates that she attempted suicide at nineteen but "didn't quite know why. . . . I just knew there wasn't any place for me to go." She married but insists that "I couldn't possibly sit up in nobody's kitchen forever baking nothing." Shange began reading her poems in bars where one evolved into the choreopoem *for colored girls.*

Funke, Phyllis. "Beneath the Surface of Shange." *Los Angeles Times* (Aug. 7, 1977): Calendar : 54.

Funke wrote her article on the eve of the opening of *for colored girls* at the Mark Taper Forum in Los Angeles. Throughout Shange's description of the genesis of her play and people's reactions to it, Funke provides a character sketch of Shange and her upcoming marriage to David Murray, a tenor saxophonist.

Futterman, Ellen. "Ntozake Shange Casts Her Eye on Texas." *St. Louis Post Dispatch* (April 15, 1987): F1, F4.

Futterman converses with Shange during her stay in St. Louis to speak at the Heart of the Arts festival. The poet/playwright talks about her latest writings and her move to Houston: "I had to go somewhere with the baby [her daughter, Savannah] that looked something like what I understood, and New York wasn't that." Very little of the article discusses Shange's work in the theater, but Shange does note that she was criticized for being "too angry and anti-men" in *for colored girls.* Shange views herself as "pro-women."

Gillespie, Marcia Ann. "Ntozake Shange Talks With Marcia Ann Gillespie." *Essence* 16 (May 1985): 122–124, 203–208.

Shange talks about what happened to her since her Broadway hit *for colored girls* catapulted her in the public spotlight ten years earlier. The success of her play with the accompanying intense attention from the media, Shange remarks, was a painful experience and "so overwhelming . . . [it] really tore a lot of my friendships apart, and they are not repaired to date." She left New York for Houston and reflects: "I've tried to figure out if I was running away. I think I would have been running away if I had stopped writing." Since her move, Shange says that she has "some new visions," such as "fight[ing] pornography and violence against women and children." Gillespie encourages Shange to talk about her daughter, Savannah, and her relationships with men, including Savannah's father: "[W]e're still friends, and we still support each other as artists and as friends."

Gomez, Jewelle. "*Belles Lettres* Interview: Ntozake Shange." *Belles Lettres: A Review of Books by Women* (Sept./Oct. 1985): 9.

On the occasion of the publication of the novel *Betsey Brown,* Gomez interviews Shange about issues related to the theater. Shange explains that she moved to Houston in 1983 to remove herself from the "hype and pressure in doing New York theater." Subsequent dramatic pieces, such as *spell #7,* lacked "theatrical fire." Gomez points out that Shange's strength is "recognizing the distinct way that Black people . . . can turn a phrase, connect words, create a syncopated pattern—the way they see society from a skewed angle that refuses sanctity to the prevailing authority." Shange admires the writers Zora Neale Hurston, Olga Broumas, Jessica Hagedorn, June Jordan, Susan Griffin, Toni Morrison, Geraldine Kudaka, and Kitty Tsui. These writers have "faced down the dragon of patriarchal language and kidnapped the king's English with an eye toward its realignment, if not its destruction."

Gussow, Mel. Three articles from the *New York Times:* "Women Write New Chapter." *New York Times* (June 8, 1979): C3; "Women Playwrights Show New Strength." *New York Times* (Feb. 15, 1981): sec. 2: 4, 24; "Women Playwrights: New Voices in the Theater." *New York Times Magazine* (May 1, 1983): 22–27.

Gussow's trio of articles is one of the earliest attempts by a drama critic from a major newspaper to survey and assess the work of contemporary women playwrights. Gussow focuses on the "proliferation" of female playwrights, which he claims was foreshadowed by Ntozake Shange's *for colored girls.* He cites several reasons for the upsurge of plays written by women, such as the women's movement, the increase in grants encouraging women to write, and the productions of the Actors Theatre of Louisville. The critic praises these new playwrights for moving away from militant themes to examining a broader spectrum of issues and concerns. Gussow also discusses individual achievements in theatrical forms and innovations in language and subject matter. The critic highlights the work of Beth Henley, Tina Howe, Ntozake Shange, Corinne Jacker, Mary Gallagher, Kathleen Tolan, J.E. Franklin, and others. In the May 1, 1983, article Gussow focuses on Marsha Norman. Gussow's choice of playwrights has been criticized by feminist theater artists for his exclusion of experimentalists such as Megan Terry, Rochelle Owens, and Adrienne Kennedy.

Horowitz, Simi. "The Playwright as Woman." *TheatreWeek* (Aug. 26–Sept. 1, 1991): 22–27.

Horowitz profiles four women playwrights: Wendy Wasserstein, Tina Howe, Marsha Norman, and Ntozake Shange. Nearly twenty years following the controversial *for colored girls,* Shange still bristles: "I'm not interested in discussions and debate. . . . I write from women in general and women of color in particular. . . . I was not cut out for combat. If you come to a work of mine, you come at your own risk, not to engage me in argument." Horowitz comments that of the playwrights she interviewed, Shange "is the most radical, surely the most angry." Shange points out that although African-American women writers are respected in academia, "in the street [they're] viewed, especially by the hip-hop community . . . as worse than breeders during the slave times. Everyone is worried about censorship, but no one seems to think it's a problem that women of color are being debased."

"[Interview with] Ntozake Shange." *The New Yorker* 52 (Aug. 2, 1976): 17–19.

The conversation with Shange took place at an unspecified restaurant near Joseph Papp's Public Theatre during a break from Shange's role in her choreopoem *for colored girls.* Between sips of coffee Shange reveals slices of her life: her childhood years in St. Louis; her close communion with the poets in San Francisco; and her loss of a "tactile or sensuous connection " to the city of New York, where she was living at the time. She concludes the conversation by talking about her writing: "I write about pain. Apathy stops me up."

Jones, Anne Hudson. "Ntozake Shange." In *Notable Women in the American Theatre: A Biographical Dictionary*. Edited by Alice M. Robinson, Vera Mowry Roberts, and Milly S. Barranger, 775–777. New York: Greenwood, 1989.

The first of its kind, this handbook focuses solely on the contributions of women in the theater. Represented here are playwrights, producers, actresses, directors, designers, critics, and managers. The entry for Shange includes a biographical sketch, a cursory discussion of selected plays, and a selected list of primary and secondary sources.

Jordan, June. "Shange Talks the Real Stuff." *The Dial* (Feb. 1982): 11–13.

Written in anticipation of the airing of a production of *for colored girls* on PBS, the poet June Jordan reminisces about her association with Shange and her reactions to a staged reading of *for colored girls* at the Public Theatre, which she was invited by Shange to attend in early 1975.

Latour, Martine. "Ntozake Shange: Driven Poet/Playwright." *Mademoiselle* 82 (Sept. 1976): 182, 226.

An intimate, if brief, profile of Shange, during a run of *for colored girls* at Joseph Papp's Public Theatre. Latour quotes Shange as saying that she is wary of all the hoopla surrounding her hit play because prior to *for colored girls*, her poetry went virtually unrecognized. Shange maintains that "had there been more respect for my poetry . . . my suicide attempts wouldn't have happened." She also talks about how she channels her "rage and alienation" into her creative work.

Lester, Neal. "At the Heart of Shange's Feminism: An Interview." *Black American Literature Forum* 24 (Winter 1990): 717–30.

Lester's interview with Shange reveals that she is a black feminist: "I use the tools that are available to me as a feminist reconstructing history. . . . Everything I write and have written comes from being a woman-centered person." Shange identifies with feminist writers such as Olga Broumas, Adrienne Rich, Audre Lorde, Barbara Smith, Shere Hite, and Andrea Dworkin. Although Shange's primary allegiance is to women, she is also deeply committed to both men and women of color. Yet she becomes angry when writers of color suggest to her that her major concern should be the liberation of oppressed people of color. Shange comments that language is crucial to understanding gender: "I'm a firm believer that language and how we use language determines how we act, and how we act then determines our lives and other people's lives. . . . [N]o matter what you put in front of people, you're going to get certain responses from men and certain responses from women—, that's a very devastating piece of information." Gender differences in language, Shange asserts, accounts for the hysterical reactions to *for colored girls* and the "silence" about her play, *a photograph.* See also Lester's "An Interview with Ntozake Shange." *Studies in American Drama, 1945–Present* 5 (1990):42–66.

Levine, Jo Ann. "'Bein' a Woman, Bein' Colored'." *Christian Science Monitor* (Sept. 9, 1976): 23.

This article anticipates the move of *for colored girls* from the Public Theatre to Broadway. Shange reflects on the consequences that the play has had on her personal life. For example, she remarks that since the play opened, she and her parents "have been going through some fairly traumatic, terribly painful discussions." Other traumatic events in her life include being bused to a white school: "I think it is unfortunate that we buffaloed ourselves into thinking that the black children who were integrated had a good time—because it was the worst time of my life." Shange talks candidly about her relations with white people: "I do have white friends. But they are very selected." She was "dumbfounded" when one reporter labeled *for colored girls* "racist." She responds, "[I]f he wanted to see me racist, he should have read the things I wrote in 1968. I have some real racist things there." But Shange claims she has "expiated all of that."

Lewis, Barbara. *"For Colored Girls Who Have Considered Suicide."* *Essence* 7 (Nov. 1976): 119–120.

Lewis's article, based on a conversation with Shange between performances of *for colored girls,* begins with Shange's reflections on her childhood. She recalls the pain she experienced because of repeated moves by her family to various cities, where the "whole ostracism [by whites] process [would begin] again." Lewis traces Shange's college days, when she developed a passionate interest in the study of the black visual arts and literature. The article concludes with Shange's description of her works in progress, such as a piece entitled *Slow Bolero Down Avenue 'C'* and *Closets,* a poem/dance piece, which Shange comments is "the underneath of *for colored girls.*"

Lyons, Brenda. "Interview with Ntozake Shange." *Massachusetts Review* 28, no. 4 (Winter 1987): 687–697.

Although the interviewer does not focus on Shange's dramatic aesthetics or her individual theater pieces, she does reveal insights into Shange's writing process, the African-American woman writer's aesthetic, and Shange's works in progress.

Newmark, Judith. "Ntozake Shange: Stuff of Legend: Where She is Now, 20 Years After *Girls.*" *St. Louis Post-Dispatch* (June 23, 1996): Magazine: 3C.

Newmark profiles Shange on the occasion of the St. Louis Black Repertory Company's second production of *for colored girls.* Shange mentions that she is working on several projects, including a history of African-American cuisine and cowriting a novel with her sister, Ifa Bayaza entitled, *Some Sing, Some Cry.*

"Ntozake Shange." In *Interviews with Contemporary Women Playwrights.* Edited by Kathleen Betsko and Rachel Koenig, 365–376. New York: Beech Tree Books, 1987.

Shange is included in this landmark volume of thirty interviews of international women playwrights who have been successful in the commerical theater. Shange's interview includes a discussion of how dance has affected her creative life: "Writing is for most people a cerebral activity. For me it is a very rhythmic and visceral experience. Dance clears my mind of verbal images and allows me to understand the planet the way I imagine atomic particles experience space." Shange also discusses her writing process, literary influences, feminism, and male critics. This interview is a must for anyone studying Shange's plays and aesthetics.

Peterson, Bernard L. *Contemporary Black American Playwrights and Their Plays: A Biographical Directory and Dramatic Index,* 417–421. New York: Greenwood, 1989.

Peterson provides a biographical sketch as well as a staging history of Shange's plays.

Shange, Ntozake. "Ntozake Shange Interviews Herself." *Ms.* 6 (Dec. 1977): 35, 70–72. Reprinted in Shange's "i talk to myself." In *nappy edges,* 17–14. New York: Methuen: 1987.

Shange indicates that she has been somewhat disappointed in herself during the myriad of interviews she has given, so she has decided to give herself "a chance to talk to myself," to have a "conversation with all [my] selves." In a highly entertaining yet perceptive self-interview, Shange responds to questions she asks herself: "how has yr relationship with the world changed since becoming an overnight sensation with *for colored girls?"*; "why did you always want to be an ikette?"; "how do you account for yr reputation as a feminist, if you listen to & get nourishment from all these men?"; "how do you explain loving some men who write . . . when yr work for almost three years has been entirely woman-centered?"; and "who did help you understand yr craft?"

Tate, Claudia, ed. "Ntozake Shange." In *Black Women Writers at Work.* New York: Continuum, 1983.

The value of this interview is that it takes place roughly ten years after Shange wrote *for colored girls.* An older, wiser Shange talks about her feminism, aesthetics, writing processes, her anger toward the theater, and her response to critics' ire over her treament of male characters. Other writers' interviews include their reactions to Shange's controversial choreopoem *for colored girls who have considered suicide/when the rainbow is enuf.*

Umrani, Munir. "Ntozake Shange: Woman Behind *Colored Girls.*" *Bilalian News* (Jan. 6, 1978): 28.

Umrani's profile focuses on Shange's creation of her choreopoem *for colored girls* and her perception of those individuals who call the play "anti-male." According to Shange, these individuals "are denying interaction among human beings more so than dealing with what kinds of things men need in terms of ego support." Furthermore, women whom Shange refers to as "male dominated" or "the executive type" dislike the play because they have assumed the "same ego structure and the same responses to the world as the people who oppress them." Umrani also touches upon how Shange's mysticism and experimentation with dance have influenced her plays.

Washington, Mary Helen. "Ntozake Shange." In *The Playwright's Art: Conversations with Contemporary American Dramatists.* Edited by Jackson R. Bryer, 205–220. New Brunswick, N.J.: Rutgers University Press, 1995.

Shange talks about the evolution of the production of *for colored girls,* from the bars of San Francisco to Broadway. She complains that when the choreopoem moved to New York, the director of the production wanted the poems to remain in the same order: "I just thought it was so horrible that they wanted me to do the same poems in the same order every night." While the director wanted set pieces, Shange wanted to create new poems and rearrange the existing ones. The interview also touches upon Shange's aesthetics, feminism, and race relations. Shange says she would like to be portrayed in theater history journals as "a passionate performer and a steady contributor of prose and poetry concerning survival mechanisms and dreams of people of color at the end of the twentieth century."

Watson, Kenneth. "Ntozake Shange." In *American Playwrights Since 1945.* Edited by Philip C. Kolin, 379–386. New York: Greenwood, 1989.

Watson provides an assessment of Shange's critical reputation, an historical survey of her productions, a brief analysis of her plays, and suggestions for future areas of study. The article includes a list of primary and secondary sources.

Wykoff, Peter C. *Houston Post* (May 26, 1985): F11.

Based on a "chat" with Shange at the Warwick Hotel restaurant in Houston, Wycoff's brief profile describes Shange's life in the Texas city, where she has been teaching drama at the University of Houston, her recently published works, and her works in progress.

Additonal Biographical Entries

Black Writers: A Selection of Sketches from Contemporary Authors. Edited by Linda Metzger, 518–522. Detroit: Gale Research, 1989.

Considine, Shaun. "On Stage: Ntozake Shange." *People Weekly* 6 (July 5, 1976): 68–69.

Current Biography Yearbook: 1978. New York: H.W. Wilson, 1979.

Ford, Andrea. "Ntozake Shange's Collection Shows She Still Has 'enuf' Polish." Detro*it Free Press* (April 19, 1987): 7C.

King, Anne Mills. "Ntozake Shange." In Criti*cal Survey of Drama: Supplement.* Edited by Frank Magill, 326–331. Pasadena, Calif.: Salem Press, 1986.

———. "Ntozake Shange: Showstoppers." Essen*ce,* 13 (Oct. 1982): 75–77.

Richards, Sandra."Ntozake Shange." In Conte*mporary American Dramatists,* 518–521. London: St. James Press, 1994.

"Trying to Be Nice." Time (July 19, 1976):44–45.

"Welcome to the Great Black Way!" Time 108 (Nov. 1, 1976): 72–76.

General Criticism

Brown-Guillory, Elizabeth. *Their Place on the Stage: Black Women Playwrights in America.* Westport, Conn.: Greenwood, 1988.

The author provides an in-depth analysis of the work of Lorraine Hansberry, Alice Childress, and Ntozake Shange, whose plays "are crucial links in the development of black playwriting in America from the 1950's to the 1980's." In her examination of these playwrights, Brown-Guillory compares their plays to the dramas of their male counterparts. She begins, however, by presenting a historical overview of the "long and vibrant" theatrical tradition from which black female playwrights evolved and devotes a chapter to the works of women dramatists identified with the Harlem Renaissance, including May Miller, Georgia Douglas Johnson, and Angelina Weld Grimké

Burke, Sally. *American Feminist Playwrights: A Critical History.* New York: Twayne, 1996.

Burke includes a survey of Shange's plays in this first sociohistorical examination of American feminist dramatists.

Gillespie, Patti. "American Women Dramatists, 1960–1980." In *Essays on Contemporary American Drama.* Edited by Bock Hedwig and Albert Wertheim, 111. Munich: M. Hueber, 1981.

This collection of essays introduces the reader to the contemporary American theatrical scene. Gillespie's straightforward essay surveys the work of women playwrights writing and producing plays from the late 1950s through the 1970s. Gillespie examines the work of Megan Terry, Myrna Lamb, Adrienne Kennedy, and Ntozake Shange. Included are a list of their major works, as well as anthologies and collections of plays.

Griffin, Susan, Norma Leistiko, Ntozake Shange, and Miriam Schapiro. "Women and The Creative Process, A Panel Discussion." *Mosaic* (Canada) 8, no. 1 (n.d.): 91–117.

Shange asserts that art is not leisure activity nor is it meant to be elitist. Instead, it is a poltical tool that Third World women artists need to use because "it is important for the survival of people." She goes on: "The kinds of things we are going to do—if we're going to write or dance or paint or sculpt—is going to have to be functional in terms of our communities. . . . [A]rt is functional."

Keyssar, Helen. *Feminist Theatre: An Introduction to Plays of Contemporary British and American Women.* Basingstoke: Macmillan, 1984.

Keyssar's book centers on her contention that feminist drama has shifted away from the "recognition scene," in which the protagonist comes to know herself and reveal that knowledge to others; instead, "the impetus is not towards self-recognition and revelation of a 'true self' but towards recognition of others and a concomitant transformation of the self and the world." In other words, the protagonist not only must know who she is but also must become aware of and transcend the constrictive roles to which she has been relegated. To do this, Keyssar contends, feminist theater must replace the traditional "recognition scene" with experimental "transformational" drama, which "inspires and asserts the possiblity of change." Thus, transformational drama focuses on the metamorphosis of self and society instead of on the revelation of self. Keyssar presents an overview of several plays, including Shange's *for colored girls* and *boogie woogie landscapes.*

Lee, Catharine Carr. *Contemporary Authors Bibliographies Series: American Dramatists,* Vol. 3. Edited by Matthew C. Roudane, 305–324. Detroit: Gale Research, 1989.

This bibliographical essay assesses the critical reputation of Shange's work. It includes a list of primary and secondary sources.

Lester, Neal A. *Ntozake Shange: A Critical Study of the Plays.* New York: Garland, 1995.

In this first full-length study of Shange's dramatic works, Lester considers the "choreopoem" as Shange's most significant contribution to the theater. Her poetic dramas "work to raise consciousness individually, socially, and artistically and center around the complex notions of identity politics." In an analysis of five of Shange's plays (*for colored girls, spell #7, a photograph: lovers in motion, boogie woogie landscapes,* and *From Okra to Greens),* Lester illuminates the close connection Shange makes between feminism and the black experience. Lester's book is vital for those seeking a critical understanding of Shange's dramas. See also Lester's article "Shange's Men: *for colored girls* Revisited, and Movement Beyond." *African American Review* 26, no. 2 (Summer 1992): 319–328.

Miller, Jeanne-Marie. "Black Women Playwrights from Grimké to Shange: Selected Synopses of Their Works." In *But Some of Us Are Brave: Black*

Women's Studies. Edited by Gloria T. Hull, P.B. Scott, and Barbara Smith, 280–290. Old Westbury, N.Y.: Feminist Press, 1982.

Miller surveys the work of several African-American women whose plays "offer a unique insight into the Black experience," including Alice Childress, Ntozake Shange, Adrienne Kennedy, Sonia Sanchez, and Martie Charles.

Roberts, Vera Mowry. "Bright Lights and Backstage: Women Playwrights in the Theatre." *Furman Studies* 34 (Dec. 1988): 26–35.

Although Roberts mainly highlights the work of female playwrights in earlier eras, she concludes her essay with a discussion of the playwrights who contributed to the formation of the feminist theater, which got its impetus from the women's liberation movement of the 1960s. Noting that dramatists such as Corinne Jacker, Megan Terry, Ntozake Shange, and Roberta Sklar collectively represent a myriad of styles and forms, the author concludes that "about the only statement possible at this time is that many women are unselfconsciously exploring what it means to be a woman in today's world."

Wilkerson, Margaret B. "Music as Metaphor: New Plays of Black Women." In *Making a Spectacle: Feminist Essays on Contemporary Women's Theatre.* Edited by Lynda Hart, 61–75. Ann Arbor: University of Michigan Press, 1989.

Wilkerson maintains that contemporary black women dramatists are redefining how music is used in drama. They have refused to conform to the conventions of the American musical because it fails to express the "deepest, unspoken . . . feelings and experiences of human existence." Wilkerson examines the plays of several black female playwrights, including Ntozake Shange and Alice Childress, in terms of how the music used as subtext for their dramas serves as "a second language that gives profound anguish and joy of their vision and experience."

Williams, Mance. *Black Theatre in the 1960s and 1970s: A Historical-Critical Analysis of the Movement.* Westport, Conn.: Greenwood, 1985.

Williams explores the contemporary black theater movement by examining its major playwrights, theater companies, and producers. Includes a brief discussion of the dramatists Alice Childress, Adrienne Kennedy, and Ntozake Shange.

for colored girls who have considered suicide/when the rainbow is enuf (New York Shakespeare Festival in association with The Henry Street Settlement's New Federal Theater at the Anspacher Theatre, 1976; Booth Theater, 1976)

Playscripts

Black Theatre U.S.A: Plays by African Americans, 1847 to Today. Rev. ed. Edited by James Hatch and Ted Shine, 771–775. New York: Free Press, 1996.

for colored girls who have considered suicide /when the rainbow is enuf. San Lorenzo, Calif.: Shameless Hussey Press, 1976. This version includes a different arrangement and poems not given in the 1976 staged publication.

for colored girls who have considered suicide/when the rainbow is enuf. New York: Bantam, 1981.

for colored girls who have considered suicide/when the rainbow is enuf: a choreopoem, ix–xvi. New York: Macmillan, 1977.

"Lady in Brown [excerpt from the play]." In Jump *Up and Say: A Collection of Black Story Telling.* Edited by Linda Goss and Clay Goss, 148–152. New York: Simon & Schuster, 1995.

Norton Anthology of African-American Literature. Edited by Henry Louis Gates, Jr. and Nellie Y. McKay, 2518–2521. New York: W.W. Norton, 1997. [abridged version]

Shange: Plays: One [with introductions by the author], xi-64. London: Methuen Drama, 1992.

Totem Voice: Plays from the Black World Repertory. Edited by Paul Carter Harrison, 223–274. New York: Grove Press, 1989.

Summary

for colored girls was the first dramatic piece written by a black woman to be produced on Broadway since Lorraine Hansberry's *A Raisin in the Sun.* The piece was also a first for black women "going public" about their tortured lives with black men. The dramatic structure of the piece does not conform to traditional dramatic realism. Instead, the organizing principle underlying the piece is what Shange calls the "choreopoem"— a series of poems set to music and dance. African traditions permeate the piece with its heritage of storytelling, rhythms, chants, and dance.

Seven black girls, whose names refer to colors of the rainbow, tell the story of growing up. The stories cover the innocence of childhood, a girl's coming of age, and conclude with the pain, rage, and disillusionment black women have experienced becuase of black men who have used, abused, and deceived them. Their stories tell of rape, abortion, violence, racism, and infidelity. However, these stories are not paralyzed in anger and rage; rather, they end with the recognition that women must accept responsibility for their situations, love themselves and each other "enough to resist oppression."

Criticism and Performance Reviews

Austin, William. "Blacks, 'the Great White Way.'" *N.Y. Amsterdam News* (Oct. 9, 1976): D11.

"It's a gem," says Austin. The critic also hopes that *for colored girls* will provide a "new attitude" toward black-oriented theater.

Bambara, Toni Cade. "On the Arts: *For Colored Girls*—And White Girls Too." *Ms.* 5 (Sept. 1976): 36, 38.

Bambara observes that although men in *for colored girls* cause pain to women, "there is no venom, no resorting to a Queen of Hearts solution—Off with his head! No godlike revenge, no godlike forgiving." Shange's women "suck their teeth, storm, sass, and get on with the miracle of living."

Barber, John."Elevating Protest Above Glumness." *Daily Telegraph* (London) (Oct. 11, 1979): 15f.

Barber believes that *for colored girls* (in a production at the Royalty Theatre, London) "could teach English playwrights a much-needed lesson—that protest theatre need not be glum, earnest or didactic." Referring to the choreopoem as "the civilised female's protest against stupid male aggression," Barber praises the piece for its elegant poetry while "remaining perfectly clear about the awfulness of the world."

Barnes, Clive. "Stage: Black Sisterhood." *New York Times* (June 2, 1976): 44.

Barnes praises *for colored girls'* poetic beauty, saying that the poems delve "profoundly and lovingly into what it is like to be black and not beautiful." As a white man, Barnes found the experience of Shange's work "humbling but inspiring." He remarks that the piece could have made him "feel guilty at being white and male. It didn't. It made me feel proud at being a member of the human race, and with the joyous discovery that a white man can have black sisters." Several New York critics shared Barnes's enthusiasm for Shange's play: Gussow, Mel. "Stage: *Colored Girls* Evolves." *New York Times* (Sept. 16, 1976): 53; Rich, Alan. "For Audiences of Any Color When 'Rex' Is Not Enuf." *New York* 9 (June 14, 1976): 62; Watt, Douglas. *New York Daily News* (Sept. 16, 1976); Wilson, Edwin. *Wall Street Journal* (Sept. 21, 1976): 24. See also Beaufort, John. *Christian Science Monitor* (Sept. 24, 1976) 62, and Catinella, Joseph. *"For Colored Girls . . . ."* *New York Times* (April 27, 1980): sec. 11: 19.

Bilowit, Ira J. "20 Years Later, Shange's *Colored Girls* Takes a New Look at Life." *Back Stage* (June 30, 1995): 15.

Bilowit talks with Shange, who is directing a revival of *for colored girls* at the New Federal Theatre at the Henry Street Settlement. As to the afteraffects of the original show, Shange muses that "it freed any number of performance artists to become who they are now, like Robbie McCauley and Jessica Haggedorn and Anna Devere Smith—even Karen Finley. . . . My peers were re-affirmed by the acceptance of my work, and were given a sense of legitimacy." Moreover, Shange feels that the piece "allowed [people of color] to be participants in discussions of gender." For the *New York Times* review of this production see Clive Barnes. "Stage," June 2, 1976. (See *for colored girls who have considered suicide/when the rainbow is enuf,* Criticism and Performance Reviews).

Bond, Jean Carey. "*For Colored Girls Who Have Considered Suicide.*" *Freedomways* 16 (3rd Quarter, 1976): 187–191.

Bond found the Henry Street Playhouse's production of *for colored girls* "a shimmering, animated painting;" however; the production at the Public Theatre is "disturbingly shrill and lacking in tonal variations . . . the actresses plow through the text like locomotives with little nuance, rarely changing pace or voice levels." As a result, the newer production amplifies the weaknesses in Shange's choreopoem. Men in the more recent production seem much more ominous and distorted. For example, the piece about Beau Willie fails to transcend his horrendous actions to the "situation's whole truth. . . . What we get is a 'crazy nigger' story that works as a theatrical showcase for Trazana Beverly's considerable acting skills but that lacks depth in its content."

Brantley, Ben. "7 Sisters Still Reflect Rainbow's Colors." *New York Times* (June 26, 1995): C11.

This revival of *for colored girls* (directed by Shange, at the New Federal Theatre) proves that this was a polemical period piece. Brantley views it as an enduring "emotional and sensual prism that refracts the light of whatever you hold it up to."

Brown, Janet. *Feminist Drama: Definition and Critical Analysis.* Metuchen, N.J.: Scarecrow Press, 1979.

Brown's volume is one of the earliest in-depth studies of feminist theater critics. Her analyses of several plays, including *for colored girls,* hinges on her idea of feminism, or the "feminine impulse," which she defines as "a woman's struggle for autonomy against an oppressive, sexist society." Brown correlates her notion of feminism with Kenneth Burke's literary theory that all fictive works have a "rhetorical or persuasive motive." Brown argues that for a play to qualify as feminist, it must have as its central rhetorical motive a woman grappling for independence in the dominant patriarchal society. In a later book *Taking Center Stage: Feminism in Contemporary U.S. Drama* (Metuchen, N.J.: Scarecrow Press, 1991), Brown states that the Burkean theory when applied to feminist drama is "somewhat constraining." She reevaluates selected plays, including *for colored girls,* in which she "searched for evidence of both a distinctly female narrative structure and a distinctively feminist rhetorical intention [then] attempted to relate the themes, structures, and values uncovered in this search with the work of feminist theorists and scholars in the same time period."

Brown-Guillory, Elizabeth. "Black Women Playwrights: Exorcising Myths." *Phylon* 68, no. 3 (Fall 1987): 230–238.

Brown-Guillory focuses on Alice Childress, Lorraine Hansberry, and Ntozake Shange, who "present a vital slice of [black] life." They offer realistic images of the black experience that differ markedly from the perceptions of black males and white writers. In effect, the images of these female dramatists smash the misconceptions of "the contented slave," "the tragic mulatto," "the comic Negro," "the exotic primitive," and "the spiritual singing, toe-tapping faithful servant." According to the author, Childress, Hansberry, and Shange use three images repeatedly in their work: "the black male in search of his manhood," the black male as "the walking wounded," and "the evolving black woman." Brown-Guillory demonstrates how Shange and Childress employ the image of the evolving black woman: Both show women as victims, disappointed and abused by their men; however, the women come to transcend their status as victims by becoming independent and learning to rely upon themselves for fulfillment.

———. "Contemporary Black Women Playwrights: A View From the Other Half." *Helicon Nine* 14 15 (Summer 1986): 120–127.

Brown-Guillory asserts that Lorraine Hansberry, Alice Childress, and Ntozake Shange consciously avoid the stereotypical images of black women that are found in the plays of black males and white playwrights. She observes the "[o]ne image which dominates their plays is 'the evolving black woman,' a phrase which embodies the multiplicity of emotions of ordinary black women for whom the act of living is sheer heroism." The "evolving woman" images in Childress's *Wine in the Wilderness* and Shange's *for colored girls* are "preoccupied with themselves" because their expectations about the men in their lives have been shattered. Rather than wallowing in self-pity or in man-hating and considering themselves perpetual victims, however, the women in these plays emerge as independent selves so as to avoid being trapped in abusive relationships.

Brunazzi, Elizabeth. "*colored girls.*" *Off Our Backs* 9 (Feb. 1979): 18.

Brunazzi reports that the female prisoners of the Federal Correctional Institution at Alderson, West Virginia, responded "intensely" to *for colored girls,* and "found [themselves] in the performances."

Calloway, Earl. *Chicago Defender* (Dec. 17, 1977): Entertainment: 2.

Calloway refers to a touring production of *for colored girls* to be performed at the Blackstone Theatre. He also discusses the staging history: "[L]ike any new or different artistic or cultural form, the genesis of [the play's] concept and development is interesting and important, historically and socially."

Christ, Carol P. " 'i found god in myself . . . i loved her fiercely': Ntozake Shange." In *Diving Deep and Surfacing: Women Writers on Spiritual Quest,* 97–117. Boston: Beacon Press, 1980. [Excerpted from *Black Literature Criticism: Excerpts from Criticism of the Most Significant Works of Black Authors over the Past 200 Years,* Vol. 3. Edited by James P. Draper, 1690–1702. Detroit: Gale Research, 1992.]

Christ states that *for colored girls* is "a search for the meaning of nothing experienced and a quest for a new sacrifice of self for the love of a man." Shange does more than merely affirm the pain of these women and their invisible selves. She depicts how the women in the play come to terms with the emptiness, which "enable[s] them to acknowledge their history while moving beyond it to the ends of their own rainbows." The poems in *for colored girls,* says Christ, "dramatize a spiritual rite of passage for these women who move through hope, defeat, and rebirth."

Clark, Rozelle. "*For Colored Girls* [Alliance Theatre, Atlanta] Unveils Raw Emotion." *Atlanta Daily World* (Jan. 10, 1980): 3, 6.

Clark hails Shange's choreopoem as a "classic . . . [that] has become synonymous with black women's experience in America."

Clurman, Harold. "Theatre." *Nation* 222 (May 1, 1976): 542. [Reprinted in *The Chelsea House Library of Literary Criticism: Twentieth-Century American Literature,* Vol. 6. Edited by Harold Bloom, 3602–3608. New York: Chelsea House, 1987.]

Clurman applauds Shange's poetic dialogue for its "literary worth." The critic remarks that the scenes in *for colored girls* are "so shattering in emotion and staggering in diction that I cried out to my neighbors in the seats around me, 'That's how Shakespeare and Euripides should be acted!'" Critics John Simon ("*Enuf* Is Not Enough."*New Leader,* July 5, 1976. Reprinted in *Contemporary Literary Criticism,* 1978. See *for colored girls who have considered suicide/when the rainbow is enuf,* Criticism and Performance Reviews) and Stanley Kauffmann ("Stanley Kauffmann on Theater." *New Republic,* July 3–10, 1976. See *for colored girls who have considered suicide/when the rainbow is enuf,* Criticism and Performance Reviews) disagree with Clurman's assessment.

Coe, Richard L."A Buoyant Assertion of Womankind." *Washington Post* (Oct. 14, 1977): F1.

Coe says that Shange's words and director Oz Scott's staging remain "a unique, moving and humorously buoyant assertion of womankind, young and black in particular." See also Coe's "In the Papp Empire." *Washington Post* (Oct. 10, 1976): F8 and *"Colored Girls." Washington Post* (Nov. 30, 1978): G18.

"*Colored Girls* and *Comments:* Separate Views." *N.Y. Amsterdam News* (Sept. 3, 1977): D7.

The writer of this article reports that poet Abiodun Oyewole (formerly Charles Davis) has written a theatrical response, titled *Comments,* to Shange's for colored girls. Oyewole represents many black men who feel that Shange's play is "a deliberate and poisonous attach on the credibility of the Black man in America." In the opinion of the writer, the tone of the Oyewole's work is one of belligerence and hostility. The power of Oyewole lies not so much in the writing but in his "preacher presence," moving his audience with "rude elements of dash and swagger." Yet both works, the writer of this article argues, are "chauvinis[tic] . . . . [B]oth authors are subjective, verging on irresponsible in the narrow and reactionary images they depict." The writer recommends that black men and women move from "the loneliness . . . competiveness . . . ego-tripping . . . [and] games" to a position in which both sexes can accept and appreciate each other.

Contemporary Literary Criticism: Excerpts from Criticism of the Works of Today's Novelists, Poets, Playwrights, and Other Creative Writers, Vol. 8. Edited by Dedria Bryfonski, 484–485. Detroit: Gale Research, 1978.

This volume offers excerpts of reviews and criticism of *for colored girls.*

Curb, Rosemary K. "Re/cognition, Re/presentation, Re/creation in Woman-Conscious Drama: The Seer, The Seen, The Scene, The Obscene." *Theater Journal* 37, no. 3 (Oct. 1985): 302–316.

Curb defines "woman-conscious" drama as being "by and about women that is characterized by multiple interior reflections of women's lives and perceptions." She draws on the ideas of authors N.O. Keohane and Barbara C. Gelpi, who distinguish three lives of women's self-consciousness: feminine, female, and feminist. The feminine consciousness is defined by male desire, that is, woman as sex object. The female consciousness, although "less inert and passive" yet still deeply rooted in the male tradition, is the "age-old experience of women in giving and preserving life, that is, woman as earth mother." And, the feminist consciousness focuses on women's experience within the patriarchal system, yet "envisions alternative levels of consciousness that operate in drama." Curb examines Ntozake Shange's *for colored girls,* Adrienne Kennedy's *Funnyhouse of a Negro,* Joan Schenkar's *Signs of Life,* Wendy Kesselman's *My Sister in This House,* Megan Terry's *Babes in the Bighouse,* Karen Malpede's *Aphrodite,* and *Daughters* by Clare Coss, Sondra Segal, and Roberta Sklar.

DeShazer, Mary K. "Rejecting Necrophilia: Ntozake Shange and the Warrior Re-Visioned." In *Making a Spectacle: Feminist Essays on Contemporary Women's Theatre.* Edited by Lynda Hart, 86–100. Ann Arbor: University of Michigan Press, 1989.

DeShazer points out that "warrior" as metaphor "is a problematic term for many feminists." On the one hand, many women writers reject its use because it "embod[ies] the destructive powers of patriarchy." On the other hand, the author has observed that "warrior" is used frequently by women writers of various races and cultures and thus has acquired new meaning. To these women, many of whom "lack class or color or heterosexual privilege, the warrior image reflects a profound commitment to combating not just sexism . . . but racism, elitist, and heterosexual oppressions as well." Therefore, the warrior image has been "re-visioned" to symbolize not destructiveness but a "source of life-preservation and enhancement." The author observes that Shange uses the warrior image in her plays. Shange dramatizes the "re-visioned" warrior—her characters' rage at their situation, as they struggle against racial, sexual, and economic oppression yet resist destruction by "nurtur[ing] . . . strong selves and communities." For example, in *for colored girls* the women rage against male domination but transcend their anger by "staking out a new country beyond this war, defined by a nurturant female community." DeShazer also discusses *spell #7.*

Dodson, Owen. "Who Has Seen the Wind? Playwrights and the Black Experience." *Black American Literature Forum* 11, no. 3 (Fall 1977): 108–116.

Dodson surveys the major works of several contemporary African-American playwrights, including Shange's *for colored girls* and Adrienne Kennedy's *Funnyhouse of a Negro.*

Drake, Sylvie. "*Colored:* Choreopoem of Passage." *Los Angeles Times* (Aug. 12, 1977): sec. 4: 1, 26.

Drake observes that *for colored girls* (Center Theater Group, Mark Taper Forum, 1977) leaves the spectators "craving [for] more . . . because it was good, because it was about being human first, then female and black." See reviews of subsequent productions: Bardacke, Frances. "Theatre." *San Diego Magazine* (Oct. 1977): 45–50; Murray, William. "Theater." *New West* (Sept. 12, 1977): SC-20; Smith, Cecil. "*Colored Girls* in Santa Barbara." *Los Angeles Times* (May 19, 1983), sec. 6: 3.

Elliot, Jeffrey. "Ntozake Shange: Genesis of a Choreopoem." *Negro History Bulletin* 41 (Jan.-Feb. 1978): 797–800.

In this profile of Shange, the playwright describes how *for colored girls* evolved.

Epstein, Helen. *Joe Papp: An American Life.* Boston: Little, Brown, 1994.

In this biography of the director Joe Papp, Epstein recounts the genesis of the Broadway production of *for colored girls,* which Papp produced. Papp describes Shange's writing as a "unique style with high flights of poetry intermixed with down-to-earth folk, black material. She has an honesty, a power which makes it dramatic. When someone says something out loud and you're moved by it—that's the first law of drama."

Evans, Everett. "Colored Girls Still Filled with Fire and Truth." *Houston Chronicle* (Feb. 7, 1994): Houston: 1.

Evans reviews the revival of *for colored girls,* as directed by Notzake Shange. He observes that the play is as relevant today as it was twenty years ago because black women continue to deal with the same problems, and "most have become exacerbated." The only difference is that child abuse, alcoholism and incest are discussed more openly than they were two decades ago. Perhaps that is the reason, Evans speculates, that the current show "takes on more edgy anger and impatience. There's an exasperation, a cynical humor to the playing of some scenes, a new urgency [on the part of the characters] to shake off the shackles of imposed limitations and get on with their lives."

Flowers, Sandra Hollin. "*Colored Girls*: Textbook for the Eighties." *Black American Forum* 15, no. 2 (Summer 1981): 51–54. [Reprinted in *The Chelsea House Library of Literary Criticism: Twentiteth-Century American Literature,* Vol 6. Edited by Harold Bloom, 3602–3608. New York: Chelsea House, 1987.]

Flowers disagrees with those spectators and critics who view *for colored girls* as a feminist harangue against the evils that black men do. Rather, Flowers contends, the play conveys Shange's compassion toward men and the "crisis between black men and women." This crisis and the nature of relationships is the focal point of the play. Shange's compassion for black men is most noticeable in the Beau Willie poem. Here Flowers demonstrates how Beau Willie is a "tragic figure," that Shange's anger is not directed toward Beau Willie as a man but toward the circumstances that compelled him to drop his children out the window. For additional articles on reactions to the portrayal of men in *for colored girls,* (10.113, 10.123)

"For Colored Girls To Play Hanna." *The Call and Post* (Cleveland)." (Dec. 3, 1977): 6A.

The article refers to an upcoming production of *for colored girls* at the

Hanna Theatre in Cleveland. For letters to the editor regarding the play, see *Call and Post* (Jan. 14, 1978): B:3.

Garner, Stanton B. *Bodied Spaces: Phenomenology and Performance in Contemporary Drama,* 198–224. Ithaca, N.Y.: Cornell University Press, 1994.

Garner examines *for colored girls* and *spell #7* in relation to the staging of the female body within its spatial and environmental relationships. Garner asserts that *for colored girls* "counterpoints the pain of diminishment, objectification, and invisibility with celebratory moments in which African American women claim their bodies as their own." Shange's use of dance, movement, and language enables the female body to transcend boundaries that have restricted it in traditional theater.

Geis, Deborah. "Distraught Laughter: Monologue in Ntozake Shange's Theatre Pieces." In *Feminine Focus: The New Women Playwrights.* Edited by Enoch Brater, 210–224. New York: Oxford University Press, 1989, and in Geis's *Postmodern Theatric[k]s Monologue in Contemporary American Drama.* Ann Arbor: University of Michigan, 1995. [Excerpted in *Black Literature Criticism: Excerpts from Criticism of the Most Significant Works of Black Authors over the Past 200 Years.* Vol. 3. Edited by James P. Draper, 1690–1702. Detroit: Gale Research. 1992.]

Geis points out that in her plays, Shange "develops her narration primarily through monologues because monologic speech inevitably places the narrative weight of a play upon its spoken language and upon the performances of the individual actors." According to Geis, Shange does not use the monologue to "define and embody [the] characters," as does Maria Irene Fornes, but instead employs the monologue to assume "multiple roles and therefore to emphasize the centrality of *storytelling.*" The author also discusses the criticism voiced by critics Erskine Peters ("Some Tragic Propensities of Ourselves." *Journal of Ethnic Studies,* 1978. See *for colored girls who have considered suicide/when the rainbow is enuf,* Criticism and Performance Reviews) and Andrea Benton Rushing ("*For Colored Girls,* Suicide or Struggle." *Massachusetts Review,* 1981. See *for colored girls who have considered suicide/when the rainbow is enuf,* Criticism and Performance Reviews) and others who complain that the play's focus is too narrow in that it deals with the personal experiences of a few middle-class black women rather than the sociopolitical ramifications that affect all African-Americans.

Gottfried, Martin. "*Rainbow* Over Broadway." *New York Post* (Sept. 16, 1976):22. Reprinted in *New York Theatre Critics' Reviews* 37 (Sept. 13, 1976): 199–202.

Gottfried applauds *for colored girls* as "good theatre." Shange's choreopoem "is the kind the stage was created for .There is no comparing the thrust and presence of its power with any other kind of art in any other medium." However, Gottfried faults the work for its lack of diversity. He argues that the playwright is too "concern[ed] with romance and sex, music and dancing, even considering that the work is about young women."

Griffin, Rita. "*For Colored Girls* [Fisher Theatre]: Shades of Emotional Upheaval." *Michigan Chronicle* (May 27, 1978): C12.

Griffin points out that while Beau Willie Brown is not the norm, he "might possibly serves to remind us that the Viet Nam nightmare has done more of a number on our men than they have done on us."

Harris, Jessica. *"Suicide/When the Rainbow Is Enuf." Essence,* 7 (Nov. 1976): 87–89.

Accompanying Harris's chronicle of the genesis of *for colored girls* is her profile of each of the seven actresses who performed in Joseph Papp's production of the piece. See also Harris's "*For Colored Girls.*" *N.Y. Amsterdam News* (Oct. 9, 1976): D10–D11.

Hughes, Catharine."Theatre." *America* 135 (Oct. 9, 1976): 214.

Hughes observes tht the most powerful and poignant material of *for colored girls* are those monologues that speak of individual human experiences.

Johnston, Laurie "*Colored Girls* Goes to Rikers Island and Hits Home." *New York Times* (Jan. 14, 1977): B2.

Johnston focuses on the reactions of the prisoners of the Women's House of Detention on Rikers Island, New York, to a performance of *for colored girls* staged at the prison.

Kalem, T.M. "He Done Her Wrong." *Time* 107 (June 14, 1976): 74.

Kalem lauds Shange for creating a "poignant, gripping, angry and beautiful piece." But many black male theatergoers may "wince," for the black male characters are "brutal con men and amorous double-dealers."

Kauffmann, Stanley. "Stanley Kauffmann on Theater." *New Republic* 174 (July 3–10, 1976): 20–21.

Unlike Clive Barnes, Kauffmann finds Shange's poetic dialogue hyperdramatic, superficial, and sentimental. However, he concedes that some of the pieces are "effective melodrama." Kauffmann uses *for colored girls* as an example of one kind of "tacit theater conspiracies." He lambastes critics, mostly white, who overpraise black plays, which to Kauffmann seems to be a "despicable kind of patronization."

Keyssar, Helene. *The Curtain and the Veil: Strategies in Black Drama,* 207–218. New York: Burt Franklin & Co., 1981.

Keyssar points out that *for colored girls* reflects a major strategy of black drama: "to warn the spectator that to place their hopes in the success of the individual, to embrace the peculiar American admiration for 'each man out for himself,' is both aesthetically and politically suicidal."

Kingston, Jeremy. "Theatre: *For Coloured Girls.*" *Times* (London) (July 6, 1990): Features: n.p.

Kingston suggests that because men are portrayed as "uniformly horrible," the subtitle for *for colored girls* (Siren Theatre Company, Battersea Arts, London) should be *colored boys who always consider rape when the girls say enuf.* Kingston praises Shange's piece for "passionate testimony [that] grips the heart."

Kroll, Jack. "Women's Rites." *Newsweek* 87 (June 14, 1976): 99. [Reprinted in *New York Theatre Critics' Reviews* 37 (Sept. 13, 1976): 199–202.]

Kroll extols *for colored girls* for being "exultingly, bitingly alive . . . Your scalp prickles at the stunning truth of [Shange's] characters."

Levin, Bernard. "Lullabies of Broadway." *Sunday Times* (May 15, 1977): 37.

Levin lauds a British production of *for colored girls* because it "transcends its locale, its background and its idiom; that, indeed, was why it made so disquieting a contrast with most of what I see here in Britain."

Levin, Toby, and Gwendolyn Flowers. "Black Feminism in *for colored girls.*" In *History and Tradition in Afro-American Culture.* Edited by Gunter Lenz, 181–193. Frankfurt: Campus Verlag, 1984.

In what might be considered a response to those critics who believe that Shange's play is a diatribe against the black male, Flowers and Levin assert that because African-American men "have little present need to be reminded of the devastating effects of racism, Shange's primary purpose is to bring to their attention the equally scathing effects of sexism on the potential for black solidarity." The article is arranged in two parts: First the principles of black feminism are discussed; in the second, each author critiques the play "as a black and a white woman, offering our independent but mutually supportive experiences with the text."

Lewis, Barbara. "Back over the Rainbow." *American Theatre* (Sept. 1995): 6.

Shange discusses the production of *for colored girls* at the Henry Street Settlement in New York. She talks of the changes she has made to the choreopoem, including adding more music and movement and making the beginning "softer, less alarming" than the original. For example instead of the characters running on stage "as though startled, frightened, terrified by something," one character, the Lady in Orange, enters alone, signifying to the audience that these "women are determined to create beauty out of ugliness." Shange comments that this production reflects her response to critics who referred to her work "in terms of sharp and jagged edges." "Who I am," says Shange, "is different from that conception. I wanted to reveal my nurturing side."

———. "Rikers Inmates Touched by *for colored girls.*" *N.Y. Amsterdam News* (Jan. 22, 1977): D7.

Lewis reports on the reactions of inmates of the Women's House of Detention on Rikers Island, New York, to a production of *for colored girls.* See also Lewis's article: *Essence* 7 (Nov. 1976): 86, 119–120.

Mael, Phyllis. "Rainbow of Voices." In *Women in American Theatre.* Edited by Helen Krich Chinoy and Linda Walsh Jenkins, 317–321. New York: Theatre Communications Group, 1987.

Mael examines three plays—Shange's *for colored girls,* Susan Griffin's *Voices,* and Eve Merriam's *Out of Our Father's House*—and how each uses the consciousness-raising group as a dramatic structure to express the individual and collective female quest for self-definition. According to Mael, consciousness-raising groups, which aim to help women become aware of how they are assigned certain roles in society, assemble women on stage, allowing "the individual voices [to] merge to speak to the collective journey of women. The distinct voices thus interact with and respond to each other."

McKenzie, Vashti. "No Punches Pulled." *The Afro-American* (March 4, 1978): 11.

McKenzie points out that although male heroes are absent from *for colored girls* (Mechanic Theatre, Baltimore), it would be trite to reduce all men to the level of cruelty and irresponsibility of Beau Willie Brown or Toussaint Jones. However, "there seems to be enough of them around for Shange . . . to stereotype black males this way. . . . If the rap fits, bear it. Otherwise, forget it."

Miller, E. Ethelbert. *New Directions* (Washington, D.C.) (April 1980): 29–31.

Miller defends Shange against critics, such as Michael Harper, who contend that her work is influenced too much by popular culture and others who criticize her for her bashing of the black male. Shange, Miller asserts, is not a radical feminist but an artist who hopes to open the eyes of black people to "the totality of [their] dilemma." Miller observes that although the women's movement of the 1970s emerged from the black movement of the 1960s, many blacks "resent the influence of the [women's movement] upon their own." To encourage Ntozake Shange, Ethelbert wrote a poem for her, "For Ntozake Shange," *Black Scholar* 10 (May/June 1979): 90.

Miller, Jeanne-Marie A. "Three Theatre Pieces by Ntozake Shange." *Theatre News* 14 (April 1982): 8.

Miller comments on Shange's dramatic pieces *spell #7, a photograph: lovers in motion,* and *boogie woogie landscapes.* Within the context of these pieces and *for colored girls,* she observes that Shange's strengths lie in the loose dramatic structures of the choreopoem, her use of language and the black idiom, and her articulation of the strong black female. Miller concludes her assessment by asserting that "Shange may well be the catalyst that the sagging American theatre so badly needs."

Miller, Lynn F. "Theatre in Review." *Educational Theatre Journal* 29, no. 2 (May 1977): 262–263.

Miller observes that *for colored girls* "culminates in the joyous affirmation of the beauty and integrity of the black woman's self. It is a rousing yet delicate, strongly felt spiritual dedicated to the earthy reality of the great goddess/mother/source-of-all-life, sincerely perceived by Shange to be a woman, probably a black woman."

Mitchell, Carolyn. " 'A Laying On of Hands': Transcending the City in Ntozake Shange's *For Colored Girls.*" In *Women Writers and the City: Es-*

says in Feminist Literary Criticism. Edited by Susan Merrill Squier, 230–248. Knoxville: University of Tennessee Press, 1984.

Mitchell examines *for colored girls* within the context of Paul Tillich's vision of the city, which "supports equality of aspiration, mobility of action, and freedom of community." Tillich's idealistic vision of urban life, according to Mitchell, excludes women because he bases it on the tenets of a patriarchal system. Clearly, Mitchell asserts, Shange repudiates Tillich's vision; her perception of contemporary city life as depicted in her theater piece lacks the characteristics identified with Tillich's model city. To the several women in Shange's play, the city represents isolation, repression, and oppression. In their city, creativity does not flourish but rather is "perverted into desperate schemes for survival." Whereas Tillich envisions the city as fostering equality at the marketplace, in Shange's world, "competition becomes the dog-eat-dog syndrome." These women neither succumb to nor are destroyed by the city. Instead, they transcend to another community that has arisen from the bleakness and horror of the city.

Narvaez, Alfonso A. "Broadway Show Is a Hit As It Goes Behind Walls of Jail." *New York Times* (April 8, 1977): sec. 2: B13.

Narvaez reports on the reactions of the inmates of Essex County Jail (Newark, New Jersey) to a production of *for colored girls* at their own "Jail Theater." One inmate, Leroy Harnette, said of the play, "It shows that we should show more kindness, consideration, and love for our women."

New York Theatre Critics' Reviews 37 (Sept. 13, 1976): 199–202.

Contains reprints of reviews by selected New York critics.

Novick, Julius. *"Colored Girls."Humanist* 37 (Jan.-Feb. 1977): 56.

Novick admits that he was skeptical of a work that consisted entirely of poems by an unknown poet with a strange name and staged by a director equally unfamiliar, but after seeing the play he "is happy to report *that for colored girls* triumphed over all [my] suspicions." For the most part, Shange's poems are "supple, unostentatious, vernacular language, very good for speaking onstage." As a white male, Novick remarks that the work was "an exotic experience, and yet at the same time it felt unexpectedly immediate. It got to me on some level beneath gender, beneath color, beneath temperament—a level, perhaps, merely human."

Olaniyan, Tejumola. *Scars of Conquest/Masks of Resistance: The Invention of*

Cultural Identities in African, African-American, and Caribbean Drama. New York: Oxford University Press, 1995.

Olaniyan examines Ntozake Shange's dramatic work within the context of the plays of Wole Soyinka, Amiri Baraka, and Derek Walcott. Underlying these authors' works is the assumption that black cultural identity speaks for black men and black women. But Shange's work challenges this assumption. The language and structure of *for colored girls* reflect the political underpinnings of Shange's exposure of black women as victims of oppression: externally by the white culture and internally by the black community.

Pacheco, Patrick. "Reviews: Theater." *After Dark* 9 (Oct. 1976): 36–37, 88.

According to Pacheco, the strength of *for colored girls* is that the pain and despair are tempered with humor, thus preventing the work from becoming "self-pitying bathos." Pacheco also comments that Shange's view toward the black man "is a curious blend of bitterness and desire."

Patraka, Vivian. "Staging Memory: Contemporary Plays by Women." *Michigan Quarterly Review* 26 (Winter 1987): 285–292.

Patraka critiques plays whose themes revolve around memory, "linking women's memory to women's history." The plays include Ntozake Shange's *for colored girls who have considered suicide/when the rainbow is enuf,* Megan Terry's *Mollie Bailey's Traveling Family Circus: Featuring Scenes from the Life of Mother Jones,* Joan Schenkar's *Signs of Life,* Marsha Norman's *'night Mother,* and Joanna Glass's *Play Memory.*

Peters, Erskine. "Some Tragic Propensities of Ourselves: The Occasion of Ntozake Shange's *For Colored Girls." Journal of Ethnic Studies* 6, no. 1 (Spring 1978): 79–85.

Peters finds the "heaps upon heaps of praises" for *for colored girls* unfortunate. He complains that the "discriminating" spectator is "overcome with a sense of disappointment and betrayal." Shange, according to Peters, portrays black men as shallow, one-dimensional "pasteboards or beasts." Furthermore, Shange reneges on her responsibility as an artist because she fails to explore the underlying "tragic circumstances" that consume the male characters.

Peters, Ida. "Colored Girls . . . No Lynching of Black Men: Trazana Beverley." *The Afro-American* (Feb. 21–25, 1978): 7.

In this interview with Trazana Beverley, who plays The Lady in Red in the National Company's production of *for colored girls,* the actress deplores the notion that Shange's play "is a vicious lynching of black men." Beverley has observed that older male theatergoers 'don't feel threatened and sympathize with the dilemma of the women characters. Yet for the younger male spectators, she says, "if the shoe fits, [they] seem to be hurt by the truth." As for female audiences, both black and white, they "get very vocal during the performances, jumping to their feet, shouting and talking back to the actresses." See also Peters's article on the Mechanic Theatre's production of *for colored girls,* "A Moving Theatre Experience About Pain." *The Afro-American* (March 4, 1978): 11. For addtional profiles of Trazana Beverley, see "The Blood and Sweat of a *Colored Girl.*" *Encore American & Worldwide News* 5 (Oct. 18, 1976): 33; "Schedule For *Colored Girls* at Blackstone." *Chicago Defender* (Dec. 24, 1977): Accent: 5; Tapley, Mel. "Trazana, Dolores and Diana Win Tonys." *N.Y. Amsterdam News* (June 11, 1977): D2.

Ribowsky, Mark. "A Poetess Scores a Hit with Play on 'What's Wrong With Black Men'." *Sepia* 25 (Dec. 1976): 42–46.

Shange comments that male spectators often "can't handle" the images of themselves in *for colored girls.* The play depicts black men "the way they can be—cruel, headstrong and patronizing to black women." However, Shange feels that many men are "being 'purified' because for the first time they can see in clear terms how ugly they can be."

Richards, Sandra L. "Conflicting Impulses in the Plays of Ntozake Shange." *Black American Literature Forum* 17, no. 2 (Summer 1983): 73–78.

According to Richards, one of Shange's most effective dramatic strategies is the dialectic of "awareness of social oppression and commitment to struggle . . . [and] a desire to transcend or bypass, through music and dance, the limitations of social and human existence." Richards sees as one aspect of the dialectic an element that Shange terms "combat breath," which the author views as the explanation "that Shange's plays not only startle and energize but also infuriate and disturb many of her audiences." *for colored girls* and *spell #7* are discussed throughout the article.

Ridley, Clifford A. "Off-Broadway, the Rainbow Is Enuf." *National Observer* (July 31, 1976): 16.

Ridley concludes his glowing review of *for colored girls* by suggesting that "Black or white, male or female, you owe this one to yourself."

Rodgers, Curtis E. "Good Theatre But Poor Sociological Statement." *N.Y. Amsterdam News* (Oct. 9, 1976): D11.

According to the reviewer, while emotion, pathos, and anger emanate from Shange's play, the work is weakened by the one-dimensional treatment of the sexes.

Rushing, Andrea Benton. "*For Colored Girls,* Suicide or Struggle." *Massachusetts Review* 22, no. 3 (Autumn 1981): 539–550.

Although seeing a production of *for colored girls* moved her deeply, Rushing realized, upon reflection, that "the play was missing something." She criticizes the "ladies of the rainbow" as being unrepresentative of black women's culture and of having a too narrow focus, that is, zeroing in on "black women's shared pain" resulting from the treatment of the men in their lives. Shange, according to Rushing, disregards other reasons for black women's suffering—tensions between women and their parents, the effect of the political and sexual liberation on women, racism, and the capitalist system, for instance. In conclusion, Rushing expresses her disappointment that Shange "reject[s] political solutions . . . in favor of young African-American women seeking their solutions in themselves and with other young women who have the same troubles and scant resources."

Shange, Ntozake. "Introduction." In *for colored girls who have considered suicide/when the rainbow is enuf: a choreopoem,* ix–xvi. New York: Macmillan, 1977.

In the introduction to the text of her play, Shange talks about the work's genesis. The choreopoem, she says, began as a series of seven poems, based on Judy Grahn's *The Common Woman,* that "were to explore the realities of seven different kinds of women." Shange also emphasizes the importance of dance to her spirit as well as her work:

"With dance I discovered my body more intimately than I had imagined possible. With the acceptance of the ethnicity of my thighs & backside, came a clearer understanding of my voice as a woman & as a poet."

———. "uncovered losses/black theater traditions." In *three pieces**New York: St. Martin's, 1981. [Reprinted in Shange's *See No Evil: Prefaces, Essays & Accounts 1976–1983.* San Francisco: Momo's Press, 1984, 18–25; Shange, Ntozake. *Black Scholar* 10 (July/Aug. 1979): 7–9.]

In her preface to *three pieces* which includes the texts of *spell #7, a photograph: lovers in motion* and *boogie woogie landscapes,* Shange observes that the American theater has become "shallow/stilted & imitative." She fears that African-Americans have succumbed to the "same artificial aesthetics" as white playwrights. Black playwrights should create their own aesthetic, which would include developing more works dealing with "the lives of our regular & precious" rather than concentrating on "our geniuses." Her discussion of the plays in this collection reflect Shange's attempts to experiment with a new aesthetic.

Simon, John. "*Enuf* Is Not Enough."*New Leader* 59 (July 5, 1976): 21, 22. [Reprinted in *Contemporary Literary Criticism: Excerpts from Criticism of the Works of Today's Novelists, Poets, Playwrights, and Other Creative Writers,* Vol. 8. Edited by Dedria Bryfonski, 484–485. Detroit: Gale Research, 1978.]

The high praise for *for colored girls,* Simon claims, "is both ludicrous and pititful." He especially derides some New York critics, such as Clive Barnes, Walter Kerr, and Alan Rich, for their exaggerated accolades for Shange' s writing. Simon complains that her poetic dialogue is no better than pop poet Rod McKuen's. He contends that such superlative treatment of Shange and other black playwrights "is not so much black talent as white guilt. . . . And what makes [Shange's] work so alluring to white guilt feelings is that she is not only black but also a woman, so that a superlative flung at her is like a quarter dropped into the hand of a beggar who is blind, allowing the donor to feel doubly pious." Simon warns that dramatists, both black or white, might be harmed by critics who overpraise their work—for example, black playwrights Melvin Van Peebles and Micki Grant. Their nondramatic medleys were "lauded to the skies," yet "their hastily concocted encores promptly failed."

Staples, Robert. "The Myth of Black Macho: A Response To Angry Black Feminists." *Black Scholar* 10 (March/April 1979): 24–32.

In the opinion of Staples, a sociologist of black sex roles, Shange shows no "compassion for misguided black men or a love of child, family and community" in her play *for colored girls.* He asserts that Shange's anger toward black men is displaced and suggests that rather than focusing on blacks as monsters she should communicate through her art ways that black men and women might reconcile their differences and confront racial and sexual discrimination. He accuses Shange of failing to explore the reason "many black men feel their manhood . . . is threatened by black women." For rebuttals to Staples's article, see Audre Lorde's "Feminism & Black Liberation: The Great American Disease." *Black Scholar* 10 (May/ June 1979): 17–19 and Yvonne Smith's "Ntozake Shange." *Essence* 12 (Feb. 1982):12. For additonal reactions by Shange, Kalamu ya Salaam, June Jordan, Julianne Malveaux, and others, see *Black Scholar* 10 (May/June 1979): 14–67.

Sullivan, Dan. "Confessions by *Colored Girls.*" *Los Angeles Times* (Feb. 7, 1977): sec. 4: 1, 11.

Sullivan praises *for colored girls* (New York Shakespeare Festival, 197 7 as "the strongest thing on Broadway just now." Shange infuses her play with such "sharp language" that "you have to buy" her statements. The dialogue, Sullivan maintains, "is some of the most alive stage writing the American theater has heard in years." See also Sullivan's "*Colored Girls*: They Can Cope." *Los Angeles Times* (July 14, 1978): sec. 4:1

Talbert, Linda Lee. "Ntozake Shange: Scarlet Woman and Witch/Poet." *Umoja* 4 (Spring 1980): 5–10.

Ntozake Shange "is preoccupied with poetcraft-as-witchcraft," says Talbert. In examining two poems from the theater piece *for colored girls (Sechita* and *A Laying On of Hands),* Talbert explores how Shange combines poetry and magic "as a mode of transforming patriarchal myths into a distinctive female mythology." In *Sechita,* for example, the dance hall girls represent "deity and slut, innocent and knowing" but their dances reflect feminine creative powers, that is, as a means of "conjurin' the spirit."

Taubeneck, Anne. "Shange's Colored Girls Still Brilliant." *Chicago Sun-Times* (April 21, 1995): Weekend: 10.

Taubeneck gives a glowing review for a revival of *for colored girls* at Chicago's Steppenwolf Theatre. See also an earlier review by Nancy Maes of the same production, "Steppenwolf Offers Telling *Colored Girls.*" *Chicago Tribune* (April 13, 1995): Tempo: 9E.

Thompson-Cager, Chezia. "Superstition, Magic and the Occult in Two Versions of Ntozake Shange's Choreopoem *for colored girls* . . . and Novels *Sassafrass, Cypress and Indigo.*" *MAWA: A Quarterly Publication of the Middle Atlantic Writers* 4 (Dec. 1989): 37–41.

Thompson-Cager explains how Shange creates a set of mythic images that "transcend the nature of traditional religious symbolism to portray an Afro-American mysticism." Shange's mythology, grounded in African-

American traditions, challenges Western political and social structures whose study of language and literature still has not moved far from the Greeks. Thompson-Cager attempts to show how Shange's characters use magic "to formulate survival strategies that may or may not make sense to anyone else."

Timpane, John. " 'The Poetry of a Moment': Politics and the Open Form in the Drama of Ntozake Shange." *Studies in American Drama, 1945–Present* 4 (1989): 91–101. [Reprinted in *Modern American Drama: The Female Canon.* Edited by June Schlueter, 198–206. Rutherford: Fairleigh Dickinson University Press, 1990.]

Timpane sees contradiction in Shange's early works. Her plays are anchored in a specific historical time and space and targeted toward specific kinds of audiences. Yet despite their exclusionary nature, her plays "remain remarkably 'open' texts. . . . [texts that are for a specific audience] throw themselves open to a multiplicity of audiences and performances."

Wallace, Michelle. "Ntozake Shange: *For Colored Girls,* the Rainbow Is Not Enough." *Village Voice* (Aug. 16, 1976): 108–09. [Reprinted in *Invisiblity Blues: From Pop to Theory.* London: Verso, 1990.

for colored girls did not disappoint Wallace, a black feminist who says that she usually "feel[s] cheated by black theatre." Wallace praises Shange's groundbreaking attempt to explore the vulnerability and pain of the "strong black woman." However, she finds the ending unsatisfying: "Why has [Shange] followed such specific ethnic information about black women with a worn-out feminist cliché like, "i found god in myself. . . . Shange offers the black woman a religious conversion to self-love as a solution to her problems." But Wallace questions whether black women's newfound sense of self can erase "the powerful forces of a profound self-hatred and a hostile environment."

Waxman, Barbara Frey. "Dancing Out of Form, Dancing into Self: Genre and Metaphor in Marshall, Shange, and Walker." *Melus* 19, no. 3 (Fall 1994): 91–106.

Waxman examines how Shange, Paule Marshall, and Alice Walker use dance to express spiritual healing, self-affirmation, and self-acceptance. Dance obfuscates traditional modes of dramatic expression. These writers "nudge readers to relinquish distinctions between personal essay and lyric poetry, between poetry and performative drama, between analytical and affective writing, between literature and music/choreography." Creating new forms of expression for these writers "is an act of rhetorical self-definition." They feel they must invent new forms to dramatize the truth of the marginal 'Other'. Waxman argues that Shange's *for colored girls* altered the course of dance and drama in America, in that she used dance "exclusively for women's pleasure, control and solidarity."

Weiner, Bernard. Vibrant 'Poems' About *Colored Girls.*" *San Francisco Chronicle* (Aug. 3, 1978): 52.

Weiner admits he arrived at San Francisco's Geary Theatre "in a blue funk," but his "spirits were raised" when he witnessed Shange's "dazzling" choreopoem. However, he relates a few disappointing aspects of the play. First, "there is the annoying tendency" to typecast whites and black men. Second, the message seems to be that there is little hope for healthy relationships. Third, gesture and movement are exaggerated "almost as though the words themselves cannot be trusted without the extra hype." For reviews of subsequent productions in San Francisco, see Weiner's article "A Weaker *Colored Girls* Returns." *San Francisco Chronicle* (Jan. 26, 1979): 57. For a review of the revival production at the Lorraine Hansberry Theatre see Steven Winn. "*Colored Girls* Home for Birthday." *San Francisco Chronicle* (Mar. 28, 1995): Datebook: E2.

Wetzsteon, Ross. *Plays and Players* 23 (Sept. 1976): 39.

Wetzsteon considers *for colored girls* to be "too fragmented and abstract" to be a theater piece; however, he concedes that Shange has "succeeded in defining black experience in America in terms of joyous self-assertion as well as frustrated rage." Wetszsteon also makes this point in his article "A Season for All Seasons." *Village Voice* (June 6, 1977): 91, 93.

Wiley, Catherine. "Theatre Review." *Theatre Journal* 43, no. 3 (Oct. 1991): 381–382.

Wiley reports that the production of *for colored girls* at the Theatre on Broadway in Denver was boycotted by black theater workers because it was directed by a white man. Her major concern about the directorial quality of the production is its "cavalier" treatment of the text. She suspects that the director inserted additional material written by Shange, some of which is of questionable quality, to simply showcase the talents of the actors. Equally intrusive and unnecessary is the director's hanging of a huge Robert Mapplethorpe photograph depicting a white male torso in the middle of the stage of a play dealing with the sexuality of black women. Wiley wonders about this attempt at universalizing Shange's play and asks if it is "possible for a white person to direct a play that does not become, on some level, a play about white people."

Willis, Ellen. "*For Colored Girls.*" *Rolling Stone* (Sept. 23, 1976):19.

As a white feminist, Willis observes that Shange's piece made her "squirm." Without compromising black experience, Shange managed to "reveal so much about [Willis's] own mask and what's under [it]." The playwright makes it impossible for a white feminist to either "sentimentalize women's shared oppression, denying the gravity of race and class . . . or by distanc[ing] herself and get off on vicariously trashing black men, which is easier than dealing with the white man sitting next to her."

Wilson, Edwin. "The Black Experience: Two Approaches." *Wall Street Journal* (Sept. 21, 1976): 24.

Wilson hails *for colored girls,* claiming that it "capture[s] the inner feelings of young black women today and . . . and achiev[es] its own kind of universality."

Winer, Linda. "Black Feminism Sparkles Under a Poetic *Rainbow.*" *Chicago Tribune* (Dec. 25, 1977): sec. 6: 2.

Winer profiles Shange shortly before *for colored girls* opened at Chicago's Blackstone Theater. Shange remarks that she developed the poems that comprise her choreopoem in bars, cafes, poetry centers, and women's studies departments, but at the time she "never considered them a single statement." Joseph Papp, who produced the play at the Public Theatre, remarked that "I was struck, first of all, with the honesty of [*for colored girls*], and then impressed with its high flights of pure poetry intermixed to such a marvelous degree with down-to-earth, folk, black material. . . . [Shange] is, in one sense, as militant as anybody can be. But she's an artist, which means she will never avoid certain truths to make another point." See also Winer's laudatory review of *for colored girls,* "Theater: On Broadway." *Chicago Tribune* (Jan. 23, 1977): sec. 6: 2–3.

Additional Performance Reviews

Barnes, Jessica. "*For Colored Girls . . .*" *N.Y. Amsterdam News* (Oct. 9, 1976): D10.

Bell, Roseanne Pope. "*For Colored Girls.*" *Black Collegian,* 7 (May-June 1977): 48–49.

Christiansen, Richard. "Cast Lends a Fierce Beauty to Shange's Colo*red Girls.*" *Chicago Tribune* (Apr. 3, 1986), sec. 2: 9.

Dodds, Richard. "Dashiki's Girls." Time*s-Picayune* (New Orleans) (Nov. 14, 1979): sec. 1: 26.

Haugen, Peter. "*Colored Girls* Gives Reason to Celebrate." *Sacramento Bee* (March 18, 1996): C3.

Higgins, John. "Theatre." *Times* (London) (April 12, 1978): 11c.

Kart, Larry. "Coarseness Takes Gold Out of 2nd Rain*bow.*" *Chicago Tribune* (Oct. 5, 1978): sec. 2: 8.

Lardner, James. "Source Theatre's for *colored girls* . . . Verse in Verse." *Washington Post* (March 3, 1981): D3.

Loynd, Ray. "Stage Beat." *Los Angeles Times* (July 31, 1987): sec. 6: 23.

Morley, Sheridan. "Theatre." *Punch,* 277 (Oct. 24, 1979): 731.

Nightingale, Benedict. "Theatre: Picnic on an Anthill." *New Statesman,* 98 (Oct. 19, 1979): 604–605.

Sumrall, Harry. "Theater." *Washington Post* (March 24, 1979): B2.

"Shows on Broadway." *Variety* (Sept. 22, 1976): 72

Taylor, John Russell. "Reviews: Stage Struck." *Plays and Players* 27 (Dec. 1979): 16–17.

"Theatre." *Players* 3 (Dec. 1976): 24–25

Trescott, Jacqueline. "Ntozake Shange: Searching for Respect and Identity." *Washington Post* (June 1976): B1, B5.

a photograph: lovers in motion

(Originally titled *a photograph: a still life with shadows/a study in cruelty;* New York Shakespeare Theater Festival, Public Theatre, 1977; revised, *a photograph: lovers in motion*, Equinox Theatre, Houston, 1979)

Playscript

a photograph: lovers in motion. New York: Samuel French, 1981.

three pieces. New York: St. Martin's, 1981.

Summary of Play

Following *for colored girls,* Shange wrote *a photograph,* a choreopoem dramatizing the ambivalence of heterosexual identity. Sean David, a struggling photographer, attempts to define himself within the contexts of his art, a racist society, and his relationship with the women in his life: Michael, who is free and unsubmissive to men; Nevada, who is educated and graceful; and the sensual Claire. As with Shange's other theater pieces, *a photograph* incorporates music and dance.

Performance Reviews

Barnes, Clive. "*Photograph* Has Beauty—& Problems." *New York Post* (Dec. 22, 1977): 39.

Barnes considers *a photograph* a silly soap opera—"Who can care about the escapist fantasies of a failed black photographer?"

Eder, Richard. "Stage: *Photograph* by Miss Shange." *New York Times* (Dec. 22, 1977): C11.

Eder feels that Shange is less a dramatist and more a troubadour. Her characters are illuminated by song-length outbursts, but the vignettes in *photograph* are weakened by a work that is "forced. The perceptions are made to do the donkey-work of holding up what attempts to be a whole dramatic structure, and they fail."

Gottfried, Martin. "Playmaking Is Not Enough." *Saturday Review* 5 (Feb. 18, 1978): 42.

Shange is a gifted poet, says Gottfried, but she is not yet a dramatist. *photograph* yields some beautiful poetic experiences, but they are presented as a recital rather as dramatic dialogue. The play lacks coherence: "The poetry is achingly lovely, but the story is pure corn." The theme of racial oppression is "trite. . . . Even the most righteous anger and sense of injustice grow wearsome when reduced to a litany of self-pity and racial chauvinism."

Loney, Glenn. "Other Stages." *After Dark,* 10 (April 1978): 80.

Shange's "poemplay" is wonderfully whole . . . [it] dramatizes that sexual exploitation is a two-way street."

Murray, Timothy. "Facing the Camera's Eye: Black and White Terrain in

Women's Drama." *Modern Drama* 28, no. 1 (March 1985): 110–124. [Reprinted in *Reading Black, Reading Feminist: A Critical Anthology.* Edited by Henry Louis Gates, Jr., 155–175. New York: Meridian, 1990.]

Murray examines Shange's *a photograph: lovers in motion* and Adrienne Kennedy's *An Evening with Dead Essex* from the perspective of the "fixating camera and desirous male, [which] come together in a performance of masculine entrapment as deeply oppressive as is the racism from which the characters all hope to escape."

Oliver, Edith. "The Theatre." *The New Yorker* 53 (Jan. 2, 1978): 48–49.

Shange's "poetic talent and passion carry the show," and her characters are given flesh and blood by the actors.

Sharp, Christopher. "Theater: Ntozake Shange." *Women's Wear Daily* (Dec. 22, 1977): 7.

Sharp considers *photograph* a much more "significant work" than Shange's *Where the Mississippi Meets the Amazon.*

Simon, John. "A Touch Is Better Than None." *New York* 11 (Jan. 16, 1978): 58.

Simon considers *photograph* just as "rotten" as *for colored girls:* The play is "inept, absurd, [and] distastefully tendentious." See also Simon's *New York* 13 (May 26 1980): 80–81.

Stasio, Marilyn. "Theatre." *Cue* (Jan. 7–20, 1978): 31–32.

Although *photograph* demonstrates Shange's sensitivity toward the black male, the play is weakened by the protagonist and the dramatist's technical treatment of him. Although the hero, Sean, is overwhelmed by pain, Stasio believes that he is "too thick-headed and narcissistic to hold our sympathies." Furthermore, Shange "hasn't got a grip on the dramatic form. . . . The play's disjointed structure—a flutter of unfocused scenes and discursive monologues—inhibits both the characters and the action from unfolding to full power."

Valentine, Dean. "On Stage: Theater of the Inane." *New Leader* 61 (Jan. 2, 1978): 29.

Valentine suspects that Shange "is making a handsome career out of being a black woman, chiefly preying . . . on the sympathies of white critics and audiences. . . . Certainly, to judge by *a photograph* . . . she has hardly a shred of talent to call her own."

spell #7: geechee jibara quik magic trance manual for technologically stressed third world people
(New York Shakespeare Festival, Public Theatre, 1979)

Playscripts
9 Plays by Black Women. Edited by Margaret Wilkerson, 239–292. New York: New American Library, 1986.

Shange: Plays: One [with introductions by the author], 65–115. London: Methuen Drama, 1992.

spell #7: A Theater Piece in Two Acts. New York: Samuel French, 1981.

three pieces. New York: St. Martin's, 1981.

Summary of Play
In this choreopoem that is staged under an enormous black face mask, several artists and performers meditate on the irony of being black in America. The group sings and dance, then withdraw into other characterizations—into monologues and dialogues of fantasies and dreams and reminiscences."

Criticism and Performance Reviews
Albright, William."Playwright Shange's *spell #7* Lacks a Little Magic." *Houston Post* (Jan. 27, 1988): B: 5.

Albright finds *spell #7* (Kuumba House Repertory Theatre) "ambitious and challenging" but it is no match for Shange's *for colored girls*—[it is] less "coherent, compelling and entertaining."

Barnes, Clive. "*spell #7* Has a Touch of Magic."*New York Post* (July 16, 1979):20

Barnes finds *spell #7* to be a strong choreopoem: it is funny, and the language is simple, spare, and succinct. Its few weaknesses are those places where Shange "seems to self-indulge in histrionic monologues, which while theatrical enough, almost too theatrical, come from the stage rather than from life."

Beaufort, John."Black Cast Electrifies Off-Broadway 'choreopoem'." *Christian Science Monitor* (June 7, 1979): 19.

Beaufort hopes that *spell #7* will be able to move to a larger theater.

Shange has successfully honed the choreopoem technique, "using it more realistically, achieving new levels of theatrical excitement."

Bess, E. Tamu. "*spell No. 7.*" *N.Y. Amsterdam News* (Jan. 5, 1980): 21–22.

Bess says that Shange "is the best of our times, particularly because she has a willingness to embrace our dark secrets." According to Bess, *spell #7* "is both fascinating in content and disappointing in form." This production is weaker than its original because of changes, "Unfortunately, the fluidity of the production and the believability of the narratives have diminished as a direct result of these [changes]."

Byrd, William. "*spell #7* at Clark." *Atlanta Daily World* (Feb. 12, 1982): 3.

Byrd remarks that this powerful play "clearly shows the spell that black people have been put under. It is a spell they have yet to come out of."

Campbell, Mary. "*Colored Girls* Playwright Weaves Her Hit New *spell.*" *Chicago Tribune* (July 1, 1979): sec. 6: 14.

Although *spell #7* is not as powerful or as overwhelmingly angry as Shange's *for colored girls,* this piece has wit, humor, "jabs of insight, and rich imagery.

Cronacher, Karen. "Unmasking the Minstrel Mask's Black Magic in Ntozake Shange's *spell #7.*" *Theatre Journal* 44 (May 1992): 177–193. [Reprinted in *Feminist Theatre and Theory.* Edited by Helene Keyssar, 189–212. New York: St. Martin's, 1996.]

Cronacher examines *spell #7* within the context of the minstrel show, a type of theater first constructed by white males in the nineteenth century. Although minstrel shows reveal nothing of the reality of the African-American experience, they tell plenty about "that dark continent of the white male phobias and desires, and the 'horror, the horror' of the white male's experience of gender and racial difference."

Eder, Richard. "Stage: Ntozake Shange's Dramatic Poetry in *spell #7.*" *New York Times* (June 4, 1979): C13.

Eder agrees with other critics that Shange is at her best when she sticks to loosely structured theater pieces, such as *for colored girls* and *spell #7.* The latter shows Shange's "wit, lyricism and fierceness. . . . She can take a common-enough image and make it do wonders." See also Eder's "*Spell #7* by Ntozake Shange." *New York Times* (July 16, 1979): C12, and "Miss Shange's Rousing Homilies." *New York Times* (July 22, 1979): D3.

Erstein, Hap. "*spell #7* Takes Us on Magical Trip." *Washington Times* (May 9, 1991): E3.

After seeing *spell # 7* Erstein wonders why Shange's plays are rarely performed. Although the play lacks the power of *for colored girls*, Erstein considers *spell* to be the work of a more sophisticated writer.

Fox, Terry Curtis. "Black Masks & White Gowns." *Village Voice* (July 23, 1979): 77–78.

Fox opines that *spell #7* is "*for colored girls* with men . . . [but] with dialogue."

Gelman, David. "This Time Shange Casts No Spell." *Newsweek* 94 (July 30, 1979): 65. [Reprinted in *New York Theatre Critics' Reviews* 40 (Nov. 19, 1979): 107–108.]

Gelman finds *spell #7* "too diffuse to bind, and Miss Shange, who has made at least one unhappy stab at straight drama, may yet find the conventional play's the thing to capture her insistent power."

Hill, Latham. "Hats Off to *spell #7*." *Norfolk Journal and Guide* (Feb. 19, 1986): 13.

Hill comments that *spell #7* (Daedalus Productions, Old Dominion University Technology Theatre, Norfolk, Va.) "is straight to the point with its message of artistic denial and creative castration for black American artists living in a racist environment."

Nelsen, Don. "Shange Casts a Powerful *spell*." *New York Daily News* (July 16, 1979). [Reprinted in *New York Theatre Critics' Reviews* 40 (Nov. 19, 1979): 107–108.]

Nelsen applauds *spell #7* for its power and poetry. He observes that it transcends being simply an angry diatribe against whites because of Shange's "ability to make the word flesh, to fuse idea and character so that it comes out humanity."

New York Theatre Critics' Reviews 40 (Nov. 19, 1979): 107–108.

Provides reprints of reviews from New York newspapers.

Oliver, Edith. "The Theatre: Off Broadway." *The New Yorker* 55 (July 16, 1979): 73.

Oliver affirms that *spell #7* "shows Shange's passion and wit and fiery talent to be unbanked, and even replenished."

Pinkney, Mikell. "Theatrical Expressionism in the Structure and Language of Ntozake Shange's *spell #7.*" *Theatre Studies* 37 (1992): 5–15.

Pinkney asserts that Shange's "choreopoems" are eclectic theater pieces that are grounded in expressionism: "In Shange's "attack on the structure of the well-made play, her personal struggle becomes one of finding objective means to project subjective ideas, while avoiding the obvious imitation of existing styles." The traditional notion of dramatic conflict is absent from *spell #7;* Shange replaces it with a series of "dramatic statements" conveyed through poems, monologues, and vignettes. Shange also replaces traditional text and dialogue with a "coded language" that best expresses the experiences of blacks and other third world people.

Richards, Sandra L. "Under the 'Trickster's' Sign: Toward a Reading of Ntozake Shange and Femi Osofisan." In *Critical Theory and Performance.* Edited by Janelle G. Reinelt and Joseph R. Roach, 65–78. Ann Arbor: University of Michigan Press, 1992.

Richards considers the intersection of African, especially Yoruban religious practices and Western cultural traditions and their synthesis in the work of Shange and the Nigerian playwright Femi Osofisan: "Through a creative deployment of the principles of Sixteen Cowrie and Fia divination, [Shange and Osofisan] construct dramaturgies that empower audiences, challenging them to impose an interpretive hegemony that can extend from the symbolic to the socio-political order."

Salaam, Yusef A. "*Spell No. 7:* Antidote For Abuse of Black Image." *N.Y. Amsterdam News* (July 3, 1992): 34.

Salaam observes that "[l]ooking back at the poisonous, reactionary *for colored girls,* which was partially a primal scream reaction to the abuse that the African woman's image has suffered in Euro-centric and Afro-centric literature, *spell #7* is an antidote which says that the African woman/African nation must look in the mirror and start liking what she /it sees."

Sharp, Christopher. "*Spell #7*: A Geechee Quick Magic Trance Manual." *Women's Wear Daily* (June 4, 1979). [Reprinted in *New York Theatre Critics' Reviews* 40 (Nov. 19, 1979): 107–108.]

Sharp criticizes *spell #7* for being "a fecund garden that badly needs trimming. . . . The best scenes are diluted by Shange's attempts to say one thing in as many different forms as she can."

Simon, John. "Fainting Spell." *New York* 12 (July 30, 1979): 57.

Simon complains that Shange exploits her blackness and femaleness—"Belonging to one formerly underprivileged class is an advantage; to two, a gold mine." *spell #7* is a "bad" play, despite the fact that, unlike Shange's previous plays, it includes men in the cast and the women seem less angry. Simon dislikes Shange's poetry as well as her playwrighting without really saying why.

Stasio, Marilyn. "Shange Casts a Mixed *Spell.*" *New York Post* (June 5, 1979). [Reprinted in *New York Theatre Critics' Reviews* 40 (Nov. 19, 1979): 107–108.]

While *spell #7* is not as powerful as Shange's *for colored girls*, the new choreopoem "offers glimpses into the passion and beauty that bubble in Shange's fertile poetic imagination." One particular "wickedly wise" vignette about African-American women desired by non-American black men, says Stasio is a brilliant comic piece. However, the vignettes' dramatic powers are overshadowed by their moralizing, such as a "shallow and politically suspect sketch about white women and a psychological[ly] murky one about infanticide." Stasio concludes by asserting that while many of the vignettes are good, they lack cohesiveness—"these dazzling fragments amuse and delight, but they don't really grab us where we live."

Wiley, Catherine. "Theatre Review." *Theatre Journal* 43, no. 3 (Oct. 1991): 381–382.

Wiley observes that the media considered *spell #7* (Studio E Ensemble, Eulipions Cultural Center, Denver) "raw." She recounts that when she made reservations for the performance, she was "warned, presumably as a white woman, that I might find the text hard to take." See Wiley's review of a controversial production of *for colored girls* in "Theatre Review." *Theatre Journal* 43, no. 3 (October 1991): 381–382.

Winn, Steven. "Shange's Sometimes Provocative *Spell.*" *San Francisco Chronicle* (March 26, 1985): 44.

Winn suggests that Shange cut most of the second act of *spell #7* (S.E.W. Productions, Lorraine Hansberry Theatre, San Francisco) because it "begins to squander the sense of tautness and urgency that propelled things along in the first act." Furthermore, the second act "turns narrow and carping. Joyce Carol Oates is indicted for assigning the same name to three different black characters [and] a cynical bit about blacks learning to speak standard English is dated."

Wood, William R. "For [Theatergoers] It's ZAP! You're Black! In Karamu's Production *spell No. 7.*" *Cleveland Call and Post* (June 6, 1981): 11B.

Wood points out that *spell No. 7* (Karamu Theatre, Cleveland) illuminates a major problem in the United States: "the plight of our black children. Because of the shallow attitudes of many women concerning motherhood, and many people concerning the role of the parent, many parents [symbolically speaking] slit their children's wrists through lack of concern, direction and understanding."

Woodis, Carole. "*Spell No. 7.*" *Plays and Players* 381 (June 1985): 28–29.

Woodis observes that "not since Dylan Thomas's *Under Milk Wood* [has] a dramatic piece that played with language with such exuberance, and structure with such daring. . . . *Spell No. 7* [Womens Playhouse Trust, Donmar Warehouse, London] takes risks." Woodis is impressed that Shange's dramatization of racism breaks from traditional theater structure in which the monologue is responsible for the piece's impact. For a summary of the reception of the play by the British press, see Lester, Neal A. *Ntozake Shange: A Critical Study of the Plays,* 122–123. New York: Garland, 1995.

Additional Performance Reviews

Bailey, Peter. "Theater." *Black Collegian* 10 (Jan 1979): 70.

Cooper, Martin. "Theatre." *Times* (London) (April 4, 1985): 11d.

"Spell #7." Variety (July 25, 1979): 106.

Other Plays by Ntozake Shange

Betsey Brown: A Rhythm & Blues Musical

(Based on Shange's novel *Betsey Brown,* with book by Shange and Emily Mann, original music by Baikida Carroll, American Music Theater Festival, Philadelphia, 1989)

Playscript

"Betsey Brown [excerpt]." *Studies in American Drama, 1945–Present,* 4, 1989, 3–20.

Reviews

Beckerman, James. "Coming of Age, on Another Stage." *The Record* (New Jersey) (Nov. 29. 1992): E12.

"*Betsey Brown.*" *Variety.* (April 12–18, 1989): 108.

Feldberg, Robert. "From Stage to Soapbox." *The Record* (New Jersey) (April 16, 1991): B5.

Gussow, Mel. "Coming of Age with Help from a Wise Troublemaker." *New York Times* (April 13, 1991): 1.

Kent, Assunta. "The Rich Multiplicity of *Betsey Brown.*" *Journal of Dramatic Theory and Criticism* 7 (Fall 1992): 151–161.

Klein, Alvin. "Overflowing Aspirations in *Betsey Brown.*" *New York Times* (April 14, 1991): sec. 12 (New Jersey): 15.

Koenenn, Joseph C. "Unoriginal Play Titles: The Musical." *Newsday* (June 7, 1990): sec. 2: 5.

Phelan, Peggy. "Reviews." *Theatre Journal* 43, no. 3 (Oct. 1991): 383–384.

Swed, Mark. "Theater." *New York Times* (April 2, 1989): sec. 2: 25.

boogie woogie landscapes
(Symphony Space Theatre, 1979)

Playscript
three pieces. New York: St. Martin's Press, 1981.

Reviews
Berson, Misha. "Dancing Through Drama." *San Francisco Chronicle* (Jan. 8, 1984): Datebook: 32–33

McLellan, Joseph. "Bungled *boogie*: Ntozake Shange's Lower-Case Editorials." *Washington Post* (June 20, 1980): C1, C6.

Martin, Judith. " A Scattered *Landscape.*" *Washington Post* (June 27 1980): 11.

Weinraub, Bernard. "A Touring Black Troupe Begins Its Journey." *Washington Star* (June 15,1980): H1.

Winn, Steven. "Lively Experiments in Ethnic Theater." *San Francisco Chronicle* (Jan. 18, 1984): 51.

Daddy Says
(1989)

Playscript
New Plays for the Black Theatre. Edited by Woodie King, Jr., 233–251. Chicago: Third World Press, 1989.

From Okra to Greens/ A Different Kinda Love Story: A Play/with Music & Dance
(Crossroads Theater Company, New Brunswick, N.J., 1992)

Playscript
From Okra to Greens/A Different Kinda Love Story: A Play/ With Music & Dance. New York: Samuel French, 1985.

Love Space Demands
(Crossroads Theater Company, New Brunswick, N.J., 1992)

Playscript
Love Space Demands: A Continuing Saga. New York: St. Martin's Press, 1991.

Shange: Plays: One [with introductions by the author], 65–115. London: Methuen Drama, 1992.

Reviews
Howard, Susan. "Ntozake Shange Again Puts Her Poetry on Stage." *New York Newsday* (March 5, 1992): 55, 81.

Klein, Alvin. "Poems on the Politics of Seduction." *New York Times* (March 22, 1992): sec. 12NJ: 16.

Mother Courage and Her Children
(Adapted from Bertold Brecht's *Mother Courage*, Public Theatre, 1980)

Reviews
Allen, Bonnie. "Review of *Mother Courage.*" *Essence.* 11 (Aug. 1980): 21.

Barnes, Clive. "American-style *Courage* Is an Asset for Public."*New York Post* (May 14, 1980): 36.

Beaufort, John. "Mother Courage and Her Children."*Christian Science Monitor* (May 19, 1980):19.

Gussow, Mel. "Stage: *Mother Courage.*" *New York Times* (May 14, 1980): C20.

Kissel, Howard. "*Mother Courage.*" *Women's Wear Daily* (May 14, 1980) [Reprinted in *New York Theatre Critics' Reviews* (Aug. 4, 1980): 183–186.]

"Mother Courage." Encore 9 (June 1980): 34.

"Mother Courage." N.Y. Amsterdam News (June 14, 1980): 33.

Munk, Erica. "*Mother Courage.*" *Village Voice* (May 19, 1980): 89.
In addition to this review, Shange briefly discusses the production of *Mother Courage* on page 40 of this issue.

New York Theatre Critics' Reviews 41 (Aug. 4, 1980): 183–186.

Oliver, Edith. "Theater." The *New Yorker* 56 (May 26, 1980): 77.

Rich, Frank. "*Mother Courage* Transplanted." *New York Times* (June 15, 1980): sec. 2: D5.

Simon, John. "Avaunt-Garde and 'Taint Your Wagon.'" *New York* 13 (May 26, 1980): 79–81.

Watt, Douglas. "Brecht's *Mother Courage* Scalped Out West." *New York Daily News* (May 14, 1980) [Reprinted in *New York Theatre Critics' Reviews* (Aug. 4, 1980): 183–186.]

Nomathemba (Noma-temba)
(Co-authored by Shange, Eric Simonson, and Joseph Shabalala, Steppenwolf Theatre Company, Chicago,1995)

Reviews
Abarbanel, Jonathan. "*Nomathemba*; Steppenwolf Theatre Company." *Back Stage* (May 12, 1995): 19.

Pareles, Jon, "A Parable of Lovers' Quest in Today's South Africa." *New York Times* (April 22, 1996): C11.

Pressley, Nelson. "Song Blossoms Into Tale of Love and Hope in New South Africa." *Washington Times* (April 22, 1996): C11.

Rousuck, J. Wynn. "*Nomathemba* Sings of Hope, Wariness." *Baltimore Sun* (April 23, 1996): 1E.

Stearns, David Patrick. "*Nomathemba:* Staging A Poem to South Africa." *USA Today* (May 22, 1995): 4D.

Shapes, Sadness, and the Witch
(Children's play, Wortham Theatre, University of Houston, Houston, 1984)

Three Views of Mt. Fuji
(New Dramatists, (1987)

Reviews

Arkatov, Janice. "Fame Came Fast with *for colored girls.*" *Los Angeles Times* (July 28, 1987): Calendar: 5

Weiner, Bernard. "Shange's *Fuji* Needs Help." *San Francisco Chronicle* (June 12, 1987): 84.

Where the Mississippi Meets the Amazon
(With Jessica Hagedorn and Thulani Nkabinde; Public Theatre Cabaret, 1977).

Reviews

Gussow, Mel. "3 Satin Sisters Spin a Poetry of Nostalgia at Stage Cabaret."*New York Times* (Dec. 20, 1977): 44.

Oliver, Edith. "The Theatre." *The New Yorker* 53 (Jan. 2, 1978): 48–49.

Sharp, Christopher. "Theater: Ntozake Shange." *Women's Wear Daily* (Dec. 22, 1977): 7.

Stasio, Marilyn. "Theatre." Cue 46 (Jan. 8–20, 1977): 31–32.

Index